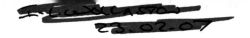

UNWANTED BEAUTY

UNWANTED BEAUTY

AESTHETIC PLEASURE

IN HOLOCAUST

REPRESENTATION

BRETT ASHLEY KAPLAN

UNIVERSITY OF ILLINOIS PRESS

Urbana and Chicago

Library of Congress
Cataloging-in-Publication Data
Kaplan, Brett Ashley.
Unwanted beauty :
aesthetic pleasure in
Holocaust representation /
Brett Ashley Kaplan.
p.   cm.
Includes bibliographical references
and index.
ISBN-13: 978-0-252-03093-2
(cloth : alk. paper)
ISBN-10: 0-252-03093-1
(cloth : alk. paper)
1. Holocaust, Jewish (1939–1945)
—Historiography. 2. Holocaust,
Jewish (1939–1945), in literature.
3. Holocaust, Jewish (1939–1945),
and art. 4. Holocaust, Jewish (1939–1945)
—Influence. I. Title.
D804.348.K37   2007
700'.458—dc22
2006000324

Anselm Kiefer, *Banner* (detail,
1990, oil, lead, ash, rock, paper, and
copper wire on canvas, 130" × 110¼"
[330.2 × 280 cm]). Used by permission
on title page and chapter openings.
Collection Museum of Contemporary
Art, Chicago. Gift of Camille
Oliver-Hoffmann in memory of
Paul W. Oliver-Hoffmann.

FOR SJH, ML

Contents

Acknowledgments

I have had the pleasure of working with and learning from many wonderful thinkers; I trust that their traces will be visible in the following pages. I will start by thanking my colleagues at the University of Illinois, especially in the Program in Jewish Culture and Society and the Program in Comparative and World Literature. The Jewish Studies group holds an exceptional workshop series at which I have presented some of the chapters of this book in earlier forms; I am grateful to all the participants in these workshops for their useful input and thought-provoking questions. From this group I would particularly like to thank Michael Shapiro, for his marvelous directorship of the program and for encouraging me to send my manuscript to the University of Illinois Press; Matti Bunzl, for discussing the structure of the book multiple times, for contributing his photograph of Whiteread's memorial in Vienna, and for always being an effective champion; and Michael Rothberg for his insightful comments on chapter 2, for generously sharing references to useful sources, and for bringing so many important and interesting scholars to our campus. Many colleagues in several departments, including Matti and Michael R., read and commented on sections of this book; thanks therefore to Jed Esty, Anke Pinkert, Zack Lesser, Rachael Delue, and Jordana Mendelson. The chair of my department, Nancy Blake, has always been supportive and encouraging, for which I thank her warmly; other members of my department (and/or dwellers in our shared office building), whose warm collegiality enlivens my days, include: Rob Rushing and Lilya Kaganovsky, Harriet Murav and Bruce Rosenstock, Kirk Freudenburg, Larry Schehr, Dara Goldman, Adlai Murdoch, Laurie Johnson and Carl Niekerk, Marilyn Booth, Stephen Jaeger, and Gary Porton.

I have been greatly influenced by the work of Marianne Hirsch, and I am grateful for her encouragement of this book and for generously reading chapter 4. Andreas Huyssen has also been influential on my thinking and I thank him for being extremely gracious during his 2003 visit to UIUC and for aiding me in my request for permission from Anselm Kiefer. I thank Susan Rubin Suleiman for her useful suggestions on an early version of chapter 2 (which she read as a then-anonymous reviewer for a journal). Other thinkers who have contributed a great deal—although they may not be aware of my debt—include James Young, Saul Friedländer, Ernst van Alphen, Geoffrey Hartman, and the late Susan Sontag. Earlier drafts of parts of this project were presented at conferences at the University of Illinois, Boston College, and Harvard University, as well as at the American Comparative Literature Association Annual Conferences; I am grateful to the audiences and co-panelists at these conferences for their lively questions. Although I have not read material from this book at the Association for Jewish Studies annual conferences—where I have presented other projects—it has been a pleasure to be a co-panelist and/or to discuss ideas with many scholars who have made AJS intellectually stimulating.

I began this book at the University of California, Berkeley, where I had the good fortune to work with Miryam Sas, who was a fabulous mentor and friend; David Cohen, who was a fount of knowledge on Holocaust history, and who extended himself generously during a multi-part visit to UIUC in 2003; Ann Smock, who was wonderfully supportive and often engaged in long, thoughtful discussions pointing me in the right direction; and Daniel Boyarin, who made many apt suggestions and who was a welcome champion. As chair of the Rhetoric Department, Judith Butler was extremely supportive and encouraging. Other debts include the late Teresa Brennan, whom I met at the New School, and whom I thank for many intense conversations about gender, science, and the universe. I owe thanks to my teachers who were then at the University of Sussex: Nancy Wood, whose course on Holocaust Representation initiated a sustained interest in the questions addressed in this book; Geoff Bennington, who was a wonderful advisor during the writing of my master's thesis on the de Man and Heidegger affairs; and Homi Bhabha and Jacqueline Rose, who offered the stimulating courses on Foucault and Freud that form the silent background of much of my work. Among the many extraordinary influences at the University of California, Santa Cruz, I would like to thank Donna Haraway, who spent endless time and energy molding a keen but unformed undergraduate, and Julianne Burton, Teresa de Lauretis, Maria LaPlace, and Hayden White.

For financial support during the writing of this book I thank the Research Board at UIUC for granting me time to write and providing a subvention for the images included herein. For research help I thank the many librarians at the Center for Jewish History in New York (especially Yivo and the Leo Baeck Institute), the United States Holocaust Memorial Museum Archives in Washington, the New York Public Library, and the Bibliothèque Nationale in Paris, who guided me toward crucial materials. Chapters 1, 2, and 5 appeared in earlier forms respectively in *Comparative Literature Studies* 38:4 (2001), *Comparative Literature* 55:4 (2003), and *Journal of Modern Jewish Studies* 2:1 (2003). I thank these journals and their editors, especially George Rowe and Lynne Rossi (of *CL*), and Glenda Abramson (of *JMJS*), for graciously granting permission to reproduce substantially revised versions of these essays. Dr. Willis Regier, at the University of Illinois Press, has been a pleasure to work with and an enthusiastic advocate of this project. I am very grateful to the two anonymous reviewers for the press, whose careful, intelligent readings have improved this book.

I heartily thank Nina Glückselig and Janet Gerson for long phone conversations about Leo Glückselig. I thank Christian Boltanski, Peter Eisenman (and Cynthia Davidson), Sir Norman Foster, Jochen Gerz and Esther Shalev-Gerz (and Anya Reichmann), Anselm Kiefer, and Susan Silas for supplying images and permission to reproduce their work. It has been a particular pleasure to have entered into dialogue with Susan Silas. Some of the works reproduced herein are housed at museums and galleries whose staff have been helpful in providing images and permissions. I therefore thank the Fonds national d'art contemporain, Ministère de la culture, Paris; Museum of Contemporary Art, Chicago; the New Museum of Contemporary Art, New York; the Center for Holocaust and Genocide Studies, Minneapolis (and Stephen Feinstein); the United States Holocaust Memorial Museum, Washington, D.C.; and Gagosian Gallery, New York.

Among the many dear friends who make the community in this small university town on the prairie so surprisingly marvelous I would like especially to thank Ania Loomba and Suvir Kaul (who are now at Penn), Zohreh Sullivan and Jim Hurt, Audrey Petty, Jed Esty and Andrea Goulet, Adam Sutcliffe (now at King's College) and Nadia Valman (Southampton). I have been graced for many years with sustaining friendships with several remarkable women who, alas, live in my former homes of New York, Berkeley, and London; I thank Lara Weitzman, Polly Pagenheart, Amy Huber, Julia Harrington, and Yasmin Mohsenzadeh for remaining so close despite geographical distance. My parents, Ann and Ralph, stepfather, Marty, and in-laws, Rod and Sandy, have all been exceptionally supportive and have offered models of engaged citizenship that I will strive to emulate. My late grandmother, Omi (Trudie), has been an enduring influence and I thank her for breaking her era's strictures limiting women and becoming a force to be reckoned with; indeed, the wonderful, huge, English family that Omi created has always offered me a second home, and for this I have been truly thankful.

It is impossible to thank my husband, Stephen Hartnett, enough; he has discussed, read, edited, and lived through every moment of this book with so much love that I consider myself blessed beyond imagination to be next to him now and for what is to come. He teaches me daily how to combine poetry with politics, activism with play, and love with the rest. Our children, Anya Helene and Melia Reyes, bring so much happiness, silliness, and plain rompishness into our lives that they have changed my perspective on everything.

UNWANTED BEAUTY

Introduction

THE POLITICS OF AESTHETIC PLEASURE IN
HOLOCAUST REPRESENTATION

Only art has the power of redeeming
suffering from the abyss. —Aharon Appelfeld

"What is this film that I have made? . . . Will it transmit the trauma of history in a way that is beneficial? Or is it a thing of exquisite, but ultimately
useless, beauty?" Thus the filmmaker in Atom Egoyan's *Ararat* wonders
whether his film about the horror of the Armenian genocide will be a useless aesthetic object or an important historical contribution.[1] This book
collapses this opposition between the beneficial and the beautiful by arguing that the unwanted beauty offered by some Holocaust representations
transforms Holocaust memory in important, enlivening, and indeed beneficial ways. I have been struck repeatedly by the fact that much prose,
poetry, visual art, and architecture representing the Holocaust is beautiful,
even though remaining mournful. While it may be counter-intuitive to
understand some Holocaust representation as beautiful, I argue that thinking about the role of aesthetic pleasure in complex and multivalent texts
opens this traumatic historical event to deeper understanding. Indeed, the
works I analyze insist that we continue to examine how the Holocaust
resides in our thoughts; because they are beautiful, these works entice our
reflection, our attention, and our questioning.

Unwanted Beauty thus asks several questions: How can we make sense of
the often contradictory claims of aesthetics and history? How can we understand the incredible beauty of much Holocaust art? And is there something indecent or unethical about this beauty? Irving Howe echoes some of
these questions when he wonders, "Can we really say that in reading a memoir or novel about the Holocaust, or in seeing a film such as *Shoah,* we gain
the pleasure, or catharsis, that is customarily associated with the aesthetic
transaction? More disquieting, can we be sure that we do not gain a sort of
illicit pleasure from our pained submission to such works?"[2] This book ex-

amines the "disquieting" sensation outlined by Howe by looking at multiple genres of Holocaust representation and reconsidering the "illicit pleasure" of their beauty.

While philosophers and others have endeavored to forge a science of aesthetics, the designation "beautiful" and its attendant "aesthetic pleasure" ultimately entail a subjective stance. In contrast to some notions of beauty as merely pretty or attractive, I use beauty to designate texts that offer ambiguous, diverse, complicated, open-ended reflections on the Holocaust. Because aesthetics is the branch of philosophy dedicated to investigating what pleases the senses, aesthetic questions generally involve pleasure; because history is the branch of the humanities that investigates social change, it often involves pain. The relationship between aesthetics and history, then, or between art and politics, has generally been vexed; yet many readers and viewers of Holocaust literature, art, and memorials confess that where the historical documentary might not affect them deeply, the aesthetic power of art encourages them to remember the Holocaust rather than shunt it aside. I therefore argue that the distinction between history and aesthetics is fluid and that beautiful representations can enhance Holocaust remembrance. As several recent works on aesthetics have observed, beauty is currently enjoying a renaissance; that matters for our understanding of the Holocaust because we must face the role of the "illicit" aesthetic pleasure of unwanted beauty in transforming memories of this important event in twentieth-century history.

Indeed, since the Second World War, survivors, artists, and scholars have been struggling with the question of how to represent the Holocaust. Some have argued that the Shoah is so traumatic that it should render words speechless and images blank; others have argued that the Holocaust is just as representable as any other historical event. Yet proponents of both views have found that attempting to represent the Holocaust, even if doomed to failure, is a crucial endeavor full of historical, political, and cultural importance. Many observers have argued, however, that there is something unethical about beauty in Holocaust literature, art, and memorials, as if crafting beautiful words or images about the Holocaust constituted a betrayal of its victims or a naïve forgetting of its perpetrators.

Three main arguments have contributed to the demonization of beauty in Holocaust literature, art, and memorials. First, because a certain kind of beauty was exploited by the Nazi regime, the very concept of beauty has been tainted by its association with fascism. Second, because of his fear of reproducing the horror of the Holocaust and a profound skepticism of the culture industry, in 1949 Theodor Adorno famously claimed that it is barbaric to write poetry after Auschwitz. Consequently, many Holocaust writers and artists have feared the ethical implications of rendering the Shoah in beautiful forms. As I discuss in more detail in chapter 1, Adorno's original maxim—despite his later modification of the claim—has had an enormous impact on artists, writers, scholars, philosophers, and theorists trying to treat the vexed question of how best to represent the Holocaust. As Irving Howe puts it, "I cannot think of another area of literary discourse in which a single writer has exerted so strong, if diffused an influence as Theodor Adorno has on discussions of literature and the Holocaust."[3] Third, because the Shoah has often been seen as historically unique, cultural theorists and survivors have clamored for an equally unique aesthetic—one devoid of beauty—that avoids the representational strategies used to depict other historical crises.

These three arguments against the beautiful in Holocaust representation have led to a series of aesthetic contortions in Holocaust literature, art, and memorials that often compromise the pedagogical and emotional aims of these texts, works, or spaces. By titling this book *Unwanted Beauty* I indicate how, in contrast to these three dominant interdictions against beauty in Holocaust representations, the unwanted beauty of such depictions encourages us to see the complexity of the Shoah in ways that conventional works fail to achieve.

Perhaps this idea of beauty in Holocaust works will strike some as sacrilegious. But survivors such as Aharon Appelfeld, who found that artistic expression seemed repellent immediately after the Holocaust, ultimately argue for sensitive Holocaust representations in order to bridge the "difficult imperatives" of the "desire to keep silence and the desire to speak." Appelfeld explains, "Artistic expression after the Holocaust seem[ed] repugnant, disgusting. The pain and suffering called either for silence or for wild outcries. Any embellishment or sweetening was jarring. Moreover, art, and not without reason, was linked in our minds with a sphere of European culture of which we had been the victims."[4]

Appelfeld here summarizes the plea for silence in the face of horror, the turning away from artistic "sweetening" or aesthetification, and the sense that an intimate link prevails between the structure of European culture and the Holocaust. But as a Holocaust artist, Appelfeld goes on to argue for artistic expression of the Holocaust, concluding that "we must transmit the dreadful experience from the category of history into that of art."[5] Appelfeld also notes that Holocaust studies has moved away from the often paralyzing debates over representation that stymied earlier generations of critics who found artistic expression "repugnant." In fact, recent works such as Susan Gubar's *Poetry After Auschwitz,* Norman Kleeblatt's collection of essays about the Jewish Museum show *Mirroring Evil,* and Shelly Hornstein, Laura Levitt, and Laurence Silberstein's collection of essays on contemporary Holocaust art, *Impossible Images,* have addressed some aspects of this new cultural turn toward unwanted beauty, thus opening up fascinating questions about the available means of Holocaust representation.[6]

Moreover, works by some historians—notably Saul Friedländer and Hayden White—argue that there is *no crisis of representation* regarding the Holocaust. Friedländer claims that "The extermination of the Jews of Europe is as accessible to both representation and interpretation as any other historical event. But we are dealing with an event which tests our traditional conceptual and representational categories, an 'event at the limits.'"[7] Friedländer thus suggests that an adequate representation of the Holocaust *is* possible, as long as we understand that the representation will be complicated by the fact that the Holocaust was a "limit" event. Similarly, White claims: "I do not think that the Holocaust, Final Solution, Shoah, Churban, or German genocide of the Jews is any more unrepresentable than any other event in human history."[8] White thus debunks the mystical appeal of the argument that because the Holocaust can be seen as "unique" historically it should be "unique" aesthetically as well. In agreement with Friedländer and White, then, historical studies now tend to argue that while the Holocaust was unprecedented in scale, other twentieth-century genocides have demonstrated that the hatreds exhibited during it were not "unique."[9]

For an example of how some have argued that the "uniqueness" of the Nazi genocide requires its own aesthetic approach, consider Elie Wiesel's claim that "The Holocaust is not a subject like all the others. It imposes certain limits. There are techniques that one may not use, even if they are commercially effective. In order not to betray the dead and humiliate the living, this particular subject demands a special sensibility, a different approach, a rigor, strengthened by respect and reverence, above all faithfulness to memory."[10]

Likewise, in reflecting on the difficulty of writing about his experience in the camps, Wiesel remarks that "All words seemed inadequate, worn, foolish, lifeless, whereas I wanted them to sear. Where was I to discover a fresh vocabulary, a primeval language?"[11] Similarly, Lawrence Langer remarks that "The universe of dying that was Auschwitz yearns for a language purified of the taint of normality."[12] Wiesel and Langer search for "fresh" words, for "a different approach," for a "purified" language so that a new aesthetic can equal the new form of historical event the Nazi genocide imposed on our history. This sense of aesthetics is thus driven by two factors: a stunned sense that language has failed and a fear of betraying the dead.

In a study of the United States Holocaust Memorial Museum (a site I discuss in chapter 5), Adrian Dannatt observes that "We are now beyond the simple platitude that the Holocaust should not be given physical form or expression. Such icy logic begins to look like 'Good Taste'—a particularly dangerous form of Modernist probity. A building, a poem, song or film . . . is surely always better than the elegant silence of superiority when it comes to dealing with the Holocaust."[13]

Dannatt's argument is opposed by those who find that some narratives are unethical because they *encourage forgetting* by seducing us into the cozy idea that these narratives are sufficient to engender Holocaust memory. Jean-François Lyotard is a representative of the group of scholars whose ideas became prevalent in the late 1980s and early 1990s, and who oppose narrative modes of representation in favor of allusive, oblique, and broken models. Lyotard insists that "It is to be feared that word representations (books, interviews) and thing representations (films, photographs) of the extermination of the Jews and of 'the jews,' by the Nazis bring back the very thing against which they work unceasingly."[14] Similarly, Geoffrey Hartman warns that "popular representations emerge that are uncomfortably close to fantasies that may have played their part in the genocide."[15] Rather than encouraging forgetting through the facile closure promised in some representations, Lyotard and Hartman argue that to avoid forgetting one must always allow the rumble of the past to persist through fragmentation and disruption. With the exception of some of the commemorative sites discussed in chapter 5, most of the works I examine in this book are effective through fragmentation and disruption yet their beauty offers an aesthetic pleasure that encourages us to grapple with the Holocaust. These works embody an argument for representation of the Holocaust and an end to the clamoring for "the elegant silence of superiority."

As a case study of the transformation from a resistance against representing the Holocaust toward an encouragement of representation, consider James Young's self-examination of his change in position from a self-proclaimed "skeptic" of the very project of building a memorial to the murdered Jews of Europe in Berlin (another site that I discuss in chapter 5) to an advocate of the project. As one of the commissioners charged with deciding which model for the memorial would be chosen, Young was immersed in the vociferous debates regarding the aesthetic, pedagogical, ethical, and political functions of the Berlin memorial that absorbed parts of the cultural and public spheres in Germany for over ten years. Young reports that initially, in 1997, when he became involved in the Berlin project, he felt that such a public and high-profile memorial would *encourage forgetting* by becoming a "hermetically sealed vault for the ghosts of Germany's past," thus "finish[ing] memory itself." Eventually, by the time Peter Eisenman and Richard Serra's design—which has finally been built, after overcoming many obstacles—was chosen in 1999, Young supported the project on the grounds that "I began to see how important it would be to add a space to Germany's restored capital deliberately designed to remember the mass murder of Europe's Jews."[16] Thus Young's position changed from the Lyotardian anti-representational form, in which closure supposedly encourages forgetting, to the pro-representational form, in which the visibility of Holocaust imagery creates meaning and therefore opens up a space for memory. Young's transformation perhaps represents the larger cultural shift away from an insistence on the absolute impossibility of Holocaust representation toward recognizing how attempts to represent it, even if flawed, can encourage complex forms of memory work.

With this welcome shift away from the paralysis of silence as the only ethical means of Holocaust representation, we need to examine how the production of Holocaust literature, art, and memorials has created meaning through the unwanted beauty feared in Adorno's original maxim. Asking about the power of unwanted beauty in Holocaust representation in turn opens up questions about the representational strategies available for making sense of the twentieth century, for the turn to unwanted beauty raises the larger question of how aesthetics—and particularly the discussion of beauty—have changed in recent humanities discourse. Adequately tracing the history of aesthetics, and in particular the vagaries of the category of the beautiful, is much beyond the scope of this introduction, yet the following comments situate the argument I make in this book about unwanted beauty in the Holocaust within the deeper question of the place of beauty in the humanities.

While debates over aesthetics and beauty can be found in Plato, Aristotle, Longinus, and a host of other philosophical and literary theorists since them, it was A. G. Baumgarten who first coined the term "aesthetics" in his *Reflections on Poetry* (1735), where he argued that "*things perceived*" are to be known by "the science of perception, or aesthetic."[17] Despite Baumgarten's desire to forge a *science* of aesthetics, the most widely read eighteenth-century treatises on the sublime and the beautiful, by Edmund Burke and Immanuel Kant, are testaments to the difficulty of deciding upon aesthetic judgments in a scientific manner. Indeed, Kant rails against Baumgarten's attempted science of aesthetics in his *Critique of Pure Reason* (1781), where Kant finds that "the abortive attempt made by Baumgarten, that admirable analytic thinker, to bring the critical treatment of the beautiful under rational principles, and so to raise its rules to the rank of a science . . . [is] fruitless."[18] The fruitlessness of this endeavor is manifest in both Burke's and Kant's discussions of the sublime and the beautiful, wherein definitions cannot hold and designations about sublimity and beauty perpetually slip into each other.

In *A Philosophical Enquiry into the Origin of Our Ideas of the Sublime and the Beautiful* (1757), Burke argues that the sublime and the beautiful may be differentiated because the former relates to terror and the latter to love. Burke finds that "whatever is in any sort terrible, or conversant about terrible objects, or operates in a manner analogous to terror, is a source of the *sublime*."[19] Kant was acquainted with Burke's text via a review written by Moses Mendelssohn in 1758, but did not read it in German translation until 1773, ten years after publishing his own treatise on the subject.[20] One of the features that differentiates the Burkian and Kantian sublimes is that for the former, the sublime engenders pain and the beautiful produces pleasure, whereas for Kant, the sublime engenders pleasure through pain.[21] Burke suggests that the sublime can generate a "delightful horror," but he is careful to distance this from pleasure. Both philosophers equate the sublime with more "masculine" attributes, such as greatness of scale, and the beautiful with supposedly more feminine attributes, such as smallness.[22] Because of the association of sublimity with greatness of scale, the sublime is often linked with the monumental; as I discuss in chapter 5, however, what constitutes the monumental can be very hard to determine. In addition to these associations of the sublime with the painful, the masculine, and the monumental, Kant also insists upon the formlessness of the sublime that is in keeping with its magnitude. Kant connects this formlessness with what is most important for this brief discussion of the sublime, namely the sublime's association with the unrepresentable.

Kant's discussions of the sublime and the beautiful in *Observations on the*

Feeling of the Beautiful and the Sublime (1763) and *Critique of Judgment* (1790) are relentlessly subjective, producing not only a great deal of cross-over between the two terms, but a great deal of confusion as well. In the *Observations,* Kant splits the sublime into three categories: "Its [the sublime's] feeling is sometimes accompanied with a certain dread, or melancholy; in some cases merely with quiet wonder; and in still others with a beauty completely pervading a sublime plan. The first I shall call the *terrifying sublime,* the second the *noble,* and the third the *splendid.* Deep loneliness is sublime, but in a way that stirs terror."[23]

Kant goes on to offer examples of the different types of the sublime, yet these illustrations always betray the interconnection between the three types of sublimity as well as between the sublime and the beautiful. Indeed, in the passage above Kant offers an example of the sublime that is pervaded by beauty. As this moment in Kant's *Observations* indicates, the sublime and the beautiful often blur into each other; it is this combined sense of the sublime and the beautiful that I find in the works discussed herein. While one might imagine a neologism that combines the two terms, there is one important distinction between them that seems to hold fast: the sublime is often associated with the unrepresentable whereas the beautiful is not. It is for this reason that I use the term "beauty."

In the third critique, *Critique of Judgment,* Kant famously proclaimed the connection between the sublime and Jewish law, and thereby between the sublime and the unrepresentable: "Perhaps the most sublime passage in the Jewish Law is the commandment: Thou shall not make unto thee any graven image."[24] Many in the legions who have interpreted and been influenced by the Kantian sublime have taken up this link between the sublime and the unrepresentable; curiously though, the opposite of this reading has also emerged, thus allowing a too-ready proclamation that a certain painting or natural object is "sublime."[25] Anselm Kiefer's paintings (which I discuss in chapter 4), for example, are often termed "sublime" even though this word also indicates the unrepresentable—and therefore connotes an entity too great to be contained within the bounds of a mere canvas. For instance, Paul Crowther remarks of Kiefer: "His canvases alluding to the disasters of German history and national identity are very much what we would expect of 'sublime' painting, as are some of his more recent works focusing on mythological or cosmological imagery."[26] Crowther, a careful Kantian scholar, has argued elsewhere that while Kant initially rejects the idea of the sublime in art, an *n*th-hour footnote indicates that he does concede its possibility;

Crowther uses this footnote as a justification for terming certain paintings sublime.[27] As Rachael DeLue pointed out, Kiefer's paintings may be seen as gesturing toward their own impossibility to represent and therefore indeed be considered "sublime" even within the Kantian limits on representation.

Nonetheless, because of the associations of the sublime with the terrifying and the unrepresentable and because art and literature do not need to terrorize in order to deepen our understanding of the Holocaust, I have been forced to employ "beauty" over "sublime" to define the aesthetic pleasure of the works discussed in this book. In other words, I chose beauty over sublime as my central theme because the aesthetics of the sublime align politically with the idea that the Holocaust is too terrible to be represented. But, as the writers and visual artists I examine throughout this text ceaselessly attest, while representing the Holocaust is difficult, associating this event with the sublime, and therefore with the unrepresentable, leads to too great a distanciation, too fearsome a project to try to remember. While the sublime is usually understood as carrying both the emotions of pleasure and of pain, we can also understand that beauty—or at least the complex forms of beauty discussed in this book—can carry both emotions as well. Beauty need not be simple, as it is often assumed to be in contrast to the sublime. Thus, while the sublime silently haunts the pages that follow, I have found beauty a more useful concept as it allows us to approach the Holocaust without feeling the chilly terror of the rigorous impossibility of understanding imposed by the sublime. It is important to hope that we can understand the Holocaust because when it is bracketed off—as it continues to be—as a demonic aberration in Western History, as an unapproachable sublime, then we cannot examine it in order to find out how ordinary people could perform extraordinarily evil acts.[28]

When Kant calls up the second commandment, against graven images, in Jewish law, he refers to a large field of inquiry, namely the place not only of representability in Jewish tradition but also of beauty in Jewish art. Indeed, there is an extensive discussion to be had about the role of beauty in Jewish art (itself a contested term) that I will not have space to address adequately here. Yet I will interject the following from Margaret Olin: "They [avant-garde artists] found the Second Commandment eminently suitable to an art world dominated by expressionism and later abstraction, where a sense of beauty was associated with dry academism."[29] Olin touches here on complex questions about the connections between Jewishness and modernism and Jewishness and the avant-garde, but what is interesting for the purposes of this introduction is that the interdiction against representation, so often evoked in examinations of ethical means of representing the Holocaust, surfaces here along with avant-garde art. Indeed, Robert Rosenblum's famous essay "The Abstract Sublime" made a plea for bridging the gap between eighteenth- and nineteenth-century Romantic paintings—which were often explicitly devoted to evoking the sublime—and the twentieth-century painters who evoked what he termed "the abstract sublime."[30] And it was within the realm of modern art that ideas about beauty began to alter significantly.

While beauty no doubt changed course multiple times in the almost century and a half between Burke/Kant and the First World War, art historians generally agree that the world war years of the last century witnessed a radical change in the place of beauty. As Neal Benezra puts it, during the two world wars "aesthetics and beauty were called to serve a wide range of masters, from utopian idealism on the left, to fascist populism on the right."[31] In the wake of the First World War, sensitive to the inadequate bourgeois banality of art in the face of the terror of the war, artists such as Marcel Duchamp began to cry out against the aestheticism at the root of artistic production. Thus, in 1917 Duchamp entered a urinal, signed by one "R. Mutt" and ironically entitled "Fountain," into the Society of Independent Artists exhibition. His "Fountain" ploy has taken on iconic status because it encapsulates his generation's distaste for the placid norms of bourgeois aesthetic production. Duchamp continued to explore artistic production divorced from aesthetics through his use of ready-mades and found objects. Because these require no "artistic" skill to produce and offer dubious aesthetic appeal, they functioned as a slap in the face to the rapidly commodifying art market, which glorified the artist and his precious signature. Of course, aesthetic judgments are ever changing and what Duchamp and his circle gleefully thought ugly, many contemporary viewers may find beautiful. Nonetheless, Duchamp's playful and mocking anti-aesthetics had wide appeal in the art world and defined one part of modern art through the Second World War and into the 1980s.

After the Second World War, and with the echo in mind of Walter Benjamin's famous 1936 claim that "all efforts to render politics aesthetic culminate in one thing: war," the fear of aesthetics derived as much from the Duchampian distaste for bourgeois banality as from a fear of the disastrous outcome of the aesthetification of politics that found its apogee in the Hitler regime.[32] Adorno's maxim against poetry after Auschwitz can be seen as a combination of Duchampian disapproval of the commodification of art and Benjamin's argument that the aesthetification of politics characterizes fascism. The artist Barnett Newman captured this postwar view of art in the December 1948 issue of *Tiger's Eye,* where he declared that "the impulse of modern art was this desire to destroy beauty."[33] As Benezra argues, Newman's approach to aesthetics was echoed in 1963 by Robert Morris's *Statement of Aesthetic Withdrawal,* and can be seen in the 1980s anti-aesthetics of artists such as Mike Kelley and Barbara Kruger.[34] This trend against beauty may be said to culminate in Hal Foster's important 1983 collection, *The Anti-Aesthetic.*[35] In short, artists and the critics who followed their work argued that traditional aesthetic concerns with beauty had become irredeemably banal and that it was therefore imperative to adopt an anti-aesthetic, an aesthetic devoid of beauty, in order to produce progressive art.

This aversion to aesthetics has begun to soften in the last ten years, and in explaining how outré beauty had been, scholars first note its debasement. For example, Alexander Nehamas, in heralding the return of the beautiful, claims that "Beauty is the most discredited philosophical notion"; and Craig Lambert notes that "beauty has been in exile."[36] Of course, the notion that beauty had ever entirely disappeared as part of humanities discourse is contestable, yet its reinvigoration nonetheless seems clear. The return to beauty can be neatly summarized by the art critic Peter Schjeldahl's phrase "Beauty is back." This sentiment has been echoed in such statements as Lambert's "beauty is rearing its beautiful head," Dennis Donoghue's "the word 'aesthetic' is no longer a term of abuse and contempt," or Liliane Weissberg's "there is, no doubt, a new obsession with beauty."[37] The refrain that "beauty is back" justifiably reverberates throughout the popular and art presses and scholarly books devoted to exploring beauty in new forms.[38] Indeed, since the mid-1990s a host of books have addressed this resurgence of beauty from different ideological positions. While these works do not form a single, unified theory of aesthetics, they do all recognize beauty's growing importance. In *The Scandal of Pleasure,* for instance, Wendy Steiner makes a plea for enjoying the pleasures of aesthetics:

> What we need is a situation in which art and the life of the mind can be enjoyed with a knowing pleasure, one that thrills to every richness art can offer, yet does not shrink from the issues art can raise. The greatest artists of the moment are undermining the dire rigors of recent criticism and the fundamentalism and literalism of extremists. It is time for the rest of us to join them—to acknowledge both the power and the pleasure of art, aware at the same time that it is still art and not something else.[39]

Steiner insists that art should not be confused with other phenomena such as politics so that, while art does not exist in an independent realm, we might imbibe its possible, even if complicated and ambivalent, pleasures without mistaking these sensations for breaches of ethical or moral norms. In discussing the term "pleasure" in this context Steiner touches upon the distinction I outlined in brief above between a sublime that encapsulates pleasure and pain and a beauty that is often thought to be limited to pleasure. By enjoining us to enjoy the pleasures of art, Steiner invites us to make a productive connection between beauty and pleasure.

In another text that welcomes the return of beauty, *On Beauty and Being Just,* Elaine Scarry corroborates Steiner's sense that the pleasures of art can expand horizons. Scarry's argument is helpful in understanding how beautiful works that treat the Holocaust can be pedagogically useful, for she argues that "beauty is a starting place for education."[40] Ernst van Alphen makes Scarry's claim concrete in the context of the Holocaust when he explains in the introduction to *Caught by History* that the endless documentaries and historical sources that he was made to imbibe as a Dutch schoolchild could not interest him in the Holocaust in the powerful way that Holocaust art encouraged him to reflect on the catastrophe. Van Alphen finds that "it was imaginative representations of the Holocaust that hooked me."[41] Similarly, one of the characters in Jorge Semprun's remarkable narrative about surviving Buchenwald, *Literature or Life,* is convinced, right after the war, that through historical accounts "la vérité essentielle de l'expérience, n'est pas transmissible" (won't contain the essential truth), and that only "par l'artifice de l'œuvre d'art" (through the artifice of a work of art) will this truth of the horror of the camps be conveyed.[42]

While the sensation of being "hooked" by the unwanted beauty of Holocaust art (whether literary, visual, or sculptural) has generated this book, I should add that the beautiful works I discuss herein are not simply part and parcel of an unreconstructed return to an idealized version of beauty. What these works negotiate can be summed up in Craig Owens's articulation of art beyond modernism: "appropriation, site-specificity, impermanence, accumulation, discursivity, hybridization."[43] The complex works that *Unwanted Beauty* examines therefore do not offer themselves to simple aesthetic evaluations; rather, their beauty evolves through the slow unraveling of their surprising, often disturbing revelations into the worst experiences.

Unwanted Beauty analyzes how aesthetic pleasure provided survival mechanisms in the concentration camps (chapters 1 and 2), how it enabled a poet to explore the Holocaust's haunting of what Marianne Hirsch terms "postmemories" (chapter 3), and how aesthetic pleasure allows postwar visual artists (chapter 4) and architects and sculptors (chapter 5) to bring the Holocaust to the forefront of our cultural consciousness.[44] While the case studies presented in this book are not organized strictly chronologically, they imply a historically inflected narrative. Moving from survivor accounts shaped by experiences immediately after the war (chapter 1), to a survivor account written two decades later (chapter 2), to a poet who was not directly involved in the Holocaust and who wrote from the 1960s to 1991 (chapter 3), to artists working in the 1980s and 1990s (chapter 4), to architects working in the late 1990s and first decade of the new millennium (chapter 5), *Unwanted Beauty* demonstrates how aesthetic pleasure has itself been transformed from its earlier use as a survival mechanism into its later use as a means of catalyzing Holocaust memory.

There are of course many interesting writers and artists who I have had to leave out of this study, not least the visual artists who produced sketches and paintings from within the camps. Some of their fascinating works were on view at the Brooklyn Academy of Art in 2003 and they offered an incredible range of art made under the worst conditions.[45] I chose the work of the Jewish, half-Jewish, and non-Jewish survivors, novelists, poets, artists, and architects addressed herein from a vast body of global Holocaust representations because these texts all speak powerfully to the central questions of this book. I have chosen works from different genres—testimony, novels, poetry, visual arts, and architecture—in order to open up the initially literary treatments of Holocaust writing to larger questions of cultural production. Moreover, many of the writers and artists I have chosen to study live hyphenated, diasporic lives that bear witness to the cosmopolitan politics of Holocaust memory.

The first chapter, "Aesthetic Survival: Paul Celan, Charlotte Delbo, and 'Living Next to Auschwitz,'" serves as an introduction to the central debates over Holocaust representation. I analyze "Todesfuge," the influential and controversial poem by the Bukovinian/Romanian Jewish survivor, Paul Celan, and explore the poem's intimate connection to Adorno's famous maxim against poetry after Auschwitz. I then focus on the work of a member of the

French resistance and a concentration camp survivor, Charlotte Delbo. Her literary testimonies read like strange love stories because she has infused them with beautiful images that help her come to terms with the troubling persistence of Auschwitz in her life. Because Delbo's theories of memory evoke Proust, I use Proust's examination of modes of voluntary and involuntary memory to reflect upon the vagaries of Holocaust memory. This chapter demonstrates that the act of representing the Shoah is haunted by a schism: these works are aesthetically pleasing, yet critics seem to argue that such texts should eschew the sensual and the beautiful in order to be truer to the experience of the Holocaust. I refuse this dichotomy and argue that the beauty of this literature actually allows it to convey the complexity of survivors' experiences of trauma. This chapter thus introduces the book's central theme of the transforming power of aesthetic pleasure in Holocaust memory while focusing in particular on beauty as a survival mechanism.

In the second chapter, "Aesthetic Memory: Jorge Semprun and 'The Bitter Residue of Death,'" I analyze *Le grand voyage* (1963), one of the literary testimonies of the Spanish/French resistance fighter and survivor, Jorge Semprun. His narrator relies upon the aesthetic pleasure offered by memories of Proust's *À la recherche du temps perdu* to transform the narrative of his horrible journey to Buchenwald into a reflection on memory itself. This chapter thus extends my discussion of Proustian modes of memory and how they contribute to understanding some Holocaust literature. Furthermore, I demonstrate how Semprun seeks comfort in aesthetic pleasure in order first to survive the concentration camps, then to come to terms with his painful memories of them, and ultimately to rewrite his experiences of the Holocaust as a literary meditation on the brutality of history. Because he demonstrates the concrete effects of the transformative power of beautiful memories, Semprun's narrative offers a template both for how aesthetic pleasure functions as a survival mechanism and how it enables successive generations of Holocaust rememberers to come to terms with survivors' traumatic experiences.

The third chapter, "Aesthetic Allusion: Edmond Jabès, 'The Page Is a Charred Field Where the Dead Would Have Written,'" examines the elliptical poetry of the Egyptian/French Jewish poet, Edmond Jabès. His poetry demonstrates that we bear an ethical, aesthetic, and historical imperative to try to grapple with the question of how the Holocaust has become embedded in Western consciousness. Indeed, by avoiding direct and clear Holocaust representations, Jabès forces his readers to recognize their own investments in the nuanced process of memory; he tempts readers to find the Holocaust for themselves in his aesthetic allusions. Jabès's extension of the problem of how beauty functions in works on the Holocaust takes a different turn than the survivors considered in chapters 1 and 2, because whereas in Delbo's and Semprun's work beauty in "the worst" functioned as a survival mechanism, in Jabès's poems beautiful and shadowy allusions to the Holocaust are layered within other concerns that the poet shares with postmodernists who wonder about the word's ability to signify, the situation of God, and the possibility of reconciliation. Jabès's meditations on the Holocaust share with some of the postwar generation the sensation that the Shoah asserts itself in the shadow of each word or image. Indeed, by forcing us to question our own desire to find the Holocaust in allusive references, and by meditating on how the Holocaust dwells within those who did not experience it directly, Jabès demonstrates the transformative power of inherited memories of the Shoah.

In the fourth chapter, "Aesthetic Mourning: Anselm Kiefer, Christian Boltanski, and 'Light Pulsing through Ash,'" I turn to two contemporary visual artists who offer fascinating cases of the aesthetic transformation of the Holocaust in postwar German and French art. By examining the role of visual pleasure in Kiefer's and Boltanski's Holocaust art (as opposed to the writerly pleasures to be found in Celan, Delbo, Semprun, and Jabès), I find that aesthetic pleasure deepens yet also complicates Holocaust memory in postmodern art. Indeed, while much of their art is arguably pleasurable, Kiefer's and Boltanski's works make many viewers uncomfortable. Kiefer's images disturb because they often blur the boundary between depiction and critique of Nazism and the German mythological sources that undergirded it. Because Kiefer projects a desire to mourn a lost Reich in the same breath as the loss of its citizens (and many others) in the Nazi genocide, his work exemplifies an uncomfortable cohabitation between victim and perpetrator. Boltanski's images disturb because he collapses specific historical losses into transhistorical traumas. Because Boltanski's photo-sculptures simultaneously expand the role of the individual survivor and efface his or her individuality, because he therefore invites us to mourn loss in general and not necessarily losses in the Holocaust, his work exemplifies the postmodern tendency toward cryptic historical references that are meaningful in an emotional rather than political or historical manner. Kiefer and Boltanski thus offer nuanced reflections on the Holocaust that challenge their audiences to grapple with the effects of the beautiful in transforming second- and third-generation Holocaust memory.

In the fifth chapter, "Aesthetic Pollution: Peter Eisenman, Jochen Gerz and

Esther Shalev-Gerz, James Ingo Freed, and 'Nazi Contamination,'" I examine the problem aesthetic pleasure poses for memorial spaces. I argue that in order to have a transformative effect, Holocaust memory-production needs to feel free to use whatever aesthetic forms will be productive and to do so without associating monumental aesthetics with fascism. This chapter develops my concept of "aesthetic pollution," or the fear that some contemporary artistic forms have been tainted by fascist aesthetics. I then discuss the political, ethical, and historical implications of aesthetic pollution in the creation of three commemorative spaces dedicated to the Holocaust. Peter Eisenman and Richard Serra's Memorial to the Murdered Jews of Europe (which opened in 2005 in Berlin), Jochen Gerz and Esther Shalev-Gerz's Monument against Fascism (Harburg-Hamburg), and James Ingo Freed's United States Holocaust Memorial Museum (Washington, D.C.) demonstrate how the fear of aesthetic pollution haunts many artists attempting to represent the Nazi genocide. In short, by examining aesthetic pollution I demonstrate how postwar memory production is transformed by the fear that unwanted beauty somehow relies on fascist aesthetics.

Taken as a whole, my treatment of the simultaneity of past pain and present pleasure in the authors, designers, and visual artists considered herein will provide lessons applicable beyond the Shoah and thus speak to theoretical questions that beset the full spectrum of historical circumstances where violence, memory, trauma, and aesthetics intersect.

Chapter 1

AESTHETIC SURVIVAL:
PAUL CELAN, CHARLOTTE DELBO, AND
"LIVING NEXT TO AUSCHWITZ"

When I would recite a poem, when I would tell the
comrades beside me what a novel or a play was about
while we went on digging in the muck of the swamp, it was
to keep myself alive, to preserve my memory, to remain
me, to make sure of it. —Charlotte Delbo

During a commemoration for French victims of Nazism in the 1950s, Charlotte Delbo, a member of the French resistance and Auschwitz survivor, was
sitting in the audience when her name was called out among the dead.[1]
Having always maintained a distinction between her Auschwitz self and her
post-Auschwitz self, the announcement seemed at first correct: she had died
there and then while surviving to live here and now. Because the pronounce-
ment of her death was thus curiously true and not true at the same time,
Delbo's experience indicates how survival often means living in multiple
times and places, returning from the camps mute yet full of words that beg
to be spoken. Delbo chose to speak the words needed to tell the story of her
incarceration by creating beautiful literary testimonies that combine drama,
prose, and poetry into reflections on her painful past and the struggle to
represent those experiences to those of us who did not live through the
horror of the camps. She thus offers us both descriptions of the past and
theories of memory that illuminate how that past continues to live next to
and in survivors.

Twenty-five years after the close of World War II, Paul Celan, a Jewish
poet from Bukovinia/Romania and work camp survivor, took his own life.
While the reasons for his suicide remain his alone, it seems that the war
continued to live next to and in Celan to an unbearable degree. Despite a
life dedicated to producing beautiful poems—many of which allude to the
Holocaust—Celan found that even his own aesthetic production could not

sustain him. Nonetheless, his work attests to the power of the aesthetic in surviving the worst and it has offered those of us who are "nonwitnesses" (to borrow Gary Weissman's phrase) insight into the experience of the Holocaust.[2] As Jorge Semprun, a witness and survivor whose work I discuss in the next chapter, remarks about Celan, "Je suis toujours tombé, au moment opportun, sur l'œuvre poétique qui pouvait m'aider à vivre, à me faire avancer dans l'acuité de ma conscience du monde. Ainsi de . . . Paul Celan" (*L'écriture ou la vie,* 219) (I inevitably find a poetic work that can help me to live, to sharpen my consciousness of the world. That's what happened with . . . Paul Celan, 166).

Although from very different positions, one Jewish and one not, Celan and Delbo share an abiding concern with the process of conveying terrible experiences and a commitment to providing readers with beautiful accounts of the worst. Indeed, because both writers embrace the use of metaphor and moving imagery to challenge us to understand the complexity of their experiences and their memorial processes, Celan's and Delbo's works exemplify the problem of how to make sense of the unwanted beauty of some Holocaust literature.

To grapple with the interpretive, historical, and ethical challenges offered by Celan and Delbo, this chapter begins by revisiting Theodor Adorno's interdiction regarding poetry after Auschwitz and its relationship to criticisms of Celan's allegedly too-beautiful poetry. Because it is one of the earliest and most renowned examples of a piece of Holocaust literature that has been both praised and acerbically dismissed for its beauty, I then analyze Celan's poem "Todesfuge" ("Death Fugue," 1944). Building upon my analysis of Adorno and Celan, I then discuss Delbo's literary testimony, *La mémoire et les jours* (1985), and trace her division of memory into Proustian intellectual and sense modes, which in turn oblige me to address Proust's philosophy of memory as articulated in *À la recherche du temps perdu.* Because Celan's and Delbo's works exhibit a bittersweet melancholic energy that often seems to act as salvation rather than sacrilege, they offer us examples of how aesthetic pleasure functioned as a survival mechanism in the camps and then how, after the war, it helped them come to terms, at least temporarily, with their traumatic experiences by creating beautiful literature. I therefore argue that the unwanted beauty in these works is precisely what provokes us to engage with them in order to deepen the search for Holocaust understanding.

No one, Georges Perec remarks, investigates "la littérature concentrationnaire" as literature, but rather in terms of how closely it reaches the imagined "it" of *le pire* ("the worst," a word that is often used as a shorthand for the experience of the Holocaust).[3] This unease with reading survivor accounts as art, and conversely with appreciating the art (and therefore sometimes the beauty) in Holocaust testimony, stems from the unease that leads critics and theorists to return ceaselessly to Adorno's statement in "Cultural Criticism and Society" (1949) that "To write poetry after Auschwitz is barbaric."[4] This return continues despite Adorno's own modification of his original claim and despite rejections of it by many poets and artists who have produced a prodigious amount of Holocaust art and literature. Adorno's haunting of attempts to represent the Holocaust hails from a sense of guilt about beauty, as though anyone who injects the beautiful into the funerary commits sacrilege. In "Commitment" (1962) Adorno specified that the fear of poetry after Auschwitz has to do with the possibility of pleasure in Holocaust representation: "The so-called artistic rendering of the naked physical pain of those who were beaten down with rifle butts contains, however distantly, the possibility that pleasure can be squeezed from it."[5] This statement gets to the heart of the nexus of beauty and pleasure that this book examines; for while I agree with Adorno that there is something ethically wrong with finding pleasure in representations of the pain of others, the works I examine here offer pleasure that derives not from the pain of others but from the complexity of artistic representations that invite us to think critically about the Nazi genocide. Thus, whereas Adorno feared crass exploitation of the Holocaust by a callous culture industry, I celebrate the tenacity of survivors and others who write movingly, and indeed beautifully, about the worst experiences.

Even though Adorno claimed in "Commitment" that he did "not want to soften [his] statement that it is barbaric to continue to write poetry after Auschwitz," he qualified his original ban on poetry after Auschwitz when, in *Negative Dialectics* (1966), he admitted that "Perennial suffering has as much right to expression as a tortured man has to scream, hence it may have been wrong to say that after Auschwitz you could no longer write poems." Yet he diminishes this modification of his earlier claim by continuing, "But it is not wrong to ask the less cultural question whether after Auschwitz you can go on living."[6] The qualification of the site of the interdiction from the specific aesthetic act of "poetry" to the sweeping existential act of "living" simultaneously allows poetry to be beautiful while extending a new question to all poets and non-poets alike. Adorno proceeds to explain the impossibility of living by linking survival with the need for the same mechanism that allowed the concentration camps to happen in the first place: "survival calls for the coldness, the basic principle of bourgeois subjectivity, without which there could have been no Auschwitz; this is the drastic guilt of him who was spared."[7] In Adorno's formulation, then, survival requires the coldness engendered by the isolation of bourgeois subjectivity, so that living itself necessarily means being riveted to the cultural norms that enabled the machinery of death. For Adorno, then, the same coldness and sterility of bourgeois subjectivity that allows one to rationalize the death camps out of sight enables postwar survival. Because poetry offers the possibility of breaking through the coldness of the contemporary world, thus allowing one to "see" or "understand" at a historical moment when seeing would blind one with inexplicable conundrums, living, in Adorno's compromised sense, requires an absence of poetry. But Adorno's sweeping condemnation of "bourgeois subjectivity" paints with too broad a brush and does not treat the specificity of historical actors who created the Final Solution. Clearly, not all "principles of bourgeois subjectivity" lead to Auschwitz, and those who survived the camps did not do so by retreating into bourgeois isolation.

Despite both Adorno's change of heart and the over-zealous breadth with which he condemns all of the mechanisms that created the conditions of possibility for the Holocaust, the idea that there is something deeply unethical in poetry (and therefore beauty) in Holocaust representation took hold. Paul Celan is very often cited in the same space as Adorno's complaint against poetry after Auschwitz because his most famous (and also most lambasted) poem, "Todesfuge," offers a beautiful meditation on the horror of the Shoah that seems to fly in the face of Adorno's original maxim. Indeed, there is some speculation that "Todesfuge" initially gave rise to Adorno's maxim precisely because of its incredible beauty; there is also contradictory speculation that this same poem encouraged Adorno to soften his original statement from "Cultural Criticism" in *Negative Dialectics.* For example, Lisa Saltzman remarks that Celan's "work is somewhat paradoxically considered at once the catalyst for and aesthetic fulfillment of Adorno's proscription"; Amy Colin argues that "Under the impact of Celan's poetry, Adorno, in *Negative Dialectics,* was moved" to alter his original claim; whereas Sidra Dekoven Ezrahi claims that Adorno's statement was "originally occasioned by a reading of Celan's 'Todesfuge'"; and Ulrich Baer reports that "Celan had been troubled by Adorno's negative verdict on the possibility of poetry after Auschwitz."[8] Thus, Adorno's maxim is powerfully, if paradoxically, linked with Celan, and Celan's poetry has thus been criticized as being "too metaphorical" or "too beautiful to confront history's greatest catastrophe."[9] This unbalance between aesthetics and history, where the "too beautiful" means that literature or art cannot be true to historical catastrophe, encapsulates the perceived problem of beautiful Holocaust representations without answering the claim that perhaps the beauty of Celan's poem allows historical consciousness to unfold.

Celan's "Todesfuge" has captured the imagination of artists, theorists, survivors, non-survivors, and others because its lyrical, musical, rhythmic structure struggles to convey horror and beauty in the same breath.[10] Before turning to "Todesfuge" I offer a brief record of Celan's life that illuminates the experiences that enabled him to write this remarkable poem. While many of the details of Celan's whereabouts during the war remain unclear, Celan scholars generally agree on the following biography: Paul Antschel was born in 1920 in Czernowitz, Romania (Bukovina before 1918), the only child of a "stern and uncultured father" and a much-beloved "refined and literate" mother.[11] Antschel adopted the name "Celan" (an anagram of the Romanian spelling of his surname, "Ancel") in 1947 when "Todesfuge" was first published in Romanian translation.[12] His family contributed to and participated in the flowering of assimilated, Germanophile Jewry in Czernowitz that flourished under the "tranquil days of the Hapsburg monarchy," when Czernowitz was known as "Little Vienna."[13] Before and after the war Celan bore a deep attachment to German, which was in keeping with the Jewish-Bukovinian focus on Vienna as the idealized center of culture and refinement.[14] Aharon Appelfeld wrote a moving description of his return to his glorified city of Czernowitz, and its neighboring village Drajinetz, where he lived until he was forced to flee at age eight. Appelfeld remembered that "German was insisted upon, as though it embodied everything good and beautiful."[15] The irony of course, is that the language that embodied the good and the beautiful should come, after the war, to signify the evil and the ugly. Yet, in spite of this irony, and in an often uncomfortable manner, Celan continued to insist upon German as his poetic language.

In 1940 the Soviet Union's occupation of Romania was met by Celan and his circle with muted approbation, as they had been sympathetic to Trotskyism, but in 1941 Germany occupied Romania and ghettoized all Jews.[16] In

1942 Celan's parents were deported from the Czernowitz ghetto to the camps in Transnistria, where his father died of typhus and his mother was shot.[17] Celan scholars differ on the mood in which Celan parted from his parents, and therefore on the burden of guilt he bore for their death. Amy Colin and Israel Chalfen claim that Celan begged his parents to leave with him and to go into hiding, but they refused.[18] According to John Simon, Celan left home "in a huff" the very weekend that his parents were deported; had he been there, Celan would presumably have been deported with them.[19] Simon thus reports that Celan shouldered lifelong guilt for having neither perished with nor saved his parents. Apparently Celan was deeply affected after the war by hearing the story of another Jewish survivor who had managed to save his mother. While I do not want to conflate biography with literary criticism, I cannot help wondering how the different versions of this story play out in Celan's poetry. Is the pain of memory so often described in his work an allusion to the painful experiences of the war or to the guilt of not having saved his beloved mother, or perhaps to both at once?

While his parents were in Transnistria, Celan was interned in a Romanian labor camp, where he shoveled stones and built roads and camps in horrible conditions until 1944, when Czernowitz was again taken over by Soviet forces. As Chalfen explains, this Soviet invasion had a very different tone than the first, as any remaining citizens were seen by the occupiers as collaborators with the fascists, even if they were Jewish.[20] After liberation Celan lived in Bucharest for about two years, where he enjoyed a career as a Russian-Romanian translator before finally making his way to his beloved Vienna. But postwar Vienna was a bitter disappointment to him and he soon returned to France (where he had spent a year as a medical student in Tours in 1938) to settle in Paris in 1948. In Paris he translated poems from a multitude of languages including Russian, French, and English; taught German at the Ecole normale supérieure; and developed an important and ongoing correspondence with the survivor and poet Nelly Sachs, who was living in Sweden.[21] Celan married Gisèle de Lestrange (a "member of an aristocratic French Catholic family that intensely disapproved of her marriage to a Jewish refugee") and had a son.[22] Thus, like so many Holocaust survivors, Celan's formative experiences were of exile and displacement, the death of his parents, and an ongoing struggle with the use of his native tongue to write poems in order to continue to survive and come to terms with his painful past.

On or near April 20, 1970, Celan committed suicide by jumping into the Seine. As is the case with many writer-survivors who lived long postwar lives only to end them at their own hands, one cannot help wondering about the connection between their art and their final decisions. Indeed, in attempting to commemorate the war, Celan remained ambivalent and skeptical as to the very nature of the poetic project that absorbed him.[23] In a conversation with Daniel Boyarin about the relationship between Adorno and Celan, Boyarin pointed out to me that as Adorno had claimed abstractly, Celan found that one could not concretely go on living after Auschwitz.[24] No one knows what led Celan to his final decision, but he had been treated occasionally for depression, had been hyper-sensitive to criticism of his work, and, despite literary accolades, remained paranoid that "prizes, publications, invitations to read or lecture had to do with attempts by Germany to assuage its bad conscience rather than with genuine recognition of his work."[25]

After his death, and perhaps partly because he had been acquainted with Jacques Derrida, Celan became, along with Edmond Jabès (whose work I discuss in chapter 3 and whom Celan read and knew in Paris), one of the poets most analyzed by French high theorists such as Derrida and Philippe Lacoue-Labarthe. Celan's concern with the machinations of language, along with his interest in Heidegger, whom Celan famously visited at the philosopher's home in the Black Forest in 1967, also attracted the French theorists to him.[26] As is by now well known, Heidegger had been a member of the Nazi party and had remained silent about his fascist involvement and reticent about his published comments on Nazism. Celan's visit to the German philosopher has thus echoed in critical discussions of his work because, as Françoise Meltzer aptly puts it, there is something "disturbing" in the meeting between these two figures.[27] Celan desperately needed Heidegger to explain himself and thus to offer a justification for his own profound interest in this philosopher; Heidegger failed to answer Celan's questions, leaving his complicated relationship both to Heidegger and to German intact. Because German is his ("guilty") language of choice, Celan's difficult relationship to this tongue resonates with his ambivalence about the possibility of poetically expressing the Holocaust; these ambivalences did not stop him from creating a body of work that often uses—to great effect—this catastrophe as its source.

According to John Felstiner, "Todesfuge," Celan's most well-known Holocaust poem, was most likely composed in 1944. It was first published in 1948 in the limited-edition collection *Der Sand aus den Urnen,* accompanied by an illustration commissioned by Celan by Edgar Jené; "Todesfuge" was then reprinted in Celan's celebrated collection of poems, *Mohn und Gedächtnis,* in 1952, and it has subsequently been reprinted in numerous collections.[28]

Celan has often been criticized for the beauty of this poem, yet Paul Auster argues that the "terrible beauty" of "Todesfuge" was a "means of survival."[29] Echoing my thesis about unwanted beauty, Auster's claim that this particular beauty could aid survival explains how the grim scene of the poem can be ethically rendered beautiful. The historical context for "Todesfuge" is the Nazi regime's use of music in the concentration camps, where death tangos were sometimes played by prisoners to accompany the murder of their fellow inmates before the musicians themselves were killed. The historical moment of the poem thus offers a horrifying example of the Nazis' use of aesthetics alongside violence. Citing the poem in full demonstrates both its beauty and how it offers a powerful description of the emotional and cultural complexity of witnessing death. I divide the poem into its four stanzas, pausing to comment after each one; I cite first the original and then Michael Hamburger's translation:

Schwarze Milch der Frühe wir trinken sie abends
Black milk of daybreak we drink it at sundown
wir trinken sie mittags und morgens wir trinken sie nachts
we drink it at noon in the morning we drink it at night
wir trinken und trinken
we drink and we drink it
wir schaufeln ein Grab in den Lüften da liegt man nicht eng
we dig a grave in the breezes there one lies unconfined
Ein Mann wohnt im Haus der spielt mit den Schlangen der schreibt
A man lives in the house he plays with the serpents he writes
der schreibt wenn es dunkelt nach Deutschland dein goldenes Haar
    Margarete
he writes when dusk falls to Germany your golden hair Margarete
er schreibt es und tritt vor das Haus und es blitzen die Sterne
    er pfeift seine Rüden herbei
he writes it and steps out of doors and the stars are flashing he whistles
    his pack out
er pfeift seine Juden hervor läßt schaufeln ein Grab in der Erde
he whistles his Jews out in earth has them dig for a grave
er befiehlt uns spielt auf nun zum Tanz
he commands us strike up for the dance[30]

The central metaphor of "black milk" has many valences. First, Celan replaces the whiteness of milk with its opposing image of blackness, thus implying that in this setting the order of things is reversed. The milk purported to be the milk of daybreak—of lightness, and even purity—is rather drunk in the evening, and, in the next two stanzas, this dark image will darken yet more when evening is replaced by night. Secondly, thirst (as I discuss in the section on Charlotte Delbo that follows) is naturally a recurring theme in Holocaust writing and thus it is ironic that the "we" in this poem—the Jews who the master commands to play and drink—are inundated with liquid, even if it is a dank substance that cannot sustain them. Thirdly, black milk represents the sourness, bitterness, and rot of the memories of the camps that survivors must drink morning, noon, and night.[31] Fourthly, this black milk can be seen as the German milk that had reared such assimilated families as Celan's, yet its blackness indicates that the milk that the "we" of the poem had suckled has been corrupted by its connection with the worst of German history. These interpretations of the metaphor of black milk are doubtless only four of its many possible readings, yet taken together these suggestions indicate that Celan struggles with the difficulty of memory and the complicated location of Germanophile Jewry vis-à-vis remembrance and recorded experience.

Indeed, Celan was simultaneously determined to continue writing in German (as a polyglot, a range of languages were equally available to him) and anxious about the implications of using German after the war. In German the movement from the fourth line, in which the inmates dig a grave in the air (or breeze, as Hamburger has it) and the fifth line, in which Celan introduces the figure of the unnamed master from Germany, echoes more closely than in translation. This echo is underscored because the generic "man" is aurally replicated by the specific "Mann," whereas in English Hamburger renders the first "one" and the second "man." In the original there is also a strong alliteration between spielt/Schlangen/schreibt that is necessarily lost when these words are translated as playing, serpents, and writing. Nonetheless, the poem in either language moves from victim to perpetrator very quickly: first a "we" must dig graves that the same "we" will eventually lie in and then a man, who echoes with the "we," commands this digging. While the Jews dig, the master writes and calls out orders; Celan thus invites us to meditate on the complex interplay between victim and perpetrator, and on the simultaneity of the movements of both. Both the actions of the digging and the ordering are carried out under the flashing stars ("blitzen die Sterne") where the "blitz" recalls both the sparkling beauty of the stars, which the master fails to see in the midst of his crude commands, and the blitzkriegs that had earlier been used by the

German army to great effect—even though the war was clearly not going well for them by 1944 when Celan wrote this poem.

In this first stanza, as with the alteration between the actions of the victim and those of the perpetrator, Celan switches between a grave dug in the sky and one dug in the earth. In the first iteration, the dead might gently lie in the clouds in the form of ash. The liberation suggested by the words "nicht eng" (unconfined) also sweetens death, as it is seen here as an end to the trauma of the concentration camp universe. But this sense of the release of not being confined comes to a crashing halt when Celan introduces the second grave, which the master commands the Jews to dig. In the penultimate line of this first stanza, the perspective shifts again from the master whistling to an "us" who receives the command. The order to dig is issued following a whistle, a form of music, and the digging will be accompanied by an orchestration, the "death fugue" of the title. Here the playing of the orchestra echoes the playing of the master as he writes; once again Celan knits the victim and perpetrator closely together while maintaining their respective guilt and innocence. As the poem progresses, the terms introduced in the first stanza are artfully merged, thus further intensifying the complexity of the text.

The second stanza again begins with "black milk," but here we drink the milk at night rather than sundown ("nachts" replaces "abends"):

Schwarze Milch der Frühe wir trinken dich nachts
Black milk of daybreak we drink you at night
wir trinken dich morgens und mittags wir drinken dich abends
we drink in the morning at noon we drink you at sundown
wir trinken und trinken
we drink and we drink you
Ein Mann wohnt im Haus der spielt mit den Schlangen der schreibt
A man lives in the house he plays with the serpents he writes
der schreibt wenn es dunkelt nach Deutschland dein goldenes Haar
    Margarete
he writes when dusk falls to Germany your golden hair Margarete
Dein aschenes Haar Sulamith wir schaufeln ein Grab in den
    Lüften da liegt man nicht eng
your ashen hair Shulamith we dig a grave in the breezes there one lies
    unconfined.
Er ruft stecht tiefer ins Erdreich ihr einen ihr andern singet und spielt
He calls out jab deeper into the earth you lot you others sing now and play

er greift nach dem Eisen im Gurt er schwingts seine Augen sind blau
he grabs at the iron in his belt he waves it his eyes are blue
stecht tiefer die Spaten ihr einen ihr andern spielt weiter zum Tanz auf
jab deeper you lot with your spades you others play on for the dance

In this second stanza the figure of Margarete, who had been introduced in the first stanza, is now juxtaposed with her Jewish counterpart, Sulamith. Celan's use of these two women, Sulamith from the Song of Songs (7:1), the most sensual part of the Hebrew Bible, and Margarete, the ruined woman from Goethe's *Faust,* contributes to the strange sensuality of the poem while further exploring the relationship between victim and perpetrator. As testament to the poet's love of Goethe, Chalfen reports that Celan received with "great joy" a beautiful edition of *Faust* on the day of his Bar Mitzvah.[32] In "Todesfuge" this figure from *Faust* takes on the iconic status of German womanhood; her blond hair survives, whereas Sulamith, the iconic Jewish woman, has black hair that turns to ash from the crematoria in the concentration camps. As I discuss in chapter 4, the German artist Anselm Kiefer created paintings dedicated to the two women in Celan's poem in the 1980s; but in Kiefer's rewriting the associations of Jewishness with Sulamith and Germanness with Margarete are reversed, thus confusing victim and perpetrator. Perhaps Celan invites this confusion through the close juxtaposition of the two sides of this war, yet Celan keeps these two figures distinct, whereas Kiefer blurs the associations properly accorded to Sulamith and Margarete. Even if Celan's oft-noted adoration of German culture surfaces in the choice of Margarete to be placed next to the sensual Jewish woman as embodied in Sulamith, this does not mean that a reversal such as Kiefer's is justified in the poem itself. I do not want to reproduce the argument in chapter 4 on Kiefer's use of Celan's poem, but I mention it here because Kiefer's interpretation contributes to the sense that the poem offers multivalent meanings that have been understood and echoed in diverse ways.

As had the first stanza, the second stanza also ends with "dance," yet the dance is intensified here, much as a piece of orchestral music might grow in intensity as it progresses. The master, now a blue-eyed master, commands that the digging of the grave be deeper (*tiefer*) thus allowing Celan to play with the multiple meaning of "deep" as at once a literal deepening of the grave and as a deepening or intensification of the intoxicating mix of music and death that gives the poem its sickly yet heady feel. The opening of the third stanza echoes the opening of the second stanza but there is a slight variation in the second line regarding the time of day that the milk is drunk:

Schwarze Milch der Frühe wir trinken dich nachts
Black milk of daybreak we drink you at night
wir trinken dich mittags und morgens wir trinken dich abends
we drink you at noon in the morning we drink you at sundown
wir trinken und trinken
we drink you and we drink you
ein Mann wohnt im Haus dein goldenes Haar Margarete
a man lives in the house your golden hair Margarete
dein aschenes Haar Sulamith er spielt mit den Schlangen
your ashen hair Shulamith he plays with the serpents
Er ruft spielt süßer den Tod der Tod ist ein Meister aus Deutschland
He calls out more sweetly play death is a master from Germany
er ruft streicht dunkler die Geigen dann steigt ihr als Rauch in die Luft
he calls out more darkly now stroke your strings then as smoke you will
    rise into air
dann habt ihr ein Grab in den Wolken da liegt man nicht eng
then a grave you will have in the clouds there one lies unconfined[33]

In this third stanza the images from the first two stanzas begin to merge into each other so that the line that had begun familiarly with "a man lives in the house" now ends with the golden hair of Margarete rather than with the master playing with his serpents; the serpents appear in the next line, mixed in with the second appearance of Sulamith. Thus the image of the blue-eyed-death-bringing master from Germany is combined with both women without break, indicating that the ashen, dead hair of Sulamith results from his deadly play with serpents. This merging of death-plans and play with the sensualized image of these two women further underscores Celan's bold mixture of sensuality and death. As were some of Delbo's works (as I discuss in the next section), Celan's devastating poem was paradoxically described by critics, in this case Leonard Duroche, in terms of love: "'Todesfuge,' too, is a lovesong."[34] Such words as "süßer" and "dunkler" (rendered by Hamburger as "sweetly" and "darkly") highlight the sensual imagery of the poem. This sensuality contributes to the beauty of "Todesfuge" and to the challenge that it offers us to locate this unwanted beauty in a death scene.

Celan introduces the quadruply repeated and now famous phrase "death is a master from Germany" in the third stanza. The phrase comes after a repetition of "death" so that the playing of the orchestra becomes a playing of death and death takes on the character of this German master. But whereas in the first two stanzas the master had commanded digging in the earth, in this stanza he commands a grave that will grow from the music ("stroke your strings then as smoke you will rise into air"). Thus, whereas at the outset Celan offers us the almost sweet image of an unconfined grave that is so much less crowded than the literal mass graves the inmates were forced to dig, he here locates the unconfined grave not, as it had been, in the voice of the Jewish diggers but in the voice of the German master. Celan thus indicates the transcendence of the inmates of the attempted confinement of the earth-bound grave through the sweetening offered by the music played to accompany death. The final stanza and closing lines read:

Schwarze Milch der Frühe wir trinken dich nachts
Black milk of daybreak we drink you at night
wir trinken dich mittags der Tod ist ein Meister aus Deutschland
we drink you at noon death is a master from Germany
wir trinken dich abends und morgens wir trinken und trinken
we drink you at sundown and in the morning we drink and we drink you
der Tod ist ein Meister aus Deutschland sein Auge ist blau
death is a master from Germany his eyes are blue
er trifft dich mit bleierner Kugel er trifft dich genau
he strikes you with leaden bullets his aim is true
ein Mann wohnt im Haus dein goldenes Haar Margarete
a man lives in the house your golden hair Margarete
er hetzt seine Rüden auf uns er schenkt uns ein Grab in der Luft
he sets his pack on to us he grants us a grave in the air
er spielt mit den Schlangen und träumet der Tod ist ein Meister aus
    Deutschland
he plays with the serpents and daydreams death is a master from Germany
dein goldenes Haar Margarete
dein schenes Haar Sulamith

The rhythmic structure of the entire poem turns on its repeated refrain and final lines: "your golden hair Margarete / your ashen hair Sulamith." This refrain invites us to question the very different fates of Germans and Jews while at the same time creating a resonance between the two figures. By thus drawing upon a series of Jewish and German themes, the poem further complicates our understanding of the imbrication of Jewish and German cultures for German-speaking Jews such as Celan, as it juxtaposes sensual imagery of a woman's golden hair with death in a crematorium. This final stanza highlights how a melancholy yet sweet tone merges with the brutality of death because its figure appears as curiously gentle yet simultaneously devastating; the sensuality of the women coupled with this unusual representation of death culminates in "Todesfuge's" unwanted beauty.

In her discussion of "Todesfuge," Shoshana Felman argues that "The violence [of the poem] is all the more obscene by being thus *aestheticized*. . . . But the poem works specifically and contrapuntally to dislocate this masquerade of cruelty as art, and to exhibit the obscenity of this aestheticization." Felman here claims first that Celan makes the violence of the poem "obscene" because of its aestheticization and then that he "exhibits" this obscenity. She continues by claiming that the ceaseless drinking of black milk indicates an "unforgettable return of what the aesthetic pleasure has forgotten."[35] Felman's reading thus at least in part agrees with many of the criticisms (that I discuss below) of the poem—namely that it problematically aestheticizes violence. Yet she also maintains that the poem deconstructs this aestheticizing gesture by unveiling its own process of problematic beautification. My reading is intended to demonstrate, in contrast, that "Todesfuge" has engaged a present but unwanted beauty in order to convey an understanding of the experience of this particular death scene that would otherwise be eluded.

Many criticisms of "Todesfuge" claim that it is simply too gorgeous for its themes—death and the Nazi orchestration of death tangos during executions—and that it therefore fails to express shame and fails to remain respectfully silent. If we accept the tenor of his most severe critics, the delicious, sensual images that make this poem so distinct demonstrate that Celan is not a poetic innovator whose approach to the worst reaches emotional registers untouched by many other treatments of the Shoah, but rather an insensitive transgressor of Adorno's maxim against poetry after Auschwitz. For example, Johannes Bobrowski goes so far as to belittle Celan as "at best a perfume factory," which is presumably meant to demonstrate his divorce from the grittiness of war through something like the overuse of elaborate metaphors.[36] Another of his critics, Günter Blöcker, puts it even more harshly, if more curiously: "Celan's lyrics only seldom correspond to an object. As a rule, they develop their verbal filigree like cobwebs out of the glands of language itself, so to speak. Without exception, Celan's store of metaphors is not won from reality nor serves it."[37] In a way, Blöcker's criticism could be seen as an unintentional compliment. His "cobwebs from the glands of language" can be read as the productive and even radical creation of a new vocabulary for expressing the worst. Regardless of how one responds to such critiques, it is clear that both Bobrowski and Blöcker rely on the perceived danger of the possibility of poetry after the camps to discount Celan's artful merging of the poetic with representations of the worst. Thus, this kind of criticism implicitly adopts the interdiction imposed by Adorno's original maxim. Indeed, the fear expressed in these criticisms derives from the threat posed by the beautiful possibilities of the poetic in the face of death.

However, the distinction that critics want to set up between metaphors culled from reality and those presumably free from the real cannot, as Felstiner argues, hold up in light of the way that "Todesfuge" manipulates the image of the fugue as both metaphor and a retelling of the reality of the brutal use to which the SS put music.[38] Indeed, the reading of "Todesfuge" presented here demonstrates that Celan's poem, on the one hand, invokes the sensual as a reproduction of the sick melange of music and death that the SS reveled in, while, on the other hand, inducing in the reader a chilling confusion as to where the pleasure in the imagery leads. The critical reactions to Celan's poem represented by Blöcker's and Bobrowski's comments seek an unbroken anti-aestheticized pain where Celan has instead created an immensely potent melange of sensuality, music, and the worst. Moreover, this mixture of pain with aesthetic pleasure made Celan himself uneasy. Ulrich Baer touches on this unease by finding that "Celan disturbingly suggests that even the most well-intentioned acts of commemoration may amount to a violation of the peace of the dead."[39] This would of course implicate Celan's acts of commemoration in violating the dead. Jonathan Skolnik similarly finds that Celan's poems often express "deep apprehension at [their] own project of aesthetic commemoration."[40] Yet, despite his discomfort, "Todesfuge," and other of Celan's poems, aesthetically commemorate the worst in provocative and illuminating ways that allow us to understand some of the complexities of unwanted beauty in Holocaust literature.

This discomfort with his own "aesthetic commemoration" haunted Celan, and, in a speech delivered in Bremen in 1958, he famously made a plea for the continued ability of language (and in his case the most problematic language of all, German) to live after the ravages of the war, to survive and to convey traumatic experience: "There remained in the midst of the losses this one thing: language. It, the language, remained, not lost, yes in spite of everything. But it had to pass through its own answerlessness, pass through frightful muting, pass through the thousand darknesses of deathbringing speech. It passed through and gave back no words for that which happened; yet it passed through this happening. Passed through and could come to light again, 'enriched' by all this."[41] Celan's dense passage underscores how language itself overcame historical ravages and nonetheless remained capable of expressing the worst, even though it initially had no means to do so. The contrast between the "darknesses of deathbringing speech" and the "light" into which language emerges highlights the challenge that poets and artists had to face in finding words to express their experiences. Thus, poetic language is haunted by this passing-through while it nonetheless struggles to articulate horror.

Celan, as the exemplar of what Adorno calls in *Aesthetic Theory* (1970) "hermetic art," recognizes the limits art must necessarily confront when treating suffering. Adorno defines hermetic art against mimetic art and against art that maintains the status quo. Following Hölderlin, who, according to Adorno, argued that "art must refuse to heed any demands for practical utility," Adorno holds up hermetic art as art that, even if "rebuked for being unintelligible," nonetheless moves aesthetics beyond the stagnating limitation of the bourgeois culture industry: "In Paul Celan, the greatest exponent of hermetic poetry in present-day Germany, the experiential content of the hermetic is the opposite of what it used to be. His poetry is permeated by a sense of shame stemming from the fact that art is unable either to experience or to sublimate suffering. Celan's poems articulate unspeakable horror by being silent, thus turning their truth content into a negative quality."[42] What Adorno indicates by "shame" here is no doubt the sense expressed by Celan that while language has in fact survived, it has passed through the "thousand darknesses of deathbringing speech." It is hard to grasp exactly what Adorno means by Celan's ability to articulate horror through silence. Is he suggesting that Celan's poems are allusive in their approach to the Holocaust? Or rather that, especially in the later work, the poems are sparse, use few words, and therefore offer the sensation of being composed of equal parts silence and speech? Whatever Adorno finds here, he goes on to characterize Celan's poetry as using a language of "stones and stars," images that appear in many of Celan's poems.

While a shift occurs in Celan's work toward ever greater abstraction and fewer words, his central images of stones, stars, snow, death/graves/blood, mother, heart, hair, eyes/iris, sleep, swimming, drinking, silence, and language remain. Many scholars have marked this transformation. For example, Zsuzsanna Osváth finds that "over the years, [Celan's] verse turned increasingly dark, more complex, more fractured, and more cryptic."[43] Shoshana Felman expresses the same change in Celan's poetry by claiming that in the later poems Celan sought to "dislocate his own aesthetic mastery."[44] And Françoise Meltzer phrases this transformation in terms of Celan's waning interest in the world: "As his belief in the world lessened, so the actual length of his lines of verse shortened and splintered."[45] These changes may have been a response to some of the criticism of the beauty of his earlier poems, yet the later poems in their spare depictions of pain are equally beautiful.

"Todesfuge" stands out even among Celan's earlier work for its density and descriptive plenitude, yet one need only compare the short and quiet poem "Das angebrochene Jahr" ("The Broached Year," published posthumously in 1971) to "Todesfuge" to get a sense of how different some of Celan's later works were to his earlier work. The entire poem reads: "Das Angebrochene Jahr / mit dem modernen Kanten / Wahnbrot. / Trink / aus meinem Mund" ("The Broached Year / with its mouldering crusts / of delusion bread. / Drink / from my mouth").[46] The effect is much starker than that offered by the crowded page and ample metaphors of "Todesfuge," yet this poem shares the central metaphor of drinking rot from the past. As with "Black milk . . . we drink you," here we drink mouldering crusts that have accumulated throughout a broached year. Thus Celan continued to focus on the transmission of the painful past into the present and continued to turn that past into beautiful poems that help us to grapple with the persistence of trauma.

In "Todesfuge" Celan examines a moment of the Nazis' use of aesthetics in order to demonstrate the intimate connection between aesthetics and history, and his beautiful depiction of trauma tackles this complex historical scene where beautiful music served horror and where beautiful poetry critiqued horror. Celan's powerful effort to articulate trauma through beauty reverberates throughout the rest of this book. As I mentioned above, Anselm Kiefer devoted a series of paintings to "Todesfuge," and I analyze two of them in chapter 4. And in chapter 5 I discuss how German fascism's use of aesthetics has had grave impacts on the postwar landscape of monuments, memorials, and museums; yet Celan's beautiful poems indicate that he has not fallen prey to the fear that reproducing some of the aesthetics dear to fascism thereby reproduces the violence of fascist history. In a strange passage, Amy Colin, whose book on Celan focuses on his early work, says of "Todesfuge" that the "aesthetic refinement of his poem carries readers away despite themselves. Inevitably, they find his verse beautiful, even if they are well aware that Celan did not intend to beautify what has happened and their interpretation is an utter misreading."[47] In other words, Colin claims that the unwanted beauty of Celan's poem must be denied to preserve the truth of the Holocaust. In contrast to these kinds of readings, my analysis has intended to show that Celan's "Todesfuge" has become such a powerful and oft-cited example of Holocaust art because the complexity of its beauty does not allow us to treat the Holocaust as a closed historical event but rather forces us to grapple with the continuing complications of memory.

CHARLOTTE DELBO: MEMORIES WRITTEN ON THE BODY

As does Celan's, Charlotte Delbo's work insists that the skins of painful memory are engraved on the bodies of survivors and that rotten memory will be involuntarily drunk, morning, noon, and night. Charlotte Delbo's oeuvre is committed to analyzing the possibilities of translating memory into literature from which nonwitnesses can learn: her mission is in part to make us see what it was like "over there"; she often discusses this imperative with the phrase "Il faut donner à voir," one must make them see.[48] The way she makes us see is through tender and beautiful images of the worst, sometimes rendered in poetry, sometimes in drama, and sometimes in prose. In his introduction to Delbo's nuanced and multi-perspectival collection of memories, *La mémoire et les jours* (1985), François Bott describes the sensual beauty in Delbo's work; after locating an extreme sweetness and tenderness in her account of her experiences he suggests that "C'est la raison pour laquelle les textes de Charlotte se lisent comme un étrange poème d'amour" (It's the reason why Charlotte's texts read like a strange love poem).[49] By working this place of tenderness, by writing about horror in ways that read like love poems, Delbo demonstrates that representing the Shoah is less a question of mitigating its horror than of coming to terms with how one creates survival mechanisms to help both in the process of surviving trauma and surviving or living next to memories of trauma. The sensuality implied in Delbo's "strange love poem" recalls the curiously sweet sensuality in Celan's "Todesfuge," which, as I noted above, had also been described as a "lovesong." Indeed, Delbo and Celan are aesthetically linked by creating beautiful, sensitive depictions of the worst, yet, as Bott's comment indicates, Delbo is not often criticized for this sensuality, perhaps because she is not Jewish and not writing in German. Indeed, as Celan was painfully aware, writing lyrically beautiful texts in German was often fraught with challenges from those who felt that German itself had been indelibly polluted by the stain of the past war. Survivors writing in French, on the other hand, often felt freer to explore literary and rhetorical devices in the construction of art that would speak to those who came after the war. The beauty of Celan's and Delbo's works contributes for both survivors to their reflections on memory and the relief that beautiful renditions of the Shoah offers.

Before turning to Delbo's *La mémoire et les jours,* I offer a brief history of her life and works that illuminates both her commitment to the French resistance and the influence of the theater (and therefore of aesthetics) on her survival. Delbo was born in 1913 near Paris; she was a student of philosophy at the Sorbonne before the war, and married Georges Dudach, who became a member of the French resistance. In 1941 Delbo was employed by the actor and director, Louis Jouvet, as his secretary; Jouvet exerted a lifelong influence on the theater aficionado Delbo. She was in Brazil with Jouvet and his theater company when she heard word that friends had been arrested as resisters. Against Jouvet's wishes, Delbo flew back to Paris to join her husband in circulating clandestine texts through the French resistance.[50] Dudach was arrested on March 2, 1942, and executed at Mont Valérain on May 23. Delbo was arrested in May 1942 and sent to Romainville on August 24, and from there was shipped to Birkenau in January 1943. Then in May 1943 Delbo was transferred to Raisko, a new, cleaner barrack, where the living conditions were more manageable. On January 7, 1944, Delbo was transferred to Ravensbrück and on January 23 she was liberated and treated by the Red Cross. After liberation she went to Sweden and then to Paris at the end of June 1945, where she remained until she died of lung cancer in 1985. Hence, as they were for Celan, the war years were characterized by a great deal of displacement and loss of loved ones. Under these trying circumstances, memory became the only thing she could carry with her. But because Delbo is not Jewish her community of survivors, other French resistance members, had access to a very different postwar perspective than Jewish survivors such as Celan.

Immediately after the war, Delbo wrote *Aucun de nous ne reviendra* (*None of Us Will Return*), the first volume of her three-part work, *Auschwitz et aprés* (*Auschwitz and After*), yet she did not begin publishing it until 1970. Delbo wrote four plays in the sixties and seventies, in addition to a fascinating account of the women with whom she was interned, *Le convoi du 24 janvier* in 1965.[51] This text contributes to the growing discussion of gender in the Holocaust as it offers testimony specifically devoted to women.[52] *Le convoi* is remarkable because it names each of the 230 women in Delbo's convoy and details as much of their lives as Delbo could remember or reconstruct. Of the 230 women, 49, including Delbo, survived. This work thus actively resists the anonymity that is the fate of many war victims. As a testimony to the growing importance and recognition of Delbo's work in France in recent years, on February 3, 1995, a group of 320 actresses read Delbo's works aloud for broadcast on France Culture during the entire night. This date was chosen because it was the fifty-second anniversary of the day in 1943 when photos were taken of the women in Delbo's convoy and subsequently reprinted in *Le convoi du 24 janvier*. In a discussion of this radio broadcast, Sylviane Gresh finds that "Charlotte Delbo a affronté la mémoire vivante en elle, et c'est parce qu'elle a creusé ce qu'il y avait de plus singulier qu'elle nous donne une chance aujourd'hui de transmettre aux nouvelles générations l'expérience tangible de l'horreur" (Charlotte Delbo has confronted living memory within her, and it is because she has examined so intensely that which was most unusual that she has given us a chance today to transmit the tangible experience of horror to the next generations).[53] Gresh's description aptly explains how Delbo's confrontation with memory is precisely what allows us, the next generation, to receive this "tangible experience of horror."

The ability of Delbo's writing to transmit these experiences of horror in part relies upon the theatrical qualities of her work. Indeed, all of Delbo's work is influenced by her interest in theater. As a young woman Delbo solicited an interview with Louis Jouvet for a journal she was working with, *Jeunesses communistes.* Apparently Jouvet was so pleased with the printed version of the interview that he asked Delbo to be his secretary. This time working for the actor initiated a long friendship between Delbo and Jouvet that was only halted by his death in 1951. Delbo apparently learned a great deal from Jouvet both through his theater classes and through her intense collaborations with him during her tenure as his secretary, from 1937 to 1940. Indeed, in a letter dated June 11, 1940, an aide of Jouvet's writes of Delbo's leaving his company, "Nous ajoutons que pendant ces trois années, Madame Delbo-Dudach a apporté à M. Louis Jouvet une précieuse collaboration, et seul le cours des événements a obligé M. Jouvet à se séparer de sa secrétaire" (We add that during these three years, Madame Delbo-Dudach brought to M. Louis Jouvet a precious collaboration, and only the course of events has obliged M. Jouvet to separate from his secretary).[54] There is a discrepancy of dates between this letter, which indicates that Delbo left her job as Jouvet's secretary in 1940, and the general scholarly consensus is that Delbo left a year and a half later.[55] But whatever the case, it is clear that much of the dramatic knowledge gleaned through Jouvet and his company contributed a great deal not only to her play writing, but also to her survival. As evidence of the importance of Jouvet to her, Delbo wrote a long, moving letter to her mentor that was published in book form under the title *Spectres, mes compagnons* (1972).

As one example among many of the power the theatrical offers to survival, Delbo cites a moment when, starving in the camps, she decided to exchange her precious ration of bread to buy a copy of Molière's *Le misanthrope*. Delbo reports that she had lived with the constant fear of losing her memory in Auschwitz and that in order to counter this fear she had recited poems that she had committed to memory. After her "purchase" of Molière's play she was thrilled that she had "toute une brochure à apprendre, tout un texte" (a whole book I could memorize, a whole text).[56] She goes on to describe how important it was to have the play, not only for herself, but for her comrades, who gave her bits of bread in exchange for hearing bits of theater:

> *J'ai appris* Le misanthrope *par coeur, un fragment chaque soir, que je me répétais à l'appel du lendemain matin. Bientôt j'ai su toute la pièce, qui durait presque tout l'appel. Et jusqu'au départ, j'ai gardé la brochure dans ma gorge.*

> I learned *Le misanthrope* by heart, a fragment each evening, which I'd repeat to myself at roll call the following day. Soon I knew the whole play, which lasted almost throughout the roll call. And until departure, I kept the play within my throat.[57]

As readers familiar with Holocaust literature know, in the context of the camps "roll call" was one of the most dreaded experiences. Inmates were often made to stand for hours in inclement weather while the camp leadership painstakingly assured that all the inmates were present; it was often an opportunity for the guards to beat the prisoners. Thus, the idea of Delbo removing herself from the horror of camp reality into the relative comfort of her memorized play furnishes a powerful example of how aesthetic pleasure offered a survival mechanism to endure the worst experiences. And, in addition to her theatrical interests, her collaboration with Jouvet may have been part of her resistance work.

While Delbo scholars have not, to my knowledge, referred to a letter I found in an archive in Paris, the letter indicates that as early as 1940 Delbo tried to

encourage Jouvet to help her free a prisoner. I do not know how much involvement in the resistance she had had prior to her abrupt return from the safety of Brazil, but on the twenty-ninth of July Delbo wrote to Jouvet:

> Je voulais aussi vous parler d'une chose que j'ai apprise ce matin: il est arrivé
> que le père d'un prisonnier obtienne de la direction d'un camp, la libération de
> son fils. Alors peut-être que vous pourriez, si vous passer voir Jean-Paul en rev-
> enant, essayer de le faire sortir—vous avez plus de chance qu'aucun autre.[58]

> I would also like to speak to you about something I learned of this morning:
> it happened that the father of a prisoner obtained the liberation of his son
> from the committee who runs the camp. So perhaps, if you happen to see
> Jean-Paul, you might be able to try to have him taken out [of the camp]—you
> have a better chance than anyone else.

While it is unclear who "Jean-Paul" is, it is interesting that as early as July
1940, a year and a half before returning to Paris to help in the resistance (and
a month after the letter from Jouvet's aide), Delbo was already thinking about
the release of prisoners. This plea indicates that her resolve to resist was already deep-seated and helps to explain why Delbo would choose to leave the
safety of Brazil to return to almost certain danger in occupied France. This
decision to leave Brazil was certainly heroic and this early letter that I have
uncovered perhaps illuminates her commitment to anti-fascist resistance
and her resolve not only to rejoin her husband but to take an active role in
fighting Nazism.

I now turn to one of Delbo's most powerful works, *La mémoire et les jours*
(1985), as it offers Delbo's theories of memory in beautiful, poetic prose. While
La mémoire was Delbo's last work, it is so intimately connected with the writing she produced right after the war that it carries the immediacy of testimony along with a more distanced reflection on the process of memory. *La
mémoire* is a collection of narratives and poems that tells the story of surviving
trauma through many, often unnamed characters, who are usually presented
in the first person. One has the sensation in reading *La mémoire* that Delbo
herself is the unnamed interlocutor of many of the stories and that she recounts
tales told to her by victims during the war and by survivors after the war. Some
of the first-person characters are Jewish teenagers or others from France or
Poland, some are Spanish or Greek prisoners trying to find their way in the
ruins of Europe after the war. One story describes a massacre in 1943 in the
Greek town of Kalvrita. The narrative unfolds as though the reader were standing on the site of the massacre and retracing the steps of those senselessly

murdered. By building a mausoleum to the dead men of the town, the town's women, often wearing double wedding bands, their own and those of their dead husbands, created an enduring monument to the massacre. This story is most likely true, but one never knows whether these intricate details are metaphorical tales depicting the process of memorialization or the twists of memory. For example, her image of these women building a mausoleum operates as a metaphor for the process of memorialization that Delbo constantly questions. Most of the stories and poems in *La mémoire* are set during or immediately after World War II, but Delbo has also included a powerful poem about the disappeared in Argentina's "dirty war" of the 1970s and a brief note about torture in Algeria in the 1960s.[59] The poem and note thus make an argument for understanding the Holocaust in the broader context of other twentieth-century catastrophes. Indeed, the composite of these different tales offers a meditation on memory across different moments of trauma, thus asking, How do survivors treat these painful memories? And how can one simultaneously remember and forget just enough to live in the present?

In *La mémoire* Delbo often addresses the reader familiarly as *tu;* this *tu* takes on different characters—sometimes an almost journalistic-sounding incredulous postwar figure who did not experience the war, and sometimes, I imagine, Delbo herself in the role of interlocutor with other victims (whose wartime conversations she remembers) and survivors. After claiming that the worst is not an image of horror, she challenges the indeterminate *tu* by suggesting that "Pour toi, la chambre à gaz, c'est le pire, n'est-ce pas?" (30) (For you the worst of all is the gas chamber, isn't it? 20). In this narrative told in the first person from the perspective of a Jewish woman, Delbo places the interlocutor in the curious position of judging experiences that he or she has never and will never feel. Taking on the voice of a Jewish victim is a bold act in the context of French resistance accounts, which often sharply differentiate Jewish and gentile experiences. As I discuss in the next chapter, another French resister and writer, Jorge Semprun (who was originally from Spain), was very sensitive to the differences between Jews and non-Jews, and Delbo, in another text, has also brought these differences to light in stark terms. This Jewish character in *La mémoire* feels that her ultimately false knowledge that her mother had died in the gas chambers was actually better than thinking that she had had to endure the denuded life of the camps; but this has to be read in the context of the explicit dialectic between fact and fiction that forms part of the narrative genius of Delbo's text.

Delbo repeats, while giving us contradictory stories, "maintenant, la vérité" (now, the truth) and she introduces the word *vérité* under the cloud: "C'est pourquoi je dis aujourd'hui que, tout en sachant très bien que c'est véridique, je ne sais plus si c'est vrai" (14) (That is why I say today that while knowing perfectly well that it corresponds to the facts, I no longer know if it is real, 4). The importance of this phrase is underscored by the fact that it reproduces, almost but not quite verbatim, the epigraph to the first volume of Delbo's trilogy, *Auschwitz et après:* "Aujourd'hui, je ne suis pas sûre que ce que j'ai écrit soit vrai. Je suis sûre que c'est véridique" (Today, I am not sure that what I have written is true. I am sure that it is truthful). In the reiteration of the epigraph in the later text (*La mémoire*), Delbo reverses the terms "vrai" and "véridique" so that the concept of truthfulness is highlighted. It is as though the passage of time between the two texts (almost forty years) means that truthfulness rather than truth takes precedence. As an indication of the importance of these terms for survivors, Semprun echoes these phrases of Delbo's in *L'écriture ou la vie,* where he asserts: "Voilà la vérité rétablie: la vérité totale de ce récit qui était déjà véridique" (55) (That's the truth of it, the whole truth behind this story, which was already a truthful account, 37). As I discuss in the next chapter, Semprun, like Delbo, is very sensitive to the vagaries of memory and the need to convey truth through fiction.

The literary effect of the slippage between fact and fiction that these phrases from Delbo and Semprun remind us of is that we learn about the experience of surviving the camps through a melange of conflicting stories. In other words, the beautiful narratives that make up *La mémoire* teach us not only about the intricacies of past experience but also about the struggle to portray those experiences aesthetically. Thus, when the survivor challenges us to claim that the gas chambers are the worst *for us,* she also challenges us to broaden and deepen our understanding of the experience of the worst beyond the confines of these stock images and into the more complex and beautiful narratives recounted and/or created by survivors.

Three passages from *La mémoire* contain the crux of Delbo's philosophy of memory; I quote them at length to manifest the texture of her language and to demonstrate the way she frames this collection of her own memories and those of imagined and real characters. *La mémoire* opens as follows:

> *Expliquer l'inexplicable. L'image du serpent qui laisse sa vieille peau pour en surgir, revêtu d'une peau fraîche et luisante, peut venir à l'esprit. J'ai quitté à Auschwitz une peau usée—elle sentait mauvais, cette peau—marquée de tous les coups qu'elle avait reçus pour me retrouver habillée d'une belle peau propre, dans une mue moins rapide que celle du serpent, toutefois. . . . Débarrassé de*

sa peau morte, le serpent n'a pas changé. Mois non plus, en apparence. Reste que . . . [ellipses in original]. Comment se défaire de quelque chose enfoui beaucoup plus profond: la mémoire et la peau de la mémoire. Je ne m'en suis pas dépouillée. La peau de la mémoire s'est durcie, elle ne laisse rien filtrer de ce qu'elle retient, et elle échappe à mon contrôle. Je ne la sens plus. (11–12)

Explaining the inexplicable. There comes to mind the image of a snake shedding its old skin, emerging from beneath it in a fresh, glistening one. In Auschwitz I took leave of my skin—it had a bad smell, that skin—worn from all the blows it had received, and found myself in another, beautiful and clean, although with me the molting was not as rapid as the snake's. . . . Rid of its old skin, it's still the same snake. I'm the same too, apparently. However . . . [ellipses in original]. How does one rid oneself of something buried far within: memory and the skin of memory. It clings to me yet. Memory's skin has hardened, it allows nothing to filter out what it retains, and I have no control over it. I don't feel it anymore. (1)

Delbo offers as the opening of her text the familiar paradox of the need to "explain the inexplicable" or "represent the unrepresentable," yet her work argues against the absolute unrepresentability of the Shoah by consistently representing trauma through different genres and in different voices, thus offering a complex symphony of sounds and images about the worst. The powerful metaphor of the rememberer of trauma living through many of memory's skins helps Delbo explain how she survived because it allows us to grasp the sensation of creating an armor against experience, an armor that is "beautiful and clean." The armor thus aesthetically protects her from the blows of Auschwitz. The possibility of explaining the inexplicable conjures the image of the snake because the inexplicable—memory of Auschwitz—is buried within, both "la mémoire et la peau de la mémoire" (memory and the skin of memory). While Delbo is free of the old skin it still sticks to her, uncontrollably, and the hard skin that memory has formed does not allow anything to escape from it. Because of this skin's inability to filter painful memories, the Auschwitz Delbo lives next to continues to be as painful as it had been in the past.

This all-containing, hardened memory strikingly reverses Freud's description of the crust that stimuli create on the surface of what he calls the mental vesicle in *Beyond the Pleasure Principle*. In his discussion of trauma, Freud argues that one wards off negative events by creating a "crust" that has been so thoroughly "baked through" by multiple stimuli that it becomes impenetrable to all modification.[60] Trauma, for Freud, occurs during moments when the negative input is either so sudden or so extreme that the stimulus breaks through the hard crust and damages the soft inner core. In contrast to Freud, Delbo describes memory's hardened skin refusing to let anything *out* rather than anything *in* ("Memory's skin has hardened, it allows nothing to filter out what it retains"), thus indicating that her model of trauma involves a mechanism for keeping negative stimuli within rather than a method of keeping trauma out.

Delbo's model for memory, then, indicates that she cannot forget. Indeed, Delbo and her characters contain internal images of the dead that are deeply permeable, flexible, and changing. One of Delbo's characters refuses death by carrying her murdered mother and sister within: "elle portait en elle sa soeur vivante par elle seule désormais" (16) (inside her she bore her sister, alive from now on through her alone, 6). The distancing "elle" (third person) forms part of the complex narrative strategies of the text: Delbo switches rapidly between first and third persons and between the living and the dead so that the narrative manifests repression and desire structurally. In other words, the repression or denial of death is rewritten as a desire for the return of the lost ones as well as a desire for survival. These strategies capture the sensation of survival mechanisms that render the "reality" of the camps more imaginable because in the figuration of the lost as still among us, Delbo's characters aesthetically redraw the realities that face them.[61]

In the second passage from the opening of *La mémoire*, Delbo describes her unending fear of the camp's ability to crack the skin of memory and recapture her:

> *Auschwitz est si profondément gravé dans ma mémoire que je n'en oublie aucun instant.—Alors, vous vivez avec Auschwitz?—Non, je vis à côté. Auschwitz est là, inaltérable, précis mais enveloppé dans la peau de la mémoire, peau étanche qui l'isole de mon moi actuel. A la différence de la peau de serpent, la peau de la mémoire ne se renouvelle pas. Oh! qu'elle durcisse encore . . . [ellipses in original]. Hélas! je crains souvent qu'elle s'amincisse, qu'elle craque, que le camp me rattrappe. Y penser me fait trembler d'appréhension. (13)*

Auschwitz is so deeply etched in my memory that I cannot forget one moment of it.—So you are living with Auschwitz?—No, I live next to it. Auschwitz is there, unalterable, precise, but enveloped in the skin of memory, an impermeable skin that isolates it from my present self. Unlike the snake's skin, the skin of memory does not renew itself. Oh, it may harden further . . . [ellipses in original]. Alas, I often fear lest it grow thin, crack, and the camp get hold of me again. Thinking about it makes me tremble with apprehension. (2)

In this model of memory, the camps continue to exist whole and entire and buried, and Delbo's desire radically splits between the need for the skin to harden further to protect her from becoming trapped again, and the need for the skin to weaken and fall away so that the shell of Auschwitz memory can release her. Yet, when she corrects her imagined interlocutor and insists that she lives *next to* rather than *with* the camp, she suggests that the impermeable skin protects her present self through isolating it from her. An echo of this sense of a double self due to these experiences can be found in Semprun's *L'écriture ou la vie*, where he asks, "Deux ans d'éternité glaciale, d'intolérable mort me séparaient de moi-même. Reviendrais-je à moi-même, un jour?" (141) (Two years of frozen eternity, of intolerable death, separate me from myself. Would I ever return to myself, one day? 104). As I discuss in the next chapter, Semprun, like Delbo, dwells on the interlocking of past and present and the creation of multiple versions of the self in order to control or locate different memories.

In the third passage from *La mémoire*, Delbo tells us that dreams are often the places where the skin of memory collapses and her camp self imagistically merges with her present self: the two women are of course absolutely dissimilar physically, yet dreams manage to combine them:

> Parce que, lorsque je vous parle d'Auschwitz ce n'est pas de la mémoire profonde que viennent mes paroles. Les paroles viennent de la mémoire externe, si je puis dire, la mémoire intellectuelle, la mémoire de la pensée. La mémoire profonde garde les sensations, les empreintes physiques. C'est la mémoire des sens. Car ce ne sont pas les mots qui sont gonflés de charge émotionelle. Sinon, quelqu'un qui a été torturé par la soif pendant des semaines ne pourrait plus jamais dire: "J'ai soif. Faisons une tasse de thé." Le mot aussi s'est dédoublé. Soif est redevenu un mot d'usage courant. Par contre, si je rêve de la soif dont j'ai souffert à Birkenau, je revois celle que j'étais, hagarde, perdant la raison, titubante; je ressens physiquement cette vraie soif et c'est un cauchemar atroce. Mais, si vous voulez que je vous en parle . . . [ellipses in original]. (14)

Because when I talk to you about Auschwitz, it is not from deep memory my words issue. They come from external memory, if I may put it that way, from intellectual memory, the memory connected with the thinking processes. Deep memory preserves sensations, physical imprints. It is the memory of the senses. For it isn't words that are swollen with emotional charge. Otherwise, someone who has been tortured by thirst for weeks on end could never again say "I'm thirsty. How about a cup of tea." This word has also split in two. Thirst has turned back into a word for commonplace use. But if I dream of the thirst

I suffered in Birkenau, I once again see the person I was, haggard, halfway crazed, near to collapse; I physically feel that real thirst and it is an atrocious nightmare. If, however, you'd like me to talk to you about it . . . [ellipses in original]. (3–4)

Because language continues to signify outside the trauma, Delbo differentiates between external memory and deep memory. She claims that if she were speaking from deep memory she would have to use another language free of everything in "usage courant" to avoid the doubling of two times, to avoid the Holocaust leaking back into the present. In praising the power of Delbo's language during a gloss on this passage, Lawrence Langer notes: "Such memory [i.e., external] . . . may allow us to imagine the worst, but only sense [i.e., deep] memory, which preserves and tries to transmit the *physical* imprint of the ordeal, enables us to approach the unthinkable."[62] We may be able to see, externally, what it was like in the camps, but we can never sense it deeply because it remains encoded in the same words we use in our quotidian lives.

The cup of tea Delbo chooses as her example of thirst evokes Proust's famous madeleine scene. Delbo refers to Proust explicitly in *Spectres, mes compagnons,* and she seems to conjure up Proust by titling her work *La mémoire et les jours,* thus echoing Proust's *Les plaisirs et les jours,* which in turn echoes Hesiod's *Works and Days.* Furthermore, Delbo's distinction between external and deep memory recalls Proust's distinction between voluntary and involuntary memory.[63] In *Spectres,* Delbo's letter to Jouvet that I mentioned at the opening of this section, Delbo engages in a long reflection on memory that refers to images from Proust, such as the magic lantern to which Marcel imaginatively returns. Delbo notes,

> *Pendant des jours et des nuits, j'ai dû m'acharner à affirmer mon être, à me saisir dans un effort extrême de conscience pour m'assurer de mon existence en face des fantômes qui voulaient l'absorber, l'engloutir. C'est ainsi sans doute que se recrée la vie intérieure, cet effort de la conscience pour embrasser son existence que Proust appelle la recherche du temps perdu.*[64]

For days and nights, I tried extremely hard to affirm my being, to take hold of myself in an extreme effort of consciousness—to assure myself of my existence in the face of the phantoms that would like to absorb me, engulf me. It is no doubt this way of recreating the interior life, this conscious effort to embrace existence, that Proust terms the search for lost time.

For Proust, voluntary memories are controlled memories that we can call up at will. Involuntary memories are powerful memories that invade the rememberer without warning and that seem to bring him/her back to the remembered moment in the past. The difference between Delbo's and Proust's theories of memory is that for Proust, dwelling in the sensations of the past through involuntary memory can often be extremely pleasurable; for Delbo, experiencing deep memory can be "an atrocious nightmare." As Delbo explained in the second passage quoted above, she lives next to Auschwitz while it continues, "unalterable, precise" yet enveloped in memory's hard skin. For Proust, involuntary memories are not next to the rememberer, they are suddenly triggered by serendipitous acts that bring the past sensually into the present, and thus into the rememberer. For survivors, this distinction between modes of memory is important because there is often an enormous desire to be able to control the reappearance of the past. As I discuss in chapter 2, Semprun also refers to Proust in order to help him in his discussion of the painful relationship between the present and this particular past. Thus when Delbo and others take up Proust's division of memory they struggle to articulate models of control over the past that also take into account the strong sense-component of Proustian involuntary memory.

THE SKIN OF MEMORY

Throughout *À la recherche du temps perdu* (1908–22), Marcel Proust's sprawling novel about aesthetics and memory as told through the eyes of Marcel, the character at the center of the novel, Proust argues for the possibility that consciousness and memory can be housed in external objects.[65] As Adorno puts it, "*Remembrance of Things Past* examines internal and external reality, using as its instrument the existence of a man without skin."[66] This image recalls Delbo's description of the skin of memory, yet reverses it: for Adorno, Proust blurs the lines between internal and external so that the narrator's skin seems to disappear; for Delbo, the skin of memory is a hard surface that does not let anything out of her. The hard surface of the skin of memory is a necessary mechanism for post-traumatic survival because it allows memories of the worst to remain contained and controllable. For an explanation of a man without skin in Proust, consider the following moment from the first volume, *Du côté de chez Swann,* from the section *Combray,* "Et avant même que ma pensée, qui hésitait au seuil des temps et des formes, eût identifié le logis en rapprochant les circonstances, lui—mon corps,—se rappelait pour chacun le genre du lit, la place des portes, la prise de jour des fenêtres" (And even before my mind, which hesitated on the threshold of time and of forms, had identified the abode in relation to the circumstances, it—my body,—remembered for each one the type of bed, the placement of the doors, the way the windows catch the light).[67] Marcel's bodily memories of the physical location of the objects around him challenge the source of memory and resist its being cast purely in the imaginative realm because *his body seems to know* where it has been, even if his consciousness often refuses the memories that his subconscious seems to desire. Memories of Combray resist opening into consciousness; they are encrypted like internal monuments to times past that can only spring open if catalyzed by curious and unpredictable triggers.

One of the most famous examples of this opening of memory—of what Proust calls involuntary memory—occurs during the madeleine scene, in which Marcel dips a madeleine (a delicate cookie) into a cup of tea and thereby enters into a sea of previously lost memories. The taste of the madeleine soaked in tea renders the narrator indifferent to life's vicissitudes, yet it still remains unclear why the memory should be so pleasurable. Indeed, the true source of this intense pleasure must be deferred for a long time, "quoique je ne susse pas encore et dusse remettre à bien plus tard de découvrir pourquoi ce souvenir me rendait si heureux" (47) (although I did not yet know and must put off until much later the discovery of why this memory made me so happy), yet Proust seems to take up the thread of this question some three thousand pages later as though there had barely been a break. In the final volume, *Le temps retrouvé*, Marcel finds himself once again looking for "la cause de cette félicité" (cause of this happiness) and remarking on the connection between the happiness and the sense of being "extra-temporel" or "en dehors du temps" (extra-temporal or outside of time).[68] Thus, the release from time itself furnishes the curious pleasure of this moment of involuntary memory. For survivors, the sense of being outside time must often have great appeal, and this perhaps deepens the explanation of why Proust's approach to memory is invoked by many Holocaust survivors who need to articulate the swirling complexity of memories of the worst.

In order to locate further the commonalities between Proust's approach to memory and Delbo's theory of memory I now cite a fragment of Proust's madeleine scene:

> *Et tout d'un coup le souvenir m'est apparu. Ce goût c'était celui du petit morceau de madeleine que le dimanche matin à Combray . . . ma tante Léonie m'offrait après l'avoir trempé dans son infusion de thé ou de tilleul. . . . Mais, quand d'un*

*passé ancien rien ne subsiste, après la mort des êtres, après la destruction des
choses, seules, plus frêles mais plus vivaces, plus immatérielles, plus persistantes,
plus fidèles, l'odeur et la saveur restent encore longtemps, comme des âmes, à se
rappeler, à attendre, à espérer, sur la ruine de tout le reste, à porter sans fléchir,
sur leur gouttelette presque impalpable, l'édifice immense du souvenir. (46)*

And suddenly the memory revealed itself. The taste was that of the little piece
of madeleine which on Sunday mornings at Combray . . . my auntie Léonie
used to give me, dipping it first in her own cup of tea or tisane. . . . But when
from a long-distant past nothing survives, after the people are dead, after the
things are broken and scattered, taste and smell alone, more fragile but more
enduring, more immaterial, more persistent, more faithful, remain poised a
long time, like souls, remembering, waiting, hoping, amid the ruins of all the
rest; and bear unflinchingly, in the tiny and almost impalpable droplet of their
essence, the immense edifice of memory.[69]

This recalls Delbo's argument that the thirst she suffered in Birkenau indicates that the simple phrase "I'm thirsty. How about a cup of tea" has been
split so that it simultaneously conjures up the "nightmare" of Birkenau thirst
and the more mundane thirst of those of us who have never been truly deprived of sustenance. By choosing a cup of tea as her example, Delbo refers
to this iconic moment in Proust. For Proust, there is also a split between the
mundane taste and smell of the madeleine and the access that its taste and
smell offers to the entirety of a lost past. Proust asserts in the madeleine scene
that in the face of the destruction of cities and the death of their peoples, the
most fragile tastes and smells contain the entire structure of possible memory. In Delbo's work it is less the tastes and smells that contain the entirety
of Auschwitz, and more the fear of the dark side of common words, the fear
that thirst will once again begin to signify the terrible thirst of her former,
deprived, self.

   In a passage that links Proust's elaboration of tastes and smells that evoke
powerful, involuntary memories with memories of the experience of the
camps, Semprun explains in *L'écriture ou la vie* how certain odors can trans-
port him through time: "L'étrange odeur surgirait aussitôt, dans la réalité
de la mémoire. J'y renaîtrais, je mourrais d'y revivre. Je m'ouvrirais, permé-
able, à l'odeur de vase de cet estuaire de mort, entêtante" (18) (The strange
smell would immediately invade the reality of memory. I would be reborn
there; I would die if I returned to life there. I would embrace and inhale the
muddy, heady odor of that estuary of death, 7). Semprun here captures the
paradox of involuntary memories of the worst experiences. On the one hand,

an older version of the self comes to life due to the trigger of a certain smell; on the other hand, the place of this coming to life is also a place of death and therefore an unstable, unwanted place for memory to wander.

Proust ends the madeleine scene with the observation that his recreation of the past, the return of Combray from the tiniest droplet, "tout cela qui prend forme et solidité, est sorti, ville et jardins, de ma tasse de thé" (47) (all of this that takes form and solidity came, city and gardens, from my cup of tea). That the tea contains the potentiality of everything that takes form explains the Proustian process through which external triggers unlock secret internal memories. For survivors such as Delbo and Semprun, the possibility that the memories of Auschwitz, Birkenau, and Buchenwald will take form offers nothing but a nightmarish fear, and they similarly find that, once unlocked from the skin of memory, this past has the terrifying solidity of the experience of reliving.

Proust builds the madeleine scene on the taunting suggestion that Combray remains forever dead to the narrator, that its secrets remain locked or encrypted because, until then, Marcel only receives voluntary, intellectual memories. The narrator has not yet been flooded, as he will be when he tastes the tea, by involuntary memories. Proust privileges involuntary over voluntary memory because the latter cannot fully attain the essence or vivid image of the past:

> Mais comme ce que je m'en serais rappelé m'eût été fourni seulement par la mémoire volontaire, la mémoire de l'intelligence, et comme les renseignements qu'elle donne sur le passé ne conservent rien de lui, je n'aurais jamais eu envie de songer à ce reste de Combray. Tout cela était en réalité mort pour moi.
> Mort à jamais? C'était possible. (43)

> But since the facts which I should then have recalled would have been prompted only by voluntary memory, the memory of the intellect, and since the pictures which that kind of memory shows us preserve nothing of the past itself, I should never have had any wish to ponder over this residue of Combray. All of that was in reality dead for me.
> Dead forever? Very possibly. (59, translation slightly modified)

Delbo's phrase, "la mémoire intellectuelle" is very similar to Proust's "la mémoire de l'intelligence," and each author qualifies his/her phrase with an additional adjective; for Delbo intellectual memory is external and for Proust it is voluntary. Intellectual memory allows Delbo to transmit her experiences of the camps because without it she would enter the nightmare of sense memory; for Proust, in contrast, access to involuntary memory—or sense memory in Delbo's term—allows his entire novel to unfold. Because the madeleine offers the potency of involuntary memory, as we have seen, through the fragile tastes and smells containing the entire structure of Combray, his childhood home is not dead to him in the least. Proust's philosophy of memory, therefore, relies on memory being involuntary—that it flood over one without effort—and that it be triggered by external sources that contain its edifice and therefore allow for its contents to be revealed. His philosophy also insists on the pleasures of temporal collapse and the construction of layers or envelopes enclosing different temporal moments. Time zones appear from the shadows of memory like—to borrow Delbo's term—so many serpents shedding their skins.

Whereas Delbo draws upon Proust's beautiful descriptions of memory to refine her theories of how survivors' memories function, Celan calls upon the beautiful music played during the most horrific moments to capture the complexity of Holocaust memory. In both cases the artists focus on unwanted beauty as a means of memory production. In the next chapter I turn to Semprun, another survivor who relies upon Proust's evocations of memory to use unwanted beauty as a survival mechanism and a call to examine the relationships between aesthetics and memory. All three survivors demonstrate how the beauty of their depictions can be enormously helpful in the long process of survival. These writers highlight the paradoxes of Holocaust representation, for in order to begin to capture the worst the representation must be beautiful, must be metaphorical, and must then, to some degree, be pleasurable. This is exactly the most impossible, the most unwanted beauty.

Chapter 2

AESTHETIC MEMORY:
JORGE SEMPRUN AND
"THE BITTER RESIDUE OF DEATH"

The only ones who will manage to reach this substance,
this transparent density, will be those able to shape
their evidence into an artistic object, a space of creation.
—Jorge Semprun

In his fascinating Holocaust novel *Le grand voyage* (1963), Jorge Semprun
juxtaposes the pleasure of reading the childhood memories offered in Marcel Proust's *À la recherche du temps perdu* with the painful and deferred
memory of his arrival at the Buchenwald concentration camp. By turning
to Proust's layered representations of childhood desires and fears, Semprun
illustrates both how his memory of Proust's peaceful (if neurotic) novel
and his own postwar consciousness have been colored by his experience of
the camps. Semprun's treatment of Proust—both through the voice of his
narrator, Gérard, in the scene of incarceration itself, and through the literary and stylistic appropriations of Proust that pepper his text—prompts us
to examine how aesthetic pleasure can offer an important survival mechanism. While Semprun's use of Proust is much more marked and explicit
than Charlotte Delbo's (whose work I discussed in chapter 1), these two
survivors share an interest in how Proust's theories of memory, including
voluntary and involuntary memory, inform the experience of Holocaust
survival and of postwar literary testimonial writing. By analyzing how Semprun's use of Proust helps him survive Buchenwald, the first section of this
chapter demonstrates how aesthetic pleasure affords a mode of coping with
traumatic memory. In the second section I focus on Semprun's rewriting
of the past through his use of Ilse Koch, the infamous Nazi commandant
suspected of perpetrating sexual crimes against the inmates of Buchenwald,
and Sigrid, the young woman who acts as Koch's counterbalance in the *Le
grand voyage*. By redrawing Koch in the much more palatable form of Sig-

rid, Semprun manipulates aesthetic pleasure not just to survive but to transform a painful past into a more tolerable present. Taken together, these two sections demonstrate how Semprun seeks comfort in unwanted beauty in order first to survive the Holocaust, then to come to terms with his painful memories of it, and ultimately to rewrite his experiences of the Holocaust as a literary reflection on the brutality of history.

Semprun, a Spaniard from a Catholic family, was born in 1923 and emigrated to France in 1938 after Franco became dictator. Adopting the pseudonym Gérard Sorel (and thus perhaps echoing Stendhal's hero Julien Sorel), he joined the French resistance in 1941 and in 1943 was arrested, tortured, and deported to Buchenwald. Semprun's bourgeois family, deeply rooted in Spanish politics and culture, prepared him well to appreciate the shimmering density of Proust's prose. His grandfather, Antonio Maura, whom Semprun describes as an "authoritarian but reformist man," was the Prime Minister under Alphonse XIII.[1] His father, José María Semprun Gurrea, was a lawyer and poet whose readings to his children Semprun fondly remembered; Françoise Nicoladzé credits Semprun's father's library with offering the writer his first experiences of the sensual relationship to literary works that the narrator of Le grand voyage later cherishes.[2] Before being arrested in Paris, Semprun had begun studying philosophy at the École Normale Supérieure. Fluent in French and German, he survived Buchenwald through being taken in by a clandestine communist group that maneuvered him into a position in the office responsible for deportee labor assignments. After World War II, under the pseudonym Federico Sánchez, Semprun returned to Paris and became active in the Spanish Communist Party in exile. He was expelled from the party in 1964, however, because of his criticisms of the Stalinist purges and other excesses of postwar communism.[3] After his break with the party he took up screenwriting, working on films with Costa-Gavras and Chris Marker, and with Alain Resnais on La guerre est finie (1966) and Stavisky (1974).[4] The appearance of Le grand voyage was met with great applause in 1963; Semprun was awarded the Formentor Prize, and the text was translated into multiple languages. Semprun was Spain's Minister of Culture from 1988 to 1991, before returning to France, where he remains an active writer and speaker. In 2003, Semprun was awarded the Goethe-Institut's Goethe-Medal. In 1994 he published the much acclaimed account of his experiences in struggling with wartime memories, L'écriture ou la vie; indeed, this later novel is almost a companion to Le grand voyage, as it explains how the earlier novel was written and illuminates some of its characters. As Isabelle de Courtivron claimed of L'écriture ou la *vie,* we can also claim for *Le grand voyage,* namely that it "attains a terrifying beauty."[5] The beauty of Semprun's work is of course a melancholic beauty, and he is acutely aware at each turn of the paradox of his own literary endeavor: that it must be beautiful to perform memory work but that its beauty will be an unwanted outcome in this context.

Throughout Semprun's postwar career he writes about his experience of living in two languages, as a Spaniard often writing about the Spanish Civil War primarily in French.[6] Having gone from Prime Minister's grandson to Buchenwald prisoner to Minister of Culture—and from Franco to Hitler to Stalin—Semprun has been an acute witness to the vagaries of twentieth-century European art and politics. Examining *Le grand voyage* offers insight not only into how Semprun was able to survive the worst but also into the larger question of how this important figure in contemporary French and Spanish culture portrays the relationship between aesthetics and memory.

FINDING PROUST IN *LE GRAND VOYAGE*

The narrative of *Le grand voyage* unfolds in many time frames, the first, and most recurrent, of which is the journey in a cramped and squalid boxcar carrying 120 resistance fighters from Compiègne, the transit camp in France, to the concentration camp Buchenwald, in Germany.[7] But the narrative only fleetingly remains in the boxcar; via sudden, unannounced temporal switches the first-person narration lurches back and forth from the time before the war, when Semprun, as a "Red Spaniard," arrived in Paris, to various times after the war. Although many of these scenes take place at the moment of liberation in 1945, others occur two, three, sixteen, or an unspecified number of years later.[8] Semprun thus shares with Charlotte Delbo the sense that the concentration camp universe lives next to him, and recurs long after the war. During the "present" time of the boxcar journey Semprun's narrator conveys his memories to an unnamed companion dubbed "le gars de Semur" (the guy from Semur). Or rather, he tells some of his memories to the guy from Semur, and others he narrates as daydreams—including dreams of Proust—that carry him through the interminable and grueling voyage. As Semprun tells us in *L'écriture ou la vie* (1994), he invented the guy from Semur because the memory of taking the horrific journey alone would have been difficult to reconstruct without an interlocutor who in this case becomes the physical embodiment of at least some of the narrator's memories.[9] Gérard informs us at the outset that this man will die before the deeply ambiguous relief of arriving at the camps.

By linking the narrator with a man who dies while carrying the narrator's memories, Semprun conveys a sensation shared by many Holocaust survivors—namely, that part of them is dead while another part—the rememberer—is very much alive.[10] As I discussed in chapter 1, Delbo felt this so keenly that she did not immediately protest when her name was called out among the dead at a ceremony for French victims of the war. In *Le grand voyage,* because so much remembering had taken place during the time and space of the voyage to the camps, and because Gérard and the guy from Semur had become so intertwined, when the narrator finally lays down the heavy and dead body of the guy from Semur, he laments "c'est comme si je déposais ma propre vie passée, tous les souvenirs qui me relient encore au monde d'autrefois" (it's as though I were laying down my own past, all the memories linking me to the world of the past).[11] The body of the guy from Semur has absorbed the identity of the narrator during the last moments before that identity must be traded in for a number in Buchenwald. The implication is that memory stops at the door of the camps, that the pleasure afforded by access to the past must end there.

Semprun thus echoes Robert Antelme's argument in his testimony *L'espèce humaine,* that the loss of name and therefore of identity was necessary for the dehumanizing mechanism of the camps to function. For Antelme, memory can be a hellish experience because of the difference between the pleasure of the past and the horror of the present: "L'enfer de la mémoire fonctionnait à plein. Pas un qui n'essayait de fixer une femme, qui ne sonnait à sa porte et n'entendait en même temps l'autre sonnerie, celle qui avait tout déclenché, quand il leur avait ouvert la porte" (The hell of memory was operating full blast. There was hardly a guy who wasn't trying to recall some woman, who wasn't ringing at his door, and who, at the same time, wasn't hearing that other ringing at the door, the one that, when he had opened the door to them, had precipitated everything).[12] Here, the pleasurable memory of a lover ringing the doorbell has been indelibly colored by the painful memory of the police or the Gestapo ringing the same bell at the moment of one's arrest.

Another survivor, Aharon Appelfeld, echoes this sentiment of Antelme's and finds that when he tries to remember family vacations during his short life before the Shoah (he was eight when first ghettoized, incarcerated, and then left as an orphaned refugee to fend for himself in Ukrainian forests), he discovers that his "most hidden childhood memories were spotted with the soot from the trains."[13] Thus Antelme and Appelfeld, and, as we will see, Semprun's use of Proust's ringing garden bell, all indicate that survivors often find that memory has been colonized by the experience of the Holocaust—that there is no way to retrieve the pleasant memory of a lover waiting at the door or the buried memories of prewar childhood vacations without simultaneously triggering the corruption of those memories by the Shoah.

Because memories of Semprun's past end with the death of the guy from Semur, he treats the time spent reminiscing on the train as the last access to the hawthorne bushes of a prewar, pre–concentration camp model for the pleasure of memory. Yet Semprun also speaks of the incredible relief he found in recounting these memories sixteen years after the end of the war. In devoting this testimony-inflected novel not to the actual experience of Buchenwald but to the experience of remembering prewar events on the way to the camp, Semprun chooses to focus on those moments when aesthetic pleasure allowed him to escape the horrors he endured. Indeed, in *L'écriture ou la vie* Semprun claims that as soon as he gets inside the camp, "quand j'y suis, l'écriture se bloque" (218) (I'm blocked and cannot write, 166). Curiously, however, much of the "remembering" that takes place in the boxcar is not memory but projection into the future, to the moment of liberation and beyond. The temporal disjunction that Semprun creates by leaping forward and backward from a present moment rendered unstable by an excess of memory at once replicates and exceeds Proustian temporal disjunctions. That is, beyond his references to Proust, Semprun also structures *Le grand voyage* around memory in a Proustian fashion, if not with a Proustian vocabulary: "Mais à présent c'est encore l'heure trouble des souvenirs. Ils remontent à la gorge, ils étouffent, ils ramollissent les volontés. Je chasse les souvenirs. J'ai vingt ans, j'emmerde les souvenirs" (30) (But now it's still the uneasy hour of memories. They rise to the throat, they choke you, they weaken the will. I expel memory. I'm twenty, I don't give a damn about memory, 29). Strikingly, Antelme had also used the image of choking on words in the opening of *L'espèce humaine*, where he tells us: "A peine commencions-nous à raconter, que nous suffoquions" (9) (No sooner would we begin to tell our story than we would be choking over it, 3). Ann Smock beautifully describes this paradox when she insists on the need to hear the choked words of Antelme and other survivors: "For we *must* speak in the sense that we must not ever forget the disaster, the immeasurable suffering of those who suffered the death camps; we must speak in the sense that there must be, among men who speak and listen to each other, a word bearing witness to the unspeakable."[14]

Similarly, in *Paroles suffoquées* (1987), Sarah Kofman explores how words that try to express Auschwitz are often choked, suffocated, stifled, and that one is caught between the imperative to tell and the difficulty of doing so. Kofman indicates the swallowing of clear speech through the experience of the Holocaust. In her text, she intersperses quotations from Antelme and Blanchot with the story of the murder of her father, killed at Auschwitz because he refused to work instead of pray on the Sabbath: "Parce qu'il était juif, mon père est mort à Auschwitz: comment ne pas le dire? Et comment le dire? Comment parler de ce devant quoi cesse toute possibilité de parler?" (Because he was Jewish, my father died at Auschwitz: how to not say this? And how to say it? How to speak before that which stops all possibility of speaking?).[15] How to *not* tell of her experience is equally treacherous as trying to say what suffocates all possibility of telling. Kofman, clearly, nonetheless tells the story: it is also clear that she indicates at every step that what she narrates is *not enough,* and that she cannot convey the full complexity of the experience. Semprun's description of memories that choke one, then, shifts the terms slightly, because whereas Antelme and Kofman feel that they are choked by the need to tell of the experience of horror, Gérard is choked by memories that involuntarily overcome him as he waits in the boxcar. Once again, as Antelme has described, memory can be hell because the pleasure of it forces one to recognize even more forcefully the pain of the present.

Whereas Antelme's *L'espèce humaine* is explicitly testimony rather than literature, Semprun's *Le grand voyage* is, like Delbo's *La mémoire et les jours,* literature based on experience; the moments of seemingly involuntary memory that Gérard experiences are staged recreations of memory that thus destabilize the location of both the narrator's and the writer's memories. While "Gérard" was one of Semprun's noms de guerre, we cannot assume an absolute correspondence between Semprun and his narrator, yet the narrator's reflections illuminate the writer's theory of memory. For example, returning to Semprun's dismissal of memory cited earlier, the word "chasse" has a double meaning: on the one hand, the narrator rejects memory; on the other hand, he hunts it down. Indeed, despite his protestations Gérard certainly does care deeply about memory, and he foregrounds the knowledge that "Dans quinze ans, quand j'écrirai ce voyage, ce sera impossible" (31) (Fifteen years from now, when I write about this voyage, it will be impossible, 29). Elsewhere Gérard claims that writing about the voyage is akin to living it all over again, "Mais en réalité, j'ai oublié ce voyage tout en sachant pertinemment qu'un jour j'aurais à refaire ce voyage" (26) (But the fact is that I forgot this voyage while realizing full well that I would one day have to take it again, 24). In Susan

Rubin Suleiman's words, Semprun "*performs* the vacillation or unreliability of memory over time" (emphasis in original).[16] Gérard's curious claims about forgetting what he so clearly remembers and about not caring about memory are Semprun's means of highlighting the *performance* of these memories of the journey to Buchenwald.

The present-time journey of Semprun's narrative leaves Gérard at the gates of Buchenwald wondering where one can find the music that would complete the staging of the camp arrival. At this point, just a few pages before the ending, the tone suddenly becomes more deeply reflective and Gérard begins to refer to himself in the third person. This closing segment produces a starkly different quality from that of the rest of the text and appears to have been written with the benefit of historical hindsight. Indeed, the concern over the correct staging of the arrival seems to refer to postwar reconstructions, such as that found in Paul Celan's poem "Todesfuge," which, as I discussed in chapter 1, refers explicitly to the grim playing of music over death. By contrast, even though we know that much of the text takes place after the war, the bulk of Semprun's novel (part 1) produces a sensation of immediacy.

Long before the explicit references to Proust appear in *Le grand voyage*, therefore, Semprun reflects on memory and its curious mechanisms, creating a Proustian narrative structure that kaleidoscopically conflates time zones.[17] Semprun is keenly aware, as was Delbo, that, painful or not, one can never inhabit the past again; the often melancholic nature of our relationship to the past depends upon its sometimes bittersweet finality and inaccessibility. Yet both survivors' decisions to turn to Proust allow them to sharpen their portrayal of the sense that, even when you do not wish to return to a painful past, you are on occasion nonetheless compelled to do so, even while remaining forever, thankfully, at a certain remove from the past. Indeed, throughout Semprun's returns to the past(s) we are often met with his own understanding of the uncanny nature of these returns. In discussing the late twentieth-century obsession with the uncanny—a term first put into wide use by Freud's 1919 essay of that name—Martin Jay notes that even in Freud's discussion of the desire to return home that marks the emergence of the uncanny, there is a sense that the longing is for "an eerily familiar home that, however, was never really inhabited and therefore can never be regained."[18] (In his choice of the word "regained" here Jay is no doubt thinking of the English translation of the final volume of Proust's novel as "Time Regained.") Thus the past that Semprun by turns avoids and wishes to wrestle with is, like the uncanniness of home discussed by Freud and Jay, never really regainable.

Some thirty years after writing *Le grand voyage,* with all of its thick references to Proust, Semprun claimed in *L'écriture ou la vie* that *Du côté de chez Swann* "ne m'avait pas vraiment intéressé. Je n'ai pas poursuivi plus avant ma lecture de la *Recherche.* C'était trop familier, trop familial presque. Je veux dire: c'était comme la chronique d'une famille qui aurait pu être la mienne" (189) (hadn't really interested me. I didn't read any more of the *Recherche* [beyond the first volume]. It was too familiar, and almost too familial. What I mean is, it was like the chronicle of a family that might have been mine, 143). Yet, despite these later protestations of disinterest in the *Recherche* (and Semprun did indeed read the rest of the novel, finally finishing in 1982!), Semprun's *Le grand voyage* shares many characteristics of Proust's novel—perhaps precisely defining the "familiarity" Semprun describes. For some examples of these echoes, consider that both novels often do not indicate typographically when the time frame shifts so that memory becomes the work of retrieving a past *and* of previewing a future. In addition, women in Semprun's narrative often serve emblematic or representative roles that reduce them to figures of imagination or male reconstruction, much as Marcel's imagination transforms female characters to fit his needs. Finally, Semprun's characters, like Proust's, seem to merge into one another, conflating their memories and narratives. By employing these classically Proustian techniques, Semprun reflects on how memory of the camps can be compared to prewar modes of memory production, and how it is interwoven into projections of the future. The aesthetic pleasure offered by memories of Proust's novel are at least doubled; the gauzy image of *À la recherche du temps perdu* itself is overlaid with memories of a prewar time when reading Proust was possible. Yet Semprun suggests that even associative links to prewar childhood memories have become colored by the memory of the Shoah.

Semprun's first direct reference in *Le grand voyage* to *À la recherche du temps perdu* is a complex representation of a reconstruction of a reconstruction:

> *J'ai passé ma première nuit de voyage à reconstruire dans ma mémoire le côté de chez Swann et c'était un excellent exercice d'abstraction. Moi aussi, je me suis longtemps couché de bonne heure, il faut dire. J'ai imaginé ce bruit ferrugineux de la sonnette, dans le jardin, les soirs où Swann venait dîner. . . . Et cette haie d'aubépines, seigneur, cette haie d'aubépines était aussi mon enfance. J'ai passé la première nuit de ce voyage à reconstruire dans ma mémoire le côté de chez Swann et à me rappeler mon enfance. (73)*

I spent the first night of the voyage reconstructing *Swann's Way* in my mind, and it was an excellent exercise in abstraction. For a long time, I too used to go to bed early. I imagined the metallic sound of the bell in the garden on evenings when Swann came to dinner. . . . And that hawthorne hedge, Lord, that hawthorne hedge was my childhood too. I spent the first night of this voyage reconstructing *Swann's Way* in my mind and recalling my childhood. (72)[19]

The repetition of "I spent the first night reconstructing" and the changes after each repeated phrase indicate that what had been an abstract exercise in the first iteration gives way to the more concrete exercise of remembering his own childhood as though that past were embedded in Proust's past. In referencing the famous opening lines of Proust's work, Semprun reverses them slightly. Proust opens with: "Longtemps, je me suis couché de bonne heure" (*Swann,* 3); Semprun echoes with: "je me suis longtemps couché de bonne heure." Proust's opening indicates that it is his habit, and has been for quite some time, to go to bed early, but the choice of the *passé composé* as opposed to the more habitual *imparfait* weakens this connection. Semprun's version also indicates the habitualness of going to bed early but deemphasizes it by opening with "je me suis" instead of "longtemps." This small syntactical change underscores the irony of the fact that all choice about bedtime has been nullified by the situation of incarceration both in the boxcar and at Buchenwald.

In this same passage Semprun recalls the sound of the bell to which Proust returns several times in his enormous novel, imagining the sound of the bell to be "ferrugineux" (metallic), which is how Proust also described it. At this stage, Semprun still associates the bell in the garden with Swann, and therefore with Proust; it has not yet become a bell he recalls from his own past. Toward the end of his novel, Proust uses the bell to reflect on the saturation of the flow of time into individual experience; he notices that even in the present, many years after he waited for his mother to kiss him goodnight, he still hears the metallic ring of the bell:

ce bruit des pas de mes parents reconduisant M. Swann, ce tintement rebondissant, ferrugineux, intarissable, criard et frais de la petite sonnette qui m'annonçait qu'enfin M. Swann était parti et que maman allait monter, je les entendis encore, je les entendis eux-mêmes, eux situés pourtant si loin dans le passé.

the noise of my parents' footsteps as they accompanied M. Swann to the door and the peal—resilient, ferruginous, interminable, fresh and shrill—of the bell in the garden gate which informed me that at last he had gone and that Mamma would presently come upstairs, these sounds rang again in my ears, yes, unmistakably I heard these very sounds, situated though they were in a remote past.[20]

While Proust's narrator hears the bell years after his life at Combray has ended, when he imagines the sound of the bell he elides the distinction between present and past in much the same way as Semprun does by moving from the squalid boxcar into reminiscence of reminiscence. When Gérard recalls the bell in the garden, he maintains Proust's description of the sound as "ferrugineux" and uses the memory of reading Proust, much as Proust uses the memory of the sound of the bell, as a reflection on the imagination's ability to elide time and to slip, years later, into the past. For Proust had first introduced the "ferrugineux" and "intarissable" sound of the bell at the very opening of his work, when Marcel distinguishes between the familiar, "ferrugineux" sound of the bell that introduces the family who reside in the house and the more timid sound that introduces others, in this case Swann, one of the family's only casual visitors at Combray:

> *nous entendions au bout du jardin, non pas le grelot profus et criard qui arrosait, qui étourdissait au passage de son bruit ferrugineux, intarissable et glacé, toute personne de la maison qui le déclenchait en entrant "sans sonner," mais le double tintement timide, ovale et doré de la clochette pour les étrangers. (13–14)*

> we heard from the far end of the garden, not the shrill and assertive alarm bell which assailed and deafened with its ferruginous, interminable, frozen sound any member of the household who set it off on entering "without ringing," but the double tinkle, timid, oval, golden, of the visitor's bell. (15)

Gérard also claims to remember a bell, and when he enters the garden guarded by his familiar bell he listens to the sound several times before confronting a female Jewish survivor lying on a chaise longue in his garden. In remembering this bell as "ferrugineux" Gérard identifies it as a familiar bell as opposed to a visitor's bell. Just one paragraph before the close of *À la recherche du temps perdu*, Proust again evokes the garden bell: "La date à laquelle j'entendais le bruit de la sonnette du jardin de Combray, si distant et pourtant intérieur, était un point de repère dans cette dimension énorme que je ne me savais pas avoir" (352) (In this vast dimension which I had not known myself to possess, the date on which I had heard the noise of the garden bell at Combray—that far-distant noise which nevertheless

was within me—was a point from which I might start to make measure-
ments, 530). The "enormous dimension" to which Proust refers is the vast
time that he surveys and that his novel has attempted to record. Semprun
also uses this bell as a vantage point from which to survey the enormity of
his past. In Proust's case, that past is a complicated series of social and
political interactions within French salon life; for Semprun's narrator, the
enormity of the past has been soaked up by the interminable experience
of traveling to and being interned in a concentration camp.

Proust's bell in the garden reappears in *Le grand voyage* when Semprun
describes a garden in Saint-Prix, which Gérard visits years after his return
from Buchenwald just to enjoy the sound of the bell at its gate: "J'ai ouvert
et fermé plusieurs fois la porte du potager, pour entendre ce bruit dont je
me souvenais, le bruit oxydé, ferrugineux, de la petite cloche" (94) (I opened
and closed the garden gate several times, to hear the rusty, metallic sound I
remembered, the sound of the little bell activated by the gate, 93–94). The
sound of this bell is also "ferrugineux"—and therefore the sound of family
entering the house—even though he encounters a strange woman in the
garden who is staking out an uncertain peace in light of her memories of
the concentration camp. Upon discovering that the woman has a tattoo from
Oswiecim (the Polish name for Auschwitz) on her arm, Gérard asks her why
the sound of the bell resonates with her, and she replies, "Parce que c'est
comme autrefois" (95) (Because it's like something from out of the past, 94).
For this woman, too, the sound of the bell is a reminder of something from
the prewar past. While Semprun blurs the details, it seems that the narrator's
family had once lived in the house to which this garden belongs and that the
garden had had a bell in it (we know nothing of Gérard's family, or what
their involvement in the resistance might have been). The woman is thus a
symbolic reminder that even the narrator's childhood has been polluted by
the memory of the camps. Proust's reconstruction of a childhood filled with
anticipation, anxious waiting, and listening for the sound of the bell in the
garden has become, for Semprun, an endless reminder of the camps. Garden
bells can no longer ring without the ghosts of the Shoah invading the hawthorne bushes, just as Antelme could not remember the bell of his lover
without the Gestapo ringing in his ears.

As do all women in Semprun's text, this woman on the chaise longue
serves a representative function. Before the war the narrator had encountered
her on the streets of Paris, anxiously deferring a question she clearly longed
to pose. The narrator had assumed the question involved a matter of life and

death, whereas, when finally posed, it was simply a request for directions to the rue Antoine-Bourdelle near the train station at Montparnasse. Gérard had escorted her to her destination, and along the way she had told him that she was a Jewess seeking refuge. Thus her worried question had been, after all, one involving life and death, and in helping her rather than reporting her, Gérard had done her a great service. However, when this woman mysteriously appears in the garden after the war, she refuses to recognize the narrator or to remember his kindness, claiming that "Personne ne m'a aidée, jamais" (96) (No one has *ever* helped me, 96). The woman goes on to explain that non-Jews cannot understand what Jews have gone through, and she is reluctant to enter into the community of survivors that the narrator offers her when he confesses that he wonders if she too had made the journey to the camps. In discussing the Jewish characters in Semprun's later work *L'écriture ou la vie,* Ruth Wisse criticizes Semprun for "treating Jews as a literary construct"—for reducing his Jewish characters to victims useful merely for the articulation of difference.[21] The woman on the chaise longue is thus a "literary construct," but only in the same way as is Sigrid, whom I will discuss below, or the guy from Semur, who is a fictional double of the narrator. While the survivor in the garden is doubly constructed as Jewish and female, her story serves more than a dual purpose in elaborating Semprun's theory of memory. First, the bittersweet Proustian memories of childhood will forever be haunted by the presence of the Shoah in these imaginary fragrant gardens. Second, the aesthetic pleasure afforded by the bell functions as a reminder of the pleasure of memory and its ability to transform crowded boxcars into peaceful gardens. Third, while Semprun often claims that one cannot understand the experience of deportation and the camps unless one has been there, the story of the woman in the garden indicates Semprun's complicated relationship to a parallel claim—namely that one cannot understand the experience of Jews in the Holocaust without being Jewish. Just as readers may want to empathize with the narrator and trust that the art of his text offers nonwitnesses a deeper understanding of the experience of deportation, so the narrator seems to want to understand the experience of Jews and to empathize with their plight.

By claiming that no one has ever helped her, this woman describes an experience very different from Gérard's, which is marked by both help and hindrance. The narrator had often been helped by others, and his narrative is full of moments of generosity when fellow inmates shared their last bits of food with him; yet the narrative is also replete with moments where no one helped him. Semprun highlights the vagaries of help in the camps by noting that "Dans les camps, l'homme devient cet animal capable de voler le pain d'un camarade, de le pousser vers la mort. Mais dans les camps l'homme devient aussi cet être invincible capable de partager . . . son dernier morceau de pain" (62) (In the camps, man becomes that animal capable of stealing a mate's bread, of propelling him toward death. But in the camps man also becomes that invincible being capable of sharing . . . his last piece of bread, 60). Thus, Semprun resists moralizing about either the endless resiliency of the human spirit in the camps or the ease with which the human spirit becomes so debased as to be unable to share. This reflection of the dual character of human nature as revealed in the camps follows Semprun's grateful recognition that the guy from Semur shared what little food he had smuggled into the boxcar with him (in this case some small apples, 61/59). Of course, this sharing is complicated by the revelation, discussed above, that the guy from Semur is Gérard's double, and a "literary construct" designed to facilitate the unfolding of the narrative. Nonetheless, the unnamed woman's experience and Gérard's are understood as radically different, and the difference clearly has to do with the fact that she is Jewish and he is not.

Unlike Jews, resistance fighters were interned in the concentration camps due to acts of will rather than genetic heritage, and, as grim as deportation and camp conditions were, members of the resistance were better treated and consequently had higher survival rates than Jewish prisoners. Semprun muses that "J'y suis librement, puisque j'aurais pu ne pas y être" (24) (I'm here of my own free will, since I could have not been here, 22). Unlike Jewish prisoners, resistance fighters chose to take the risk of deportation. Semprun reports that while resisters were horribly cramped in cars with 119 other people, Jewish prisoners were transported in groups of 200 in the same space (98/97). In fact, the presence of Jewish prisoners haunts Semprun's novel and he often remarks that later, after the war, he found out that the Jewish inmates had had an even more devastating experience than the resistance fighters. In a conversation with Elie Wiesel, published as *Se taire est impossible* (*Remaining Silent Is Impossible,* 1995), Semprun opens the discussion by noting the different experiences they had had in the same camp because one was Jewish and the other was not: "nous n'avons pas la même expérience du camp" (we did not have the same experience of the camp). In responding, Wiesel echoes Semprun's understanding that Semprun was in the camps freely because he chose to resist and reminds him that "tu savais pourquoi tu étais là, tu étais résistant, tu te battais, tu faisais partie de la Résistance. Moi j'étais 'un musulman,' comme on disait à l'époque n'est-ce pas, j'étais un objet" (you knew why you were there, you were a resister, you fought, you were a member of the Resistance. I was a "musulman," as we said then, I was an object).[22] In articulating the difference between non-Jewish resisters and Jews (whether resisters or not), Wiesel emphasizes many Jews' status as *muselmänner,* people whom Primo Levi and others describe as figures near death, who are no longer properly human because they have no human concerns other than sustenance.[23] By figuring himself as an "object," Wiesel insists on Jewish prisoners' radical lack of agency.

Charlotte Delbo, who was a non-Jewish member of the French resistance (as discussed in chapter 1) and a survivor of Auschwitz, also reflects in her memoirs upon the difference between the experience of resisters and that of Jewish inmates. As a prisoner, Delbo noticed the harsher treatment of Jews in the camp, but she also often resented these other victims for intruding into the tight-knit group of women that enabled her survival. At one point in her three-volume account of her experiences, *Auschwitz et àpres,* Delbo notes:

> *les juives croient qu'elles sont plus battues que nous et viennent se glisser entre nos robes rayées. Elles nous font peine. Elles nous font peine à cause de leur accoutrement. . . . Elles ont de l'épouvantail et du pingouin, avec les manches à l'envers qui embarrassent les bras. . . . Un comique terrifiant. Elles nous font pitié mais nous ne voulons pas nous séparer.*

> the Jewish women, believing they are taking more of a beating, slip in between our striped dresses. We are sorry for them. Sorry on account of their attire. . . . They have something of the scarecrow and the penguin, with their sleeves, wrong side out, hampering their arms. . . . A terrifying comedy. They fill us with pity but we do not want to be separated from each other.[24]

And so, in a passage of terrible and brutal honesty, Delbo not only reports that the Jewish women were worse off than the non-Jewish resisters, but also acknowledges that her little group of resisters would not help the Jewesses by letting them into their huddle, and would not then protect them from the surrounding blows of the SS and kapos. Delbo's admission helps us understand why Semprun's woman in the garden feels that no one has ever helped her; she thus refuses to be sentimentalized as she had been in the earlier scene on the rue de Vaugirard, where Gérard gallantly helps her reach refuge. While her presence in the garden represents the disruption that the presence of Jewish survivors of the Shoah injects into attempts to return to a prewar mode of memory that can recall an unclouded childhood, her refusal to remember the help the narrator had given her intensifies the impossibility of nostalgic remembrance. Thus, while this woman, as a "literary construct," plays such an important role in Semprun's narrative, she also disrupts Semprun's musings on the search for aesthetic (and in this case literary) pleasure amid the ruins of memory, which is why it is so important that this Jewish survivor interrupts Semprun's nostalgic musings on the comforting sound of the garden bell.

Before the scene in the garden, Semprun makes the link between the appearance of the woman in the garden and Proust's gardens explicit:

> *je guettais le départ de Swann, qui s'attardait à bavarder dans le jardin. Je me retournais dans mon lit, dans cette chambre d'hôtel allemande à Eisenach, et je cherchais un réconfort dans ma mémoire. C'est alors que je me suis rappelé cette femme israélite de la rue de Vaugirard. (88)*

> I listened for the departure of Swann, who was lingering in the garden, talking. I was tossing and turning in my bed, in that German hotel room at Eisenach, and I was hunting for something comforting in my memory. It was then that I remembered the Jewish woman at the rue de Vaugirard. (87)

It is comforting for the narrator to remember a moment when he helped someone even though the woman denies his help and refuses to remember him. Semprun continues to enact the disruption of comfortable memories that his comparisons to Proust make material. For example, by rewriting Proust's famous madeleine scene (which I cited in chapter 1), Semprun seems to mock the suddenness of an involuntary memory that takes place some years after the journey to the camp, while he is recovering from the war:

> *Alors, ce goût de pain noir, un peu acide, cette lente mastication du pain noir, grumeleux, ont fait revivre en moi, brutalement, ces instants merveilleux où l'on mangeait notre ration de pain, au camp . . . je ne pouvais quand même pas lui dire que j'étais en train de mourir, en train de défaillir de faim, très loin d'eux, très loin du feu de bois, des paroles que nous prononcions. (126–27)*

> Then, the slightly acid taste of the black bread, the slow mastication of this gritty black bread, brought back, with shocking suddenness, the marvelous moments when, at camp, we used to eat our ration of bread. . . . Obviously I couldn't tell her [i.e., the woman on whose farm he recovers] that I was in the throes of dying, dying of hunger, far from them, far from the wood fire and the words they were saying. (126)

As I discussed in chapter 1, in Proust's madeleine scene, the convergence of the madeleine and the tea releases a flood of memory and transports Marcel back to the feelings of his childhood that had been inaccessible to him prior to the taste of the tea. Here, black bread rather than a sweet biscuit catalyzes memory. But while Semprun describes the memory of the moment in the camp as "marvelous," he immediately belies this description by remembering dying of hunger. The paradox that eating should remind one of dying of hunger underscores the paucity of what passed for rations in the camps; food can only remind one of dying if it is always in short supply. Semprun's rewriting of the madeleine scene also recalls Delbo's discussion of the doubling of thirst. Many survivor accounts, including Semprun's, describe moments where, because the food may be so unclean as to sicken the prisoners, eating is physically worse for the inmates than abstaining. This black bread, then, in reproducing while radically transforming Proust's madeleine, once again underscores Semprun's argument that memory after the camps—involuntary or not—can no longer offer the comforts of Proust's "immense edifice." Thus, as I discussed in chapter 1, Proust's division of memory into voluntary and involuntary memory helped Delbo articulate the means through which painful memories often return uninvited; Semprun more closely echoes Proustian scenes in order to demonstrate how different memory has become for survivors.

In another reflection on the insertion of painful memories into the aesthetic pleasure offered by pleasant Proustian ones, Semprun explicitly links the interminable journey on the train with both the interminable night at Eisenach after liberation, and Marcel's interminable waiting for his mother's kiss in *Du côté de chez Swann:* "La nuit n'en finissait pas . . . comme n'en finissaient pas les nuits d'enfance à guetter le bruit de l'ascenseur, qui annoncerait le retour des parents, à guetter les conversations dans le jardin lorsque Swann venait dîner" (87–88) (The night refused to end . . . like the childhood nights of listening for the noise of the elevator announcing that my parents had come home, of listening to the conversations in the garden when Swann came to dinner, 86). Gérard here assimilates himself completely with Marcel; there is no separation between waiting for the elevator and listening to the conversations with Swann. In Proust, the almost endless anticipation of waiting for his mother's return heightens Marcel's anxiety; when she does return she often stays with him so fleetingly that he resumes a posture of waiting for her immediately after her departure. Thus, in Proust the moment of arrival of the mother does not offer the satisfaction that the reader, much less Marcel, might have hoped for. Semprun in effect doubles this Proustian moment: the guy from Semur complains that the night of the boxcar journey will never end, yet this night that refuses to end is also the interminable night at Eisenach. It is curious that Semprun associates the tortured waiting in the boxcar with the waiting at Eisenach for the dawn of a new Europe, and both with the anxiety of a neurotic child lavishly ensconced in a comfortable bed obsessively waiting for a glimpse of his mother. Yet the comparison underscores the impossible structure of anticipation that marks both texts. In both Proust and Semprun, arrivals achieve nothing: there is no relief to the endless anticipation and waiting that controls both narratives, because both are structured by this insistence on non-arrival. While the force of narrative closure compels us to find in the arrival at the camp some relief, Semprun's echo of the Proustian structure of non-arrival reminds us that there is no relief for the Holocaust victim. As the Jewish woman in the garden would have it, no one has ever helped; she rejects the memory of receiving help from the narrator because that might sweeten the worst memories of deportation and incarceration. Her forgetting of his help is thus linked to his willful forgetting of the most painful of his wartime memories.

Perhaps in willing himself to forget about the boxcar journey, Gérard had in fact merely set it aside, and it would take many years after the journey for another piece of black bread to bring these repressed memories to light. In commenting on the differences between Semprun's *Quel beau dimanche* and *Le grand voyage,* Robert Boyers reflects on Semprun's dialectic between memory and forgetting: "Semprun remembers whatever he can about Buchenwald and about the Nazi period generally because he wishes to put it all behind him. Compelled to remember, to bear witness, he continues to imagine that it will be possible eventually to do justice to the central truths of the holocaust experience without rehearsing over and over, for all time, the particular components of that experience."[25] Indeed, Semprun has remarked several times that forgetting is a necessary condition of remembering. As Beckett, in speaking of Proust, puts it: "The man with a good memory does not remember anything because he does not forget anything."[26] The structure of memory is complex: the narrator colors the time of the journey with other memories and projections so that he spends a great deal of time remembering when he remembered something else: "Plus tard, je me souviens—c'est-à-dire, je ne m'en souviens pas encore ... puisque ce n'est pas encore arrivé" (36) (Later, I remember—that is, I don't yet remember ... since it hasn't yet happened, 34). While Semprun does not here refer explicitly to involuntary memory (although he does to voluntary forgetting), his descriptions clearly conjure up a mode of memory in which the past suddenly takes one over and the gap between present and past evaporates: "Au fil des années, il faut dire, des souvenirs m'ont assailli, parfois, d'une parfaite précision, surgissant de l'oubli volontaire de ce voyage, avec la perfection polie des diamants que rien ne peut entamer" (126) (As the years went by, I was sometimes assailed by memories, absolutely vivid memories that arose from the willful oblivion of this voyage with the polished perfection of diamonds that nothing can impair, 126). These involuntary memories that assail "l'oubli volontaire," into which the narrator casts himself, are strikingly different from those memories on the train that seem to be willful acts of self-creation by which the narrator fashions a usable past full of aesthetic pleasure to lift himself out of the grim present.

Maurice Blanchot notes that in the moments in Proust when time collapses, "le temps est aboli . . . non pas un passé et un présent, mais une même présence qui fait coïncider en une simultanéité sensible des moments incompatibles, séparés par tout le cours de la durée" (time is abolished . . . not a past and a present, but one single presence that causes incompatible moments, separated by the entire course of lived life, to coincide in a palpable simultaneity).[27] This description could apply equally well to the structure of Semprun's writing, because he moves between modes of voluntary and involuntary memory, while always struggling with the question of control over the past. In those moments when he casts away memory, claiming it has no hold on him, he tries to make all memory voluntary, yet in other moments he admits that he is "assailed" by memories that he cannot control. Thus, when Gérard's mastication of a piece of black bread suddenly brings back a series of memories, they come in the form of involuntary memories that assail him throughout the narrative. Semprun thus represents the structure of traumatic remembering as memories that get written over by forgettings so that the palimpsest of reminiscence is an ever-turning tablet.

SIGRID REDRAWS ILSE KOCH

Semprun records a moment of involuntary memory, ten years after the war, when he dances with Sigrid, a young German woman, in a Paris bistro. Before the memories that wake him out of the "dream" in which he had been living assail him, he flirts with Sigrid, and asks pointed questions about where her father had been during the war. Sigrid's unwanted beauty functions to "faire oublier le corps et le visage d'Ilse Koch" (148) (make us forget the body and face of Ilse Koch, 148). Koch was an SS officer's wife whose sick games with concentration camp inmates epitomized the deranged practices of the Nazis, and who became famous after the war as the "bitch from Buchenwald." Indeed, the postwar American press was littered with articles with titles such as "The Bitch Again" (*Time*, October 4, 1948) and "The Witch of Buchenwald" (*Newsweek*, July 28, 1947), and Koch was featured as a torturess in a series of films beginning with *Ilsa, She-Wolf of the SS* (1974).[28] In discussing women such as Ilse Koch, Claudia Koonz, in her groundbreaking study of women in Nazi Germany, speculates that "perhaps the few [women] who ended up on camp assignments were more apt to be depraved or deranged than the men. Or perhaps women guards *seemed* more cruel because their behavior deviated farther from our conceptions of 'feminine' models than men guards' behavior departed from stereotypes about men."[29] The sexual sadism of Ilse Koch haunts Semprun's *Le grand voyage*, and it seems that both aspects of Koonz's speculation are in play here. On the one hand, Koonz's analysis of women in Nazi Germany finds that while there were many committed anti-Semites and pro-Nazi women, the majority of German women were not actively political. On the other hand, a woman who sexually and sadistically toys with male inmates becomes even more monstrous than her male counterparts, who were no doubt equally cruel and depraved. In Semprun's imagination, Ilse Koch—whose memory the beautiful young Sigrid provokes—is evil incarnate and glories in mixing sexual pleasure with death:

> elle avait fait entrer, souriante, le déporté choisi comme instrument de plaisir, doublement, dans l'acte même du plaisir, d'abord, et ensuite pour le plaisir bien plus durable de sa peau parcheminée, convenablement traitée, ivoirine, zébrée par les lignes bleutées du tatouage donnant à l'abat-jour un cachet inimitable. (148)

> she had smiled at the deportee brought in first as the chosen instrument of pleasure, a twofold pleasure, first in the act of pleasure itself and then for the much more durable pleasure of his parchment-like skin, properly treated, the color of ivory, crisscrossed by the bluish lines of the tattoo which gave the lampshade its inimitable stamp. (149)

This horrific image, combining the pleasure of sex with the pleasure of murder, indicates that Koch glories in this double pleasure and shares it with her male SS counterparts. Granted, this scene might have more to do with fantasies of sadism in Nazi Germany than it does with historical validity; the Koch case is surely very complex and the interpretation of her actions has been fraught with controversy. Alexandra Przyrembel, who examined a vast number of documents relating to Koch, including both of her war trials, has even suggested that it was the idea—and not the reality—of a woman as perverse as Koch that caught the imagination of the press, which reveled in making her a monster. However, in concluding that these images of Koch stemmed from "misogynistic clichés about female violence," Przyrembel may be dismissing too quickly the claims made by inmates.[30] For example, when she notes that detailed stories told by prisoners at Koch's trial were not eyewitness accounts, Przyrembel seems to overlook the fact that Koch's victims and any witnesses would most likely have perished in the camps. As Primo Levi so famously argued, "we, the survivors, are not the true witnesses," the true witnesses "have not returned to tell about it or have returned mute."[31]

Thus, while I agree with Przyrembel's and Koonz's feminist arguments that accounts of a sexually sadistic SS wife may have captured the popular imagination for misogynist reasons, I want to maintain that inmates' testimonies should be taken seriously and that the structure of the camps militated against the survival of what Levi calls the "true witnesses." In any case, what is important for my analysis is not Koch's innocence or guilt but the fact that Semprun uses Koch as an emblem of the monstrosity of Nazi evil (although she is certainly not his only example) and the aesthetically pleasing Sigrid as the counterbalance to the sick weight of this history. Thus, whether artifice or not, Semprun's depiction of Koch reveals his understanding of historical progress: the pain of the past can be soothed by a changed present. In this case, the aesthetic pleasure offered by a beautiful young German woman reconfigures an earlier generation of German women who contributed to the horrors of the war.

In Semprun's later novel about his experiences during the war, *L'écriture ou la vie* (1994), Semprun argues, as I discussed in the introduction, that to tell a story well ". . . de façon à être entendus. On n'y parviendra pas sans un peu d'artifice. Suffisamment d'artifice pour que ça devienne de l'art!" (165) (. . . so as to be understood. You can't manage it without a bit of artifice. Enough artifice to make it art! 123). In an analysis of this subsequent novel, David Carroll agrees with Semprun that artifice is "necessary to stimulate the imagination of listeners or readers" when representing the Shoah.[32] It is important that the artifice Semprun chooses in *Le grand voyage* to stimulate the reader's imagination involves sensual and sexual pleasure mingled with death, because he uses this scene paradoxically: the most damning of monstrous figures—Ilse Koch—serves at the same time as part and parcel of his attraction to the young Sigrid. Finding her in Paris, Gérard suspects that Sigrid has fled Germany in order to obliterate the wartime past about which she wanted to know nothing. Since the scene with Sigrid takes place ten years after the war, and since we know she was young when they met, we can assume that Sigrid was a relatively small child during the Holocaust and was therefore probably shielded from information to which adults were privy. In any case, this woman who is trying to forget catalyzes the involuntary memory that pierces the dream-oblivion of the narrator:

> *Quand cette soirée sera finie et que je me souviendrai de cette soirée où, tout à coup, le rappel aigu de ce passé si bien oublié, si parfaitement enfoui dans ma mémoire, m'a réveillé du rêve qu'était ma vie, quand j'essayerai de raconter cette soirée confuse . . . je vais réaliser que la jeune Allemande aux yeux verts, Sigrid, prend un relief particulier dans le récit . . . peut-être tout naturellement parce qu'elle est, de toutes ses forces elle essaye d'être, l'oubli de ce passé qui ne peut s'oublier, la volonté d'oublier ce passé que rien ne pourra jamais abolir, mais que Sigrid rejette . . . avec son bonheur de chaque instant présent, sa certitude aiguë d'exister, opposée à l'aiguë certitude de la mort que ce passé fait suinter comme une résine âpre et tonifiante. (147)*

> When this evening is over, and when I recall this evening during which, suddenly, the acute memory of this forgotten past, this past so perfectly buried in my memory, waked me from the dream which was my life, when later I shall try to relate this chaotic evening . . . I'll realize that Sigrid, the green-eyed German girl, assumes a special significance in the story . . . perhaps . . . quite natural[ly] . . . because she is . . . the oblivion of this past which cannot be forgotten, the will to forget this past which nothing can ever erase but which Sigrid rejects . . . with her happiness of every passing moment, her acute certainty of being alive, as opposed to the acute certainty of death which oozes out of this past like some bitter, bracing resin. (147–48)

As Proust tends to do, Semprun also marks this moment of involuntary memory with a "tout à coup," an explosion of sudden memory that irrevocably transforms the present. Because Semprun uses Sigrid as the figure to erase the memory of Ilse Koch, and because Sigrid is described as the ultimate female figure who makes all men desire to "possess" her, he sexualizes Koch in a manner that reverses the popular image of her as a sexually predatory woman. While Sigrid, as part of the postwar generation of Germans intent on forgetting the Holocaust, is explicitly posited as the figure designed to erase the memory of Koch, she will perform this erasure by evoking desire that is not tainted by the perversion and sadism of the earlier generation embodied in Koch. Yet as Sigrid's own attempt to forget exemplifies, the bitter residue of death leaks out of her even while she tries to repress it. As with the Jewess on the chaise longue in the garden, Sigrid's presence in the narrative is only important insofar as she acts as a catalyst for the narrator's memory. She represents all of Germany in the way that the unnamed Jewess represents all Jews. Gérard pretends to know the suffering of the first, only to be rebuffed, and pretends to know the complicity of the second, only to be rebuffed once again. When Gérard tries to interpret the numbers on the Jewish woman's arms, and even lightly touches them as though reading braille, she snatches her arm away, claiming that he cannot possibly know what she has gone through. She therefore rejects her position as someone who has "special significance" in the narrative by refusing to play the role of representative victim assigned to her. Sigrid similarly rebuffs the narrator with the question "Pourquoi tu me traites comme ça?" (142) (Why are you treating me like this? 142) when he asks her if she might not be secreting a former Gestapo, Waffen SS, or Nazi party father at home in Germany. Yet the narrator nonetheless reabsorbs her into the narrative and paradoxically uses this figure of willful oblivion to break through his own willful oblivion.

It remains unclear how much the narrator of *Le grand voyage* remembered before this moment of involuntary memory, ten years after liberation, because many scenes in the novel that take place shortly after liberation seem to suggest that his memory was intact at that time. Indeed, Semprun builds *L'écriture ou la vie* around the choice between literature, or memory, and life, or forgetting. He repeats the link between the pain of memory and its enactment through writing and the forgetting that can allow life. However, his beautiful literature is replete with life and he himself perhaps recognizes this, as can be glimpsed through a (Freudian) slip in this later novel. As Semprun recounts, after he finally accepted an invitation to take a trip to Buchenwald for the first time in forty-seven years, he finds that he should return to the book he had delayed writing, only here he (accidentally?) titles the work *L'écriture ou la mort* (*Literature or Death*) instead of its published title *L'écriture ou la vie* (*Literature or Life*) (358/280). This slip implies that instead of associating literature with forgetting, the mistaken title (*Literature or Death*) associates art with memory. Thus even though one way of reading Semprun's argument is to accept that for some survivors, remembering the Shoah means being plunged into the company of death, another reading suggests that the beautiful memories conveyed in some survivor literature contribute to sustaining life.

Indeed, Semprun claims in *L'écriture ou la vie* that he lived for fifteen years after the camps in "la béatitude obnubilée de l'oubli. Rares auront été les fois où le soudain souvenir de Buchenwald aura perturbé ma tranquillité d'esprit" (293) (the blissful fog of this amnesia. Rarely did the memory of the camp suddenly shatter my hard-won peace of mind, 226).[33] The moment of involuntary memory catalyzed by the black bread in *Le grand voyage*, cited above, takes place some time after liberation. Semprun's structure of memory thus recalls the model of traumatic memory wherein, as Cathy Caruth claims, "trauma is not locatable in the simple violent or original event in an individual's past, but rather in the way its very unassimilated nature—the way it was precisely *not known* in the first instance—returns to haunt the survivor later on."[34] In Caruth's formulation, trauma occurs over time and re-traumatizes the victim as he/she relives the experience through memory. Similarly, Gérard moves in and out of oblivion through moments of involuntary memory and then relives the entire memory of deportation when he writes the book we read.

SURVIVING TRAUMA THROUGH AESTHETIC PLEASURE

Semprun's use of Proust and Proustian methods enables him to speculate on the differences in memory between pre-Holocaust retellings of bourgeois, "decadent" memories (as Semprun refers to Proust, *Le grand voyage*, 74) and bitter memories of the Shoah. Semprun claims that the structure of memory remains unchanged even while the content of survivors' memories will forever be haunted by the concentration camps. By using Proustian involuntary memory as a model, Semprun beautifully captures the always incomplete rendering of the past that unwilled memories conjure up. By layering Germany's guilt with his own survivor guilt—his own "regret" (97/96) at not being Jewish and therefore at not having access to Jewish memory and experience—and an analysis of the structure of memory itself, Semprun's work, along with Celan's and Delbo's, offers a subtle and complex evocation of the experience of deportation. Moreover, Semprun suggests that the mechanisms of involuntary memory so skillfully analyzed by Proust can assist an understanding of the survival mechanisms available to the sufferers of trauma, and that a literary work such as Proust's can offer a means of imaginative escape from the worst conditions. Indeed, when Semprun travels through the Proustian frame to recover the peaceful memory triggered by hearing a comforting bell, he is confronted by the presence of a survivor whose Jewishness has meant that her experience of the Holocaust has been much worse than his. Semprun thus indicates that all attempts at prewar modes of memory will fail to allow one to escape into nostalgic reminiscence free of the worst. By using Proust in this way, Semprun thus joins the group of Holocaust survivors and artists discussed in this book whose focus on the modes of memory turns their testimonies, literature, and art into powerful examinations of how to survive trauma by seeking respite through aesthetic pleasure.

In the next chapter I discuss the unwanted beauty of the poetry of Edmond Jabès, whose allusive descriptions force us to question our postmemories of the Holocaust. Jabès extends the questions Semprun, Celan, and Delbo raise about the specificity of Jewish concentration camp experience and the ways this experience differs both from that of non-Jewish survivors and from Jewish nonwitnesses. Like Semprun, Jabès lived a life in multiple nationalities and languages and this exilic, diasporic, cosmopolitan existence is reflected in his meditations on displacement. Jabès is often linked with Celan—another poet in Parisian exile, and an acquaintance of his—as both writers struggled to represent the Holocaust through beautiful, unusual poetry. Like Delbo, Jabès often adopts and speaks through many different figures, creating a polyphonic web of competing empathic voices.

Chapter 3

AESTHETIC ALLUSION: EDMOND JABÈS, "THE PAGE IS A CHARRED FIELD WHERE THE DEAD WOULD HAVE WRITTEN"

[Jabès] recalls the day when Celan came to see him with a copy of *The Book of Questions*, heavily annotated in the margins. They talked about the book. Suddenly Celan said: "No, I will not translate you." Edmond is a bit taken aback: "But—" Celan interrupts, vehemently: "No, I cannot."
—Rosmarie Waldrop

Throughout more than a dozen works of allusive, elliptical, postmodern poetry, the French/Egyptian Jewish poet Edmond Jabès develops a complex web of memory that enables us to consider the intractable problem of representing the Holocaust that I have been analyzing vis-à-vis the unwanted beauty of some of the most painful survivor memories. From *Le livre des questions* (1963–73) through *Le livre des limites* (1982–87) and beyond, a series of themes flood Jabès's work: ashes, Judaism, Jews, exile, the desert, the sea, the book, writing, forgetting, questioning, memory, liberty, God, death, love, the Messiah, the Shoah. This list of concerns could also describe the questions that Celan, Delbo, Semprun, and (to some degree) Proust have been raising for us in the previous two chapters of this book. Jabès continues to question the pleasure of memory, the time distortions and character transformations that I have been examining in light of these authors' lives and works. Yet Jabès's poetry also demonstrates that we bear an ethical, aesthetic, and historical imperative to try to grapple with the question of how the Holocaust has become embedded in Western consciousness. Indeed, by avoiding direct and clear Holocaust representations Jabès forces his readers to recognize their own investments in the nuanced process of memory, and thus to find the Holocaust for themselves in elliptical moments where it might not be clearly represented.

The division between "direct" and "oblique" Holocaust representation is to some degree artificial because one can never transmit directly the experience of the Holocaust, and the desire for oblique representations has been prevalent among writers who represent the Shoah. This divide between oblique and direct representations often becomes a divide between aesthetics and documentary. As one of the most important poets illustrating the former of these two strategies of Holocaust representation, Jabès's allusive poetry illustrates how memory works both *on us* and *within us* so relentlessly that it paradoxically may seem to become our living memories of a past we could not have or did not experience. Thus, Jabès offers another example of the transformation of character across impossible times that I discussed in chapters 1 and 2. Delbo's characters, as we saw vis-à-vis *La mémoire et les jours,* often take on different first-person roles, experimenting with experiences not shared by Delbo such as that of Jews in the camps. With the exception of Celan's "Todesfuge," the works I have been examining have been prose texts wherein characters often have more solidity than the sometimes more free-floating poetic "I"s of modern verse. As Semprun and Proust's characters moved across times within the narrative itself, Jabès's characters both move across times within the poems and outside of the poems to implicate us in the process of what Marianne Hirsch calls "post-memory," or those memories inherited by subsequent generations.[1]

Jabès's poetry thus contributes to the blossoming field of memory studies triggered by Pierre Nora's influential *Les lieux de mémoire* (1992). In the paradigm described by Nora, the two modes of treating the past, history and memory, are antagonistic because history threatens the "eradication of memory." History is the "reconstruction, always problematic and incomplete, of what is no longer," whereas "Memory is always a phenomenon of the present, a bond tying us to the eternal present; history is a representation of the past."[2] In this formulation, memory lives vibrantly in the present, whereas history remains in the ossified and static dregs of an always inaccessible past. Although Nora does not quote Jabès here, Nora's theory of memory serves as a perfect explanation for Jabès's elliptical Holocaust representations, because instead of tackling the narrative or structural aspects of the Holocaust via traditional "historical" method, Jabès's poetry depicts how fleeting yet reiterated memories of the Holocaust proliferate through a series of interlocking images, including ashes, Judaism, exile, the desert, and writing. While employing such ambiguous terms, Jabès's work with memory clearly revolves around the following questions: How can we remember or retain the past (cultural or personal) in the face of exile? How can we remember Judaism or Jewish culture, after the Holocaust, or even after the diaspora? How can we remember in the "desert," without either symbol or memorial? How can writing enable remembering when it—at least traditionally—falsely tries to solidify fleeting thoughts? In short, the problem of memory cannot be dissociated from questions of forgetting and writing. For Jabès, then, memory and forgetting are not opposed to each other so much as mutually implicated possibilities within the writing process itself.

Jabès's merging of remembering and forgetting, of recovering and inventing, of the literal and the symbolic, creates a rich field of representational possibilities within which each word doubles as a marker of elliptical memory and a more literal history. Jabès thus warns us that all words are "enveloppés d'ombre" ("enveloped in shadow").[3] The experience of reading Jabès may at times be joyful and at other times difficult, and some of Jabès's poetic and philosophical insights are sublime, yet we must also grapple with the question of aesthetics versus history that Jabès's texts confront us with; for while Jabès explores the question of how memory works powerfully and beautifully, he takes the specificity of historical moments and displaces them onto poetic actors. Thus Jabès's extension of the problem of aesthetic beauty in Holocaust representation that I examined in the first two chapters takes a different turn when he eschews historical specificity in favor of aesthetic pleasure. For Celan, Delbo, and Semprun, beauty amid and as a postwar reflection on painful experiences functioned as a survival mechanism, while for Jabès, as a secondary witness, the beautiful representation of the Holocaust assimilates the event to other concerns that Jabès shares with postmodernists who wonder about the word's ability to signify, the situation of God, and the possibility of reconciliation. Jabès is of approximately the same generation as Celan, Delbo, and Semprun (Jabès was born in 1912, Celan in 1920, Delbo in 1913, and Semprun in 1923); yet his work anticipates the second generation of Holocaust works by those writers and artists born at the end of the war, such as Christian Boltanski and Anselm Kiefer, to whom I turn in chapter 4. Even though Jabès claims that "je me considère comme un survivant" (I consider myself a survivor), he lived alongside the war, and is thus not a survivor in the same way as Celan, Delbo, and Semprun; his meditations on the Holocaust share with some of the second generation the just-off-the-page sensation that the Holocaust asserts itself in the shadow of each word.[4]

While we need to be sensitive to the place of history in these examples of allusive Holocaust art, as I discuss in chapter 4 vis-à-vis the work of Christian Boltanski, I nonetheless disagree with some attacks on the field of memory studies, which argue that memory involves magic and religion to the detriment of the more scholarly and rational concerns of history. This kind of critique takes the difference between aesthetics and documentary and remaps it into a difference between memory and history that privileges the latter at the expense of the former. One of the most vociferous of these attacks was launched by Kerwin Lee Klein in an article in *Representations,* "On the Emergence of *Memory* in Historical Discourse." While Klein does not mention Jabès, he would clearly include Jabès among those twentieth-century artists and theorists whom he argues either use memory for "explicit religiosity" or infuse it with a "theological resonance." Klein offers a scoundrel's list of terms that contribute to such religiosity and remarkably resembles the cluster of terms that interest Jabès: "*Aura . . . Messianic, trauma, mourning, sublime, apocalypse . . . identity, redemption . . . cure, witnessing, testimony.*" Klein dismisses these phrases, arguing that "This is not the vocabulary of secular, critical practice." In fact, as Thomas Laqueur puts it, Klein claims that memory is a "quaisi-religious, metahistorical category that insidiously undermines critical history and is all the more worrisome because it hides its true, premodern, colors behind the mask of postmodernism."[5] Klein thus indicts memory for being a premodern creature hiding behind a mask of postmodernity; what he offers to replace it is a secular, critical practice that can be reduced to a science. In contrast to this critique of the use of memory, Jabès's complex Holocaust representations, which focus explicitly on memory, help us to reevaluate the place of the Holocaust in our history, and are therefore essential to the writing of "critical history" regarding the Holocaust and Judaism. That is, while Jabès clearly focuses on memory, his use of the past, rather than being, as Klein would have it, merely metaphysical, contributes to secular history by zeroing in on the complex process through which history exerts itself on the present.

Readers familiar with Jabès's difficult poetry may balk at the suggestion that one study it as a "Holocaust representation." For on the one hand, the Holocaust appears in Jabès's poetry mostly through a series of allusive words including "ashes," "burning books," and "ghetto," which gesture toward but do not directly engage in Holocaust representation. On the other hand, Jabès surrounds these ambiguous terms with references to "Auschwitz" and other words that clearly designate the Holocaust.[6] For example, when he evokes the image of a burning book, one immediately thinks of the 1933 Nazi book burnings of Jewish and other "subversive" authors, yet the burning book also symbolizes the poststructural concern with the historical tenacity of writing and with the way in which reading consumes the page. Thus, Jabès's poetry simultaneously represents the Holocaust and reflects on other concepts such as the nature of writing.[7] One must therefore resist the temptation to delimit the aim of Jabès's poetry to commentary on the Holocaust. As we will see in the next chapter, Boltanski also suffered through this reduction of his work to the Holocaust when he initially wanted to be viewed as an artist concerned with broader themes. Obviously, Jabès's repeated use of terms such as "Judaism" in conjunction with "Auschwitz" offers great temptations to delimiting the meaning of his works to the question of Jews and their destruction. But this type of reading narrows the field too quickly, and assumes an unproblematic relationship between Jewishness and memory—precisely the historical dilemma that Jabès tries to complicate rather than restrict.

In Jabès's work, as in Semprun's and Proust's, time zones merge, words multiply signification, identities crack and regroup, and memories are assumed for readers arriving for the first time in Jabès's deserts. In describing these curious congruences, Mary Ann Caws expresses beautifully how Jabès presents memories that should somehow impossibly also be *our* memories: "The tale is given as if I knew it and were being reminded of it, but I never knew it and could not have."[8] Caws's reading helps explain how many of the questions Jabès's poetry raises derive from both the specificity of his biography and from the connection between Judaism and exile. For example, Jabès's interest in exile refers both to his own exile from Egypt to France (beginning in 1957) and to the post-diasporic global Jewish exile. As Zohreh Sullivan suggests in her fascinating collection of Iranian diaspora stories, perhaps the ability to embrace multiple times and places simultaneously is fostered by national displacement. When asked whether she is "'*really* Iranian, Pakistani, or American,'" Sullivan replies, "'None of the above, all of the above, and the relation between all three.'"[9] Similarly, as Caryn Aviv and David Shneer phrase it, "for global people, home is constantly moving."[10] This diasporic logic delineates an important part of the Jabèsian poetic method, and demonstrates that questions of identity, place, and memory often demand contradictions that Jabès poetically enacts.

In order to address the questions Jabès raises for us, this chapter is organized into three parts. To analyze how Jabès positions the Holocaust, it is important to determine how Jabès's work conceives of its victims; the first section thus addresses the paradoxes of Jabès's portrayal of Jewish identity.

The second section examines whether or not Jabès's elliptical evocations can be termed Holocaust representations. The chapter closes with a section that addresses the paradoxical relationship between memory and forgetting in Jabès's work. Taken as whole, these three sections enable me to forward Jabès as a case study in how the complex language of allusive poetry can contribute to our historical understanding of the Holocaust even while complicating our sense of what it means to remember the worst through unwanted beauty.

THE PARADOX OF JEWISH IDENTITY

The paradox startles us into thinking. —Rosmarie Waldrop

Edmond Jabès was raised amid the French-dominated literary world in Egypt, in a Jewish family that had obtained Italian citizenship in 1929. The reasons for this bizarre citizenship are recounted in Rosmarie Waldrop's wonderful memoir about Jabès, *Lavish Absence*.[11] Waldrop reports that in 1929, Egyptian citizenship was offered to anyone who could prove that his or her family had been in Egypt since 1848 and had been issued an Ottoman birth certificate. The Jews of Egypt, many of whom had been there for ages, had birth certificates issued by Jewish religious authorities that were not recognized by the Egyptian government. An official in the Italian Embassy apparently realized that it could be most profitable to issue Italian citizenship to the Jews of Cairo, and thus capitalized on the fact that an Italian town hall had just burned down, taking all birth records with it. Because, during the war, Egypt was initially under the control of the British, when Italy joined the war against the allies, all Italian citizens—Jabès among them—were arrested. Luckily, Jabès had written anti-fascist pamphlets and, with the help of his father-in-law, was able to secure a release. In 1942 Jabès was evacuated by the British with other anti-fascists to Palestine, where he spent the remainder of World War II. After the war, Jabès returned to Egypt, where he worked as a stockbroker under the increasingly hostile conditions suffered by Jews and other "foreigners." Thus, while Jabès lived through and was deeply affected by the Holocaust, he did not experience it as did other Holocaust writers addressed in this book.

Although raised in a Jewish milieu, Jabès did not identify strongly with Judaism until 1957, when Gamal Abdel Nasser evicted all Jews from Egypt. In reaction against Israel's aggressive military strategies, the new Egyptian government made life extremely difficult for Jews living within its borders by confiscating their property and imposing other restrictions. In response, many Egyptian Jews emigrated to Israel, Canada, or the United States; Jabès chose to move to France, where he found anti-Semitism alive and well in some quarters, but where he also settled into a rich intellectual and artistic climate. Jacques Derrida, Maurice Blanchot, and other poststructuralists began to take note of his work and he became, along with Paul Celan, with whom he was acquainted, one of the darling poets of high theory. Indeed, Sidra DeKoven Ezrahi notes, "Edmond Jabès is reported to have discovered Celan returning the manuscript of *The Book of Questions* to Jabès's mailbox, stating that the publication of such an unabashed treatment of Jewish themes would only bring new disasters upon them all."[12] His years in France produced many volumes of poetry, right up until his death from a heart attack in 1991. His exile in France transformed the metaphoric contours of his poetry; once the desert was removed from his sight, the endless sand, the heat and emptiness of the desert, and the dry state of exile transformed from elliptical references to enter the center of his poetic vision. Similarly, the forced move to France opened up for him a series of questions about the meaning of Jewish identity. Until identified as a Jew by a hostile Egyptian political scene, he had not felt himself to be Jewish in a significant way. His poetry thus meditates on the definition of Jewishness and offers a multitude of questions about the construction of Jewish identity.[13]

Even while discussing his biography, Jabès evinces a distaste for critical readings of poetry that rely on biographies, yet he nonetheless admits that in his case the facts of his displacement from Egypt to France and the change that this exile created in his poetry bear examination. In a series of interviews conducted with Marcel Cohen, *Du désert au livre* (1980), Jabès offers a truncated biography that formally represents his distaste: "De 1912 à 1918. Petite enfance sûrement heureuse. Ciel bleu. Sans souvenirs" (From 1912 to 1918. Childhood surely happy. Sky blue. Without memories).[14] Nonetheless, as the interviews with Cohen progress, Jabès admits that many key events in his life affected the structure and content of his poetry. For instance, when Jabès was twelve, his cherished sister died. This traumatic event becomes for him a scene of loss to which his poetry ceaselessly returns; in other moments of doubling, he often combines the trauma of the loss of his sister with the trauma of the loss of victims of the Nazi genocide, thus doubling personal loss with social loss. In describing his emotions about his sister's death, Jabès extends his feelings to a disgust at all death: "Je me sentais comme anéanti. J'étais à la fois révolté contre l'injustice que représente toute mort . . . et passif" (I felt annihilated. At the same time I revolted against the injustice that all death represents . . . and remained passive). And, in a formulation that exemplifies the poetic method at work here, just as he had expanded the death of his sister into the injustice of all death—including deaths in the Holocaust—he expands the simultaneity of revolt-passivity into a characteristic of Judaism: "Imprégné de ce fatalisme par ses origines orientales, le judaïsme, au fond, a fait de la dualité passivité-révolte son lieu même. Sa révolte est devenue interrogation angoissée" (Impregnated with this fatalism by its oriental origins, Judaism, at its heart, has made its place in the same passive-revolt duality. Its revolt became anguished interrogation).[15] Thus, Jabès's poetic procedure involves synecdochal projection: one death represents all deaths and one Jew's reactions stand in for a trait of Judaism itself. His poetic method is thus similar to Semprun's use of characters as representative. As I discussed in chapter 2, for Semprun, Sigrid, the young German woman, stands in for an entire generation of Germans, and the Jewish survivor in the garden stands in for all Jewish survivors in much the same way as one death represents all death for Jabès.

Indeed, the poetic methodology Jabès uses radically rewrites the usual sense of synecdoche as a part-to-whole representation. His method takes a singular entity and transforms its meaning while simultaneously carrying its symbolism extremely far. For example, Jabès often takes a loaded word such as "God" and explains that it symbolizes any number of meanings that one would not usually associate with the divine. In one of his poetic works, *Le soupçon le désert* (1978), Jabès analyzes his use of repeated words and explains, among others, God and Jew: "Dieu, comme Nom extrême de l'abîme. Juif, comme figure de l'exil, de l'errance, de l'étrangeté et de la séparation; condition qui est aussi celle de l'écrivain" (God, as an extreme name for the abyss. Jew, as a figure of exile, or wandering, of foreignness and of separation; conditions that are also that of the writer).[16] Thus, in the case of what one would perhaps mistake for the religious concept of God, Jabès insists that it merely names the abyss and that "Jew" does not represent the historical people but rather symbolizes exile.[17] By insisting in *Du désert au livre* that God is a "métaphore du vide" completely divorced from its traditional theological sense, Jabès invokes the word "God" even while expanding its traditional meaning.[18] Thus the metaphorical values of synecdochal projection are also brought into play in the extension of God into a metaphor for emptiness. The same separation between sign and meaning occurs for the rest of the central themes in his works, so that each concept one might associate with a particular, culturally recognizable definition is rather infused with an endless series of meanings.

In a study of the connections between literature and theology, Arthur Cohen asks: "What does it mean for a Jewish writer to write either theology or literature, or to write either one 'Jewishly'? How is the Holocaust to be assimilated, not only into Jewish literature but into Jewish liturgy as well?"[19] As if responding to Cohen's questions, Jabès contemplates the relationship between writing and Judaism, and therefore what writing "Jewishly" means. Like Cohen, Jabès reflects on the possibility for "assimilating" the Nazi genocide into literature, and creates a method to weave the event into language and therefore into all writing. Can we imagine, on a poetic level, that writing requires a certain level of displacement? That is, reading poetically and bracketing, for the moment, history, can we learn something from the suggestion that writers and Jews share certain characteristics? This is the heart of the problem and the pain and joy of reading Jabès. He evokes so much without leaving us recourse to determine what to do with these beautiful, difficult, poetic evocations. His work thus shares with the art of Kiefer and Boltanski (to whom I turn in chapter 4) a hermeneutic ambiguity that allows reflection on Jewishness and the Holocaust to extend toward reflections on a host of other questions of modernity and beyond. When he sometimes essentializes Jews into figures of exile or creatures associated with writing, with the book, Jabès lays himself open to the criticism Ruth Wisse had leveled at Semprun for using Jews as mere literary constructs; yet Jabès also works to resist these essentializations by playing on our own associations and evocations surrounding words such as "Jew."

As an instance of a particularly rich poetic evocation, Jabès wonders what it would be like to separate the name "Jew" from Jews. He wonders if persecution adheres to the very name: "C'est dans le mot JUIF que nous sommes poursuivis. 'Si JUIF pouvait, tout à coup, s'écrire JUYFFE ou JOUYFFE, peut-être cesserions-nous d'être persécutés'" (It's in the word JUIF [Jew] that we are hunted. "If JUIF could be, suddenly, written JUYFFE or JOUYFFE, perhaps we would no longer be persecuted"). The answer to this question cannot be "yes"—without their name Jews would not be persecuted—because that would leave the burden of identity purely in the symbolic rather than the phenomenal realm. To the question about the un-anchoring of the name "Jew" a fictional rabbi replies: "Nous serions doublement persécutés . . . dans l'alliance avec le mot et dans sa démence" (We would be doubly persecuted . . . in the alliance with the word and in its lunacy).[20] Thus, the transformation of the sign "Jew" into another sign would not offer any relief. In fact, the double persecution would be due to the resemblance of the word to "Jew" in addition to the dementia of the new, twisted, word. Jabès thus suggests that as a phenomenal reality, persecution occurs both through an alliance with Jewishness and through any attempt to twist that alliance.

The desire to escape persecution by symbolic or real transformations of Jewish identity replicates the familiar identitarian double-bind described, for example, by Jean-Paul Sartre in *Réflexions sur la question juive* (1946), where avoidance of Jewish identity doubles rather than alleviates persecution. Either one is damned for being too Jewish and not, in this case, "French enough," or one is damned for trying to be French when one can only ever be Jewish. "Car le Juif inauthentique fuyait sa réalité juive et c'était l'antisémite qui le faisait Juif malgré lui; au lieu que le Juif authentique *se fait juif* lui-même et de lui-même, envers et contre tous" (The inauthentic Jew escapes Jewish reality yet the anti-Semite *makes him a Jew* despite himself; but the authentic Jew *makes himself a Jew* in the face of all and against all).[21] Thus, for Sartre, a comfortable relationship to Judaism is impossible: if you do not feel yourself to be Jewish, anti-Semites will nonetheless recognize you as such; if, on the other hand, you behave "Jewishly" anti-Semites will charge you with not wanting to assimilate. Jabès's play on JUYFFE, then, echoes his biography: just as the "inauthentic Jew" in Sartre's text fails to recognize his Jewishness until marked by anti-Semitic pointing, Jabès found himself marked as Jewish only when Nasser made it impossible for Jews to live in Egypt.

The speakers in Jabès's poetry often ask themselves, or various fictional rabbis ask them, how they can lay claim to Jewishness when it was something they only fully realized they owned at the moment of external marking. This perhaps explains the desire, so evident in his work, to combine the symbol of the Jew as writer or figure of exile or figure of the forgotten with the people *qua* historical beings. What Sartre would term the "inauthenticity" of Jabès's portrayal of the Jew stems from the sense that it was, paradoxically, anti-Semitism that sparked his interest in Judaism. Yet I would argue that Jabès's poetic method complicates Sartre's identitarian formulation: the fact that Jabès's interest in Judaism increased due to outside persecution does not mean that his reflections on Jewishness are "inauthentic."

In a short piece that opens the special edition of *Studies in Twentieth Century Literature* devoted to Jabès, the poet expands upon this theme of the displacement between the symbols "God" and "Jew" and their historical referents: "It is true, the word 'Jew,' the word 'God,' are metaphors for me: 'God,' the metaphor for the void, 'Jew,' for the torment of God, of the void. In parallel, I also try to close in as much as possible on the historical sense of these words; 'Jew' and 'God,' joined in one and the same becoming. Do creature and creator not prepare, together, the coming of a new world order?"[22] Jabès's insistence on the metaphorical nature of "God" and "Jew" recalls the difference Freud maps out between mourning and melancholia, where mourning represents the work of getting over loss and melancholia represents an inability to overcome loss.[23] Rather than being mired in an endless melancholia, these Jabèsian metaphors contribute to the work of mourning—the coming to terms with the past—so necessary for the treatment of Holocaust memory. Jabès lays claim to a desire to simultaneously maintain the symbolic and the historical qualities of the words "God" and "Jew." We might think that one would occlude the other, or that it would not be possible to be both metaphorically exemplary and historically specific, yet Jabès tries to do precisely that. To make sense of this merging, one must accept Jabès's desire to rewrite the word "history." Indeed, when Jabès claims that he chooses the "historical sense" of the words "Jew" and "God," the word "historical" is hard to grasp because he wants to treat the theological concept of God as a historical concept. Jabès does not attempt to portray the historical diversity of Judaism because, for him, "Jew" symbolizes a range of themes such as void, exile, foreignness, separation. Indeed, the "Jew" for Jabès is the quintessential Jew of the book, the people of the word, the Jew tied to rabbinic and Halachic law; yet, by evoking this figure Jabès challenges our own associations of Jewishness and the book.

One might imagine that Jabès could be subject to some of the same criticisms that Rachel Whiteread suffered for her monument to the Holocaust in Vienna (fig. 1). This monument, which opened in October 2000 on the Judenplatz, depicts a library turned inside out so that only the edges of the paper, not the binding that names the book and author, are visible. Whiteread claimed that, in light of Austria's wartime history and postwar tendency to deny its guilt, she did not want to simply put "a Band-aid on the situation" and rather wanted to be "quite brutal about it."[24] Whiteread's monument participates in the counter-monumental aesthetic, which I will discuss in chapter 5, because it functions on reversal and thereby attempts to dislocate the grandeur of much monumental design. While many viewers find Whiteread's vision apt and even moving, many critics find that by using the stereotype of the Jewish connection to learning and the book as the exemplar of Judaism, she excludes the many Jews who are illiterate or who do not feel a particular connection to "the book."

As Michael Kimmelman reports, some "felt that Ms. Whiteread's project was a cliché: Jew as the people of the book. Weren't the deaths of Jewish bakers and housewives as tragic as those of Jewish intellectuals?"[25] Of course, the criticism Kimmelman cites is equally subject to the charge of stereotyping, as there were doubtless many "bakers and housewives" who were highly literate and deeply attached to the book. Against the criticism cited by Kimmelman, some scholars, such as James Young, praise Whiteread's monument as representing Jews through their connection to the book: "Rather than monumentalizing only the moment of destruction itself, Whiteread's design would recall that which made the 'people of the book' a people: their shared relationship to the past through the book."[26] Thus, the different readings of Whiteread's controversial monument could apply equally well to Jabès's allocation of Jews with the book, or with writing. By insisting on the simultaneity of allegorical and historical "Jews," Jabès's symbols appear to be beyond history, and one has the sensation that they do not refer to anything we can name, yet they do nonetheless poetically evoke profound questions about Jewish identities. Whereas the genre of the monument dictates that Whiteread's project is in some way referential, the complexity of poetic description allows Jabès much more flexibility in representing Jewishness in all of its ambiguous and contradictory meanings.

Like the figure of the book, Jabès relies upon the figure of the wandering Jew in his evocations of Jewishness. Saul Friedländer discusses the limitations of the description of Jews as endlessly wandering through his development of the idea of redemptive anti-Semitism. Friedländer describes how this ideology became so seductive during the Nazi regime and notes:

> These images are the undistorted echo of past representations of the Jew as endlessly changing and endlessly the same, a living dead, either a *ghostly wanderer* or a ghostly ghetto inhabitant. Thus the all-pervasive Jewish threat becomes in fact *formless and unrepresentable;* as such it leads to the most frightening phantasm of all: a threat that looms everywhere.[27]

The "ghostly wanderer" Friedländer so aptly identifies resembles the ghostly, lost, figure of the Jew to which Jabès ceaselessly returns. Thus we can see that the image of the Jew as exilic wanderer that Jabès so complexly captures has been co-opted by this form of anti-Semitism that Friedländer identifies. Rather than a threat, of course, in Jabès the figure of the wandering Jew, while it may also be "formless and unrepresentable," is not frightening but rather by turns melancholy, exhilarating, and full of possibility.

To further demonstrate how Jabès continually questions Jewish iden-

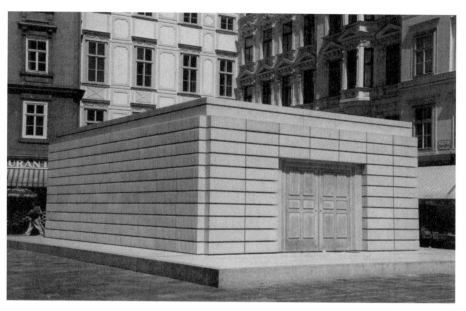

FIGURE 1. Rachel Whiteread, *Holocaust Memorial,* Judenplatz Vienna, 2000. Photograph by Matti Bunzl.

tity, we can turn to *Le livre du partage* (1987), where Jabès differentiates Judaism in general from any particular or one particular Judaism: "S'il t'arrive d'évoquer ma relation au judaïsme, ne dis jamais *le* judaïsme, mais *ce* judaïsme" (If it falls to you to evoke my relation to Judaism never say Judaism but *this* Judaism).[28] Thus Jabès commands his interlocutor to distinguish between the general abstraction of Judaism and *this* one. But he leaves the question open as to whether this specific designation is an *experiential* Judaism or one culled or created from the Talmud, the law, or the past. The demand to speak only of *this* Judaism treats the question of Judaism very differently than in *Le livre du dialogue* (1984), where both the *juif* and *judaïsme* are almost always tied in with the question *qua* question: "Il disait que lorsqu'on se pose une question on est, d'une certaine manière, juif parce que le juif s'est déjà, plus d'une fois, posé la même question" (He said that when one poses a question one is, to a certain degree, Jewish because the Jew has already, more than once, posed the same question).[29] That Jabès never ceases posing questions, then, in his formulation, names him *juif,* even while he continually puts that naming into question. Thus, as with the linking of the figure of the Jew with the book or exile or wandering, the figure of the Jew-as-questioner connects Jabès's image of Jewishness to the somewhat essentialized image of the ceaselessly questioning Jew. In short, Jabès's synecdochal connection of the symbol Jew to Jews as historical beings, while poetically evocative, also entails a great deal of historical reductionism even while it is a powerful mythologizing act wherein the figure of the Jew is inserted into modern/postmodern culture as an essential part of it, rather than a marginalized figure.

In *Le livre du dialogue* Jabès asks what allows him to label himself Jewish: "Ah qu'est-ce qui, à travers mes paroles et mes actes, m'autorise à me considérer juif? Qu'est-ce qui, dans mes livres, indique que je pense, écris, à l'ombre ou à la lumière du judaïsme?" (Ah what, across my words and my actions, authorizes me to consider myself Jewish? What, in my books, indicates that I think, write, under the shadow or in the light of Judaism?).[30] The designation "Jewish" is here self-imposed and is not, as in the case of Nasser's conferring it on Jabès and other assimilated Jews, a means through which the external world interpellates the subject. To underscore the importance of this question, Jabès also asks it in *Le parcours* (1985): "La question qui obsède le juif est celle-ci: 'Qu'est-ce qui m'autorise à me considérer juif?'" (The question that obsesses the Jew is the following: "What authorizes me to consider myself Jewish?").[31] Jabès thus questions what *authorizes* him to self-identify as Jewish in the same breath as asking which *signs* demonstrate that he works under the shadow of Judaism. Thus Jabès questions Jewish identification and its relationship to choice as a mirror image of the way that Semprun had noticed that, precisely because he is not Jewish, he could choose not to be in the camps.

It is in *Partage* that Jabès takes these questions of Jewish identity specifically into the realm of memory. Through his articulation of the necessity of memory for the Jews, Jabès at first seems to link Jews to their destruction: "Peuple juif, contemporain d'un passé et d'un avenir auxquels tu as dédié ta voix. . . . À la fidélité de ta mémoire, tu dois ta pérennité" (Jewish people, contemporaneous with a past and with a future to which you have dedicated your voice. To the fidelity to your memory, you owe your perpetuity).[32] Memory is the historical glue ensuring the future of this people. Nonetheless, Jabès suggests in *Partage* that his obsession with Judaism amounts to nothing more than a detour: "Et, peut-être que, pour moi, le détour par le judaïsme n'aura été que le plus court chemin du particulier à l'universel et de l'universel au particulier" (And, perhaps that, for me, the detour via Judaism would have been nothing but the shortest path from the particular to the universal and from the universal to the particular).[33] Thus Jabès toys with the idea of being more interested in the theoretical question of the relationship among the universal and the particular than in the cultural question of Judaism as an actual historical phenomenon. As we saw with the doubling of losses of his sister with the loss in the Nazi genocide, the particular and the universal are deeply connected for Jabès. A comparison between these two phrases ("À la fidélité de ta mémoire" and "le détour par le judaïsme") suggests that rather than owing their continuity to memory, the detour via the Jew passes through a nothingness, a *trou, abîme, néant, rien:* "Il n'y a pas de détours—le détour est trou de mémoire" (There is no detour—the detour is a hole of memory).[34] While raising the question that Judaism may be nothing more than a detour, Jabès declares that detours are nothing more than memory-holes: "L'oubli n'est pas trou de mémoire, mais trou dans l'originaire secret d'où jaillit la source" (Forgetting is not a hole in memory, but a hole in the originary secret from which the source spurts out).[35] When Jabès corrects the portrayal of the forgotten as a gap in memory so that the forgotten takes its place at the source, he then insists that memory and forgetting, rather than antagonistic opposites, interweave intimately.

Jabès thus has it both ways: on the one hand, "Jew" functions as a shorthand for describing the problem of the bulk of the forgotten past because Jews are supposed to be a people who would cease to exist without conscious acts of memory that necessarily take the place of national security. On the other hand, Jews function as the force behind the question, as the impetus to ask the question of writing, and as the heart of a series of texts that take the desert as their metaphorical center. Thus, Jews are linked phenomenally with the space of the desert, which is also figured as the space of the forgotten. The fact that Jabès manages to maintain the dual symbolic structure of the thing as itself (Jews = Jews) *and* the thing as its allegorical representative (Jews = amnesia, lostness, aspatiality, desert) outlines his refusal of a direct representational link between sign and referent. Jews/Judaism, unhinged from spatial and temporal certainty, here poetically represent both racial/cultural phenomena and the very loss of place that defines them.[36]

Like the figure of the Jew as a metaphor for exile, many of the voices in Jabès's works are imaginary rabbis who join the stream of poetic queries. These rabbis are not intended to invoke rabbinical doctrine; rather, they voice aspects of the lost Jewish world that haunts the Jabèsian imagination. Waldrop jokes that Jabès himself, while friends with several rabbis, seemed to have an allergic reaction to some of the rabbis to whom the eager Jewish communities in America were often anxious to introduce him.[37] In "Edmond Jabès et la question du livre," Derrida discusses these imaginary rabbis in the context of Jabès's relationship to the Jewish community: "[Jabès] doit alors s'expliquer avec ses frères de race et des rabbins qui ne sont plus imaginaires" (Jabès must then explain himself to his blood brothers and to rabbis who are no longer imaginary). Derrida gently teases Jabès for his use of imaginary rabbis as a means of anticipating what real rabbis would have to say about his use of them as allegorical and poetic devices (or indeed as, to return to Wisse's complaint regarding Semprun, cited in chapter 2, mere "literary constructs"). In imagining the criticism Jabès might suffer, Derrida anticipates that "Tous lui reprocheront cet universalisme, cet essentialisme, cet allégorisme décharnés; cette neutralisation de l'événement dans le symbolique et l'imaginaire" (Everyone will reproach him for this universalism, this essentialism, this emaciated allegorization, this neutralization of the event in the symbolic and the imaginary).[38] For Derrida, "event" in this context can be read as "history" in the way I have been using it here. Derrida further argues that, should the rabbis launch such a critique, they would be both right and wrong about how Jabès treats the Jew. That is, the Jew (and Jewish culture) functions *both* as symbolic metaphor and literal signifier so that "Le Juif est brisé et il l'est d'abord entre ces deux dimensions de la lettre: l'allégorie et la littéralité" (The Jew is split and he is split first of all between these two dimensions of the letter: allegory and literality).[39] This is part of what can be both so wonderful and so difficult about reading Jabès. On the one hand, the allegorical dimension to the representation of the Jew entices one, but on the other hand, one cannot help associating the imaginary rabbis with rabbis who have known historical existence, thus finding it difficult to keep the allegorical and the historical equally imaginary.[40]

Rosmarie Waldrop reports that Jabès was influenced by Derrida's text, that it "sharpen[ed] Jabès's eye to the implications of his work."[41] Indeed, Jabès almost seems to be answering Derrida's concerns over how his use of history will be perceived when he claims that "I am aware how arbitrary, how insupportable, the use of the word 'Judaism' in the expression 'Judaism after God' may seem to some—though a number of rabbis, and true ones, have not taken the least offense. I am obviously thinking of conformist Jews. I have never intended either to shock or to join them. For my part, however, I think I must understand our tradition, if possible, in its most original and daring aspects."[42] Rather than finding, as Derrida had worried, that Jabès will come under severe attack from rabbis outraged by his whimsical use of the words

"Jew" and "rabbi," Jabès reminds us that "real" rabbis have not been at all offended because they have recognized his use of "Jew" as part of a religious tradition defined by flux. For these rabbis, the concept of Jewishness forever changes shape and Jabès's work takes part in these transformations.

Susan Handelman's "'Torments of an Ancient Word': Edmond Jabès and the Rabbinic Tradition" tackles the relationship between Jabès's evocation of Jews, rabbis, mystical Jewish concepts, and the Talmud. Handelman argues that "The identification of Jew and writer is not, for Jabès, merely a convenient analogy or apt metaphor; it is the essence of his vision. In a godless and secular century stunned by its glimpse of the void, Jabès uncovers the haunting ghosts of theology long thought to have been laid to rest."[43] Handelman thus connects Jabès's identification of writer and Jew with the theological concepts one supposes were destroyed by modernism. Handelman describes Nietzsche's death of God (1887) as the determining moment for this "glimpse of the void," and further connects this absence with the Holocaust: "Man, in turn, must now contend with both his bereavement over the death of the comforting God and the onslaughts of this 'negative' side of God. And obviously, for the Jew after the Holocaust, this issue is not merely academic."[44] Thus God's death is associated with the postmodern void, and, for Handelman, this absence is connected with a particularly Jewish God, as delineated in the Kabbalah and as destroyed amid modernity. She further suggests that Derrida and other critics relegate the Kabbalistic idea of the negativity of God to a side-note and thereby underplay its importance to the heart of Judaism.[45]

This analysis of the Kabbalah forms part of Handelman's examination of the intense similarities between Jabès's work and certain Jewish texts. Handelman claims that Jabès's texts are *formally* similar to the Talmud because they comprise a chorus of competing opinions and voices; she compares *Le livre des questions* to the Talmud because in both texts "rigid temporal and spatial distinctions collapse," enabling rabbis to "speak" to each other across vast temporal and geographical divides. Because the Talmud is not punctuated, "One already has to know the text and its peculiar way of speaking, its style and shorthand, in order to read it."[46] Handelman continues by noting that a paradoxical relationship dominates that between the Old Testament and the Talmud because they both claim to be sacred, yet the Talmud contradicts itself so much, and offers so many opposed readings of biblical narratives, that it cannot possibly dictate divine law.[47] Thus for Handelman the Talmud's endlessly self-contradictory nature resembles Jabès's self-contradictions. As

I discuss in chapter 4, Christian Boltanski, too, is enticed by what he finds as Judaism's ability to assimilate self-contradiction; although the artist bears a much more tenuous relationship to Judaism than does Jabès, it is this particular trait of Judaism to which Boltanski lays claim. Thus the uses of various constructs of Jewishness serve different functions for the diverse writers and artists I examine in this book. Celan calls upon Sulamith to stand in for Jewish women and by extension Jews; Delbo takes up the position of various Jewish women and children to explore her experience from the other side; Semprun uses an anonymous Jewish woman to represent symbolically the sometimes difficult relationship between Jewish and gentile Holocaust survivors. Handelman's reading of Jabès's use of Jewish tradition insists that both subversion and support are possible and that it is the very contradictions Boltanski finds inherent in Jewishness that allow both one and the other.

Handelman's essay grapples with the question of whether one can simultaneously subvert and support the Book. Ultimately her answer is, *yes* this simultaneity is possible, because the Jewish tradition, and especially the Kabbalistic tradition, relies on what she calls the "heretic hermeneutic." This heretic hermeneutic "continues even as it abrogates tradition; it is a complex of identification and displacement inextricably linked to a Jewish scriptural and exegetic tradition, which it inverts yet which somehow retains a compelling power."[48] According to Handelman, then, Jabès both subverts and supports a Jewish tradition with which he has always maintained an uncomfortable yet profoundly productive relationship. Indeed, like Derrida, Handelman notices Jabès's tortured relationship to the Jewish community: "Jabès constantly affirms his solidarity with Jewish history and with the sufferings and yearnings of the Jewish community, and continually expresses his painful love for other Jews." Yet she adds that Jabès had been "pained by their [the Jewish community's] rejection of him and that he therefore felt the need to 'defend his Judaism.'"[49] Derrida similarly finds that Jabès always tries to *justify* his relationship to the Jewish community. Derrida discusses this need for justification or explanation in the context of the way "the Jew" always exists in a heteronymous state, so that he never merges with the land in which he resides. The Jew always speaks, like a poet, from a non-place: "en Jabès le poète et le Juif nous paraissent si unis et si désunis à la fois; et que tout *Le livre des questions* est aussi une *explication* avec la communauté juive vivant dans l'hétéronomie et à laquelle le poète n'appartient pas vraiment" (in Jabès the poet and the Jew seem to us so united and so disunited at the same time; and all of the *Book of Questions* is also a justification to the Jewish community living in heteronymity and in which the poet doesn't really take part).[50] For Derrida, then, Jabès needs to explain himself to other Jews because the poet can already anticipate the criticism that he will in fact suffer for appropriating images from Jewish culture while not being sufficiently religious, and while living in exile from Judaism; for Handelman, on the other hand, Jabès struggles to cement his solidarity with a culture from which he feels rejected.

As with the complex question of Jewish identity and its representation in Jabès's poetry, the question of the Holocaust suffers a similarly slippery fate regarding the historical and allegorical dimensions of this work. Because Jabès did not experience the Holocaust directly, the question of Jewish identity necessarily leads him to the Shoah, for this has become one of the defining spaces of Jewish identity.[51]

JABÈS'S HOLOCAUST

Over the course of his works, Jabès's treatment of the Holocaust has changed so that a subtle representational transformation takes place between his early works, such as *Le livre des questions* (1963–73, seven volumes), where an (albeit attenuated narrative) depicts a couple, Yukel and Sarah, coping with the Holocaust, and the much later *Le livre des limites* (1982–87, four volumes), where the word "Auschwitz" surfaces a handful of times without a supporting historical narrative. That is, the somewhat more direct, more narratively driven evocations in the earlier texts have been transformed in the later texts into shadows and reflections. This does not indicate a teleological change, and the memory of the earlier works inflects the later works. Considering that *Le livre des limites* treats the Holocaust rarely and only in decontextualized passages, how may one speak of these books as Holocaust representations? The range of evocative terms used here, including *cendres, exhumé, mort* (ashes, exhumed, death), might tempt us to argue that Jabès *really* deals with the Shoah, yet that conclusion limits the curious Jabèsian flux that allows us to see multiple, and often contradictory, references in each word.

Like "God," and "Jew," the word "Auschwitz" takes on a more than synecdochal force when it comes to represent not only all other camps, but all other horror. In one of the places where Jabès does name this camp he focuses on the radical contingency of the guard's right thumb: "À Auschwitz, tous les regards des déportés alignés étaient fixés sur le pouce droit du gardien gradé. À gauche, la mort; à droite, provisoirement, la vie" (In Auschwitz, all the gazes of the lined up deportees were fixed on the right thumb of the guard. To the left, death; to the right, provisionally, life).[52] A simple gesture or sign that defines the future as possible or not possible has captured the insane contingency of the camps, and the insane contingency of the gesture or the sign. Through this historical representation of a moment familiar to Holocaust survivors, Jabès indicates poetically the haphazard rules of survival. This is one of the few times when Jabès seems to be citing Holocaust testimony, and it reminds me of other testimonial moments. For example, Hillel Seidman, in his Yiddish testimony, *Tog Buch fun Varshever Geto*, describes a scene in which he waits for German guards to determine his fate: "Bey di 'selektsies' hobn zey nisht gekukt oyf keyn shum papirn, amt fun dem batrefndikn ongeshteltn, nor bloyz gevorgn a blik oyfn menshen, un— vi azoy zeyr kapriz hot zey gezogt. Mit ayn bavegung mit der hand hobn zey detsidert vegn lebn oder toyt" (At the "selections" they did not look at any papers, nor did they consult with the office of employees, they merely cast a glance over people and—with a mere caprice they decreed. With a motion of their hands they determined life or death).[53] Because of its similarity to survivors' experiences, such as this experience of Seidman's, the moment in *Le livre du partage* where Jabès describes the right thumb of the guard is striking because it is one of the rare instances where he offers a recognizable Holocaust representation. In allegorizing this historical moment Jabès enacts the complex combination of the allegorical with the historical that characterizes the many moments of memory-production that pepper his texts.

Jabès links the Holocaust as much to memory as to Jewishness, for one of the most persistent questions in his work revolves around how to remember so much loss. From the beginning of his series of multi-volume tomes, memory exerts a profound influence. By focusing so intensely on the mechanics of memory, Jabès forces us to wonder about our (imagined) memories of the concentration camps. One of the two main characters in the first series of books produced after Jabès's exile in France, *Le livre des questions,* is Sarah, a Holocaust survivor whose experience in the camps has rendered her mad. The madness from which she cannot free herself traces her survival; the Holocaust exerts a tremendous force on her and her lover, Yukel.[54] Bearing witness to the Shoah has meant that she cannot tell her story because she can no longer sustain narratives. Because no one living has properly born witness to it, no one *expects* to understand; the word "Auschwitz" cannot signify because its utterance is always set up under the sign of failure.[55] Thus, by portraying a Holocaust survivor as a mad woman whose madness consists of an inability to offer testimony, Jabès helps explain the difficulty of Holocaust representation. In making the poetic enactment of her pain beautiful, Jabès tackles the same problem of unwanted beauty in the worst as confronted by Celan, Delbo, and Semprun. As Waldrop puts it, despite the "anxiety" present in many of Jabès's works, there is also a "truly contagious" pleasure.[56]

In a fascinating methodological article, simply entitled "My Itinerary," Jabès helps to explain what the word "Auschwitz" signifies for him:

> There is something horrible about observing suffering and also about saying that it has its positive side. But what would the Jew have left if he could not at least hope that his history, his suffering, his anxiety would turn out to have been a ferment, an *exemplary experience*, which each must turn to account? To remain a moment with this experience, it is there to rouse a consciousness in danger of falling asleep. Our whole Western culture is at stake. *Any questioning which avoids Auschwitz, for example, passes by the essential.*
>
> Auschwitz has radically changed our way of seeing. What had been unthinkable before is not so much the degree of cruelty, but rather the almost total indifference of the German as well as the Allied populations, which made Auschwitz possible. This indifference continues to defy any serious notion of what is human. Auschwitz has considerably aggravated the feeling of solitude which all beings have. Today all trust is lined with a consuming distrust. We know it is unreasonable to expect anything from another. We still have hope even so, but it has a *buried* quality which keeps reminding us that the thread is broken.[57]

Jabès insists on facing Auschwitz, even while doing so in aesthetically allusive ways. His statements here support the claim that even where not named explicitly, the Shoah occupies a central place in his work. His desire to use the horror as a wake-up call to a deadened West indicates a political agenda not always easy to trace in his works. Thus, a gap yawns between Jabès's extra-poetical dictates on poetic practice, and the contents (and form) of his poetry. By claiming that "Auschwitz has radically changed our way of seeing," Jabès cannot help but bring to mind Adorno's theories, as I discussed in chapter 1, on the aesthetic change rendered by Auschwitz. Indeed, in *Du désert au livre* Jabès responds to Adorno directly: "A l'affirmation d'Adorno: 'On ne peut plus écrire de poésie après Auschwitz' . . . je serais tenté de répondre: oui, on le peut. Et, même, on le doit. Il faut écrire à partir de cette cassure, de cette blessure sans cesse ravivée" (To Adorno's affirmation: One cannot write poetry after Auschwitz, I would reply: yes, one can. And, even, one must. One must write from now on about this caesura, about this wound that ceaselessly reopens).[58] By affirming that all questioning must question

Auschwitz, and by replying to Adorno's interdiction by claiming that one *must* write about the Holocaust, Jabès declares that beautiful, poetic allusions to the Holocaust are necessary, even if their beauty is unwanted, and further that the endless questions in his text *do* in fact refer to the Holocaust. Yet do the questions stop there? Do they not refer to the Holocaust and writing and exile and a whole series of other concerns? Is there a gap between Jabès's avowed intentions and the practice of his poetic discourse?

In *Le parcours* (1985) Jabès echoes this insistence on the questioning of Auschwitz when he claims that the camp will be found in all names: "Dans tout nom, il y a un nom dérangeant: *Auschwitz*" (In each name, there is a disturbing name: *Auschwitz*).[59] The disturbing name of Auschwitz recalls Jabès's distortion of the name "Juif" into other, nonsensical sounds, because both transformations entail an indelible association. The haunting of both the future and the past becomes visible here: each name contains the prediction of the future while all names contain the torque, the twisting effect of our disturbing past. As Semprun's memory of a garden bell had been distorted by the presence of the Shoah, so Jabès argues that all names have been polluted by Auschwitz. This utterance of Jabès's in *Le parcours* about Auschwitz surprises us, falling as it does in the middle of a series of reflections on writing, on the role of the writer, and on the role of the past as something that can only be fleetingly captured: "Il écrit la minute éphémère, enfouie dans l'éternité qui lui échappe. Il écrit l'abyssale absence" (He writes the ephemeral minute, buried in the eternity that escapes him. He writes the abyssal absence).[60] That at the moment we discover the endless effects of the name Auschwitz, we are already wondering how to deal with our history, demonstrates that the ambiguities of Jabès's texts can be evocative and powerful. Thus, the divide between aesthetics and documentary once again breaks down as these beautiful renderings of the worst work through Holocaust memory and our investments in it.

In "Writing-the-Holocaust: Jabès and the Measure of History," Berel Lang addresses the question of whether or not the Holocaust is a historical or a metaphorical event for Jabès. Lang argues that Jabès answers the question "Is writing about or writing the Holocaust possible?" with a "yes," despite the fact that Jabès denudes Holocaust representation in his writing. For Lang, at least in *Le livre des questions,* the Holocaust becomes nothing more than a *personae dramatis* along with Sarah and Yukel. Thus Lang, echoing Wisse's critique of Semprun, finds fault with Jabès's approach on the grounds that the reader must determine the authenticity of the historical apparatus that he or she constructs (in the absence of the author's having done this for the reader). Lang further suggests that Jabès assumes that the twentieth-century Holocaust resembles a series of holocausts that have always beset the Jews: "the Holocaust is no more than an instance of 'holocaust'—with holocaust the pattern that has given shape to Jewish history." Ancient and modern holocausts, then, "occupy a single, virtual present."[61] Lang also discounts the idea that is so prevalent in Jabès's texts, that the Jew can or should be represented as alien, other, or wanderer. In fact, Lang traces the delineation of this series of characteristics to external, anti-Semitic utterances, hence suggesting that Jabès simply reproduces anti-Semitic stereotypes.

Lang therefore faults Jabès for historical inaccuracy on two counts. First, because of his reliance on allegory, Jabès has failed to see the twentieth-century Holocaust as historically unique.[62] Lang thereby misunderstands Jabès's attempt to open up the historical Nazi genocide into a larger series of reflections on Judaism and loss; Jabès uses his poetic method to argue against the idea that the Nazi genocide was unique. Second, according to Lang, Jabès failed to see that he willfully and uncritically adheres to a negative, historically imposed series of stereotypes when he associates the Jews with exile. Lang thus concludes that "Jabès is right; the history of the Jew and the life of language *are* closely linked. But Jabès is wrong; or to see either the one or the other as symbolized or epitomized in the Holocaust is to fail all three: Jew, language, Holocaust."[63] Lang identifies Jabès's refusal to separate allegory from history as a great failure. For Lang, Jabès has subsumed the question of language and the figure of the Jew into a vague holocaust, and thereby failed to represent each term in its historical specificity. Lang therefore criticizes Jabès for walking the tightrope between allegory and history. While it is hard not to recognize the power of Lang's critique, it also seems clear that Lang's refusal to allow the Jabèsian play to do anything other than "fail" downplays the deeper question of how the mechanics of this particular form of poetic writing work in terms of history. Indeed, I argue here that Jabès's difficult, beautiful allusions to the Holocaust rather challenge our desire to reduce Jewishness to its destruction. Through the unwanted beauty of his texts, he does not allow such easy conflations.

In another examination of Jabès's use of the Holocaust, Eric Gould asks: "What does writing do once it is disabused of the belief that words resemble anything? How does one recount again the impossible-to-tell story of the Holocaust?" Thus, in his introduction to a series of articles on Jabès, Gould links the Holocaust with the impossibility of its representation. By adhering in this way to Adorno's maxim, Gould indicates that the Holocaust has something to do with the end of the word's power to make meaning. Gould further claims that "Jabès is beyond the literal repetition of the physical horrors of the Holocaust and the trials of ethnicity. He has centered the issue of Jewish identity on the Jew's relationship to the Word, divine and human."[64] What does it mean to be "beyond" physical horror and why are "trials of ethnicity" something the poet can get beyond when his own biographical history had forced him into exile because of his ethnicity? How, finally, does the "issue of Jewish identity" being centered on the "divine and human" Word mean that Jabès's texts are beyond ethnicity?

Gould further examines the process of representing the Holocaust in Jabès's work: "The God who can let the Holocaust happen by being absent coincides with the Word that can never be exhausted; the writer who is writing is the reader absent from, yet making, his or her own book; the moralist must rely on the aesthetic to attempt to disperse the horror of genocide."[65] Does morality actually require *aesthetics* to disperse the horror of genocide? Dispersion is a casting away, breaking apart, getting rid of; if this is the case then, alas, Adorno (in his initial, but later modified maxim) would have been right: there can be no poetry after Auschwitz because it would disperse the horror. On the contrary, I see Jabès, far from being "beyond" the mere physical horror, as using the aesthetic to shift our understanding of its effects. Unwanted beauty in the worst, rather than dispersing horror, allows us to fully *realize* (in the largest sense of that word) the ways in which the Holocaust lives with us, in our language, in our emotions, always there even if in trace form.

In furthering his claim about how Jabès travels "beyond" physical horror, Gould argues that "Jabès avoids the easy emotion, the (impossible) catharsis of the Holocaust, by insisting that reflection upon death, exile, God, silence, and so on, not only exists in its uncertain articulation in the book, but is absorbed by the *play* of the word."[66] As I discussed in the introduction, the fear of many attempts at Holocaust representation is that they offer an impossible catharsis. By setting up the binary between different representational strategies so that direct depictions of physical horror stay on one side, and Jabèsian play on the other, Gould has limited the ideal mode of representation to the allusive, indirect, elliptical, lyrical. Yet seeing images, for example, of the physical horror, or reading testimonies gruesome in their level of descriptive detail, do not evoke "easy" emotions. Those emotions can be disturbing, and the remainder of any catharsis persists.

Even though Jabès avoids physical description, Gould argues that the poet's work is not a "mere aestheticizing of pain" because *Le livre des questions* centers itself on the scream, "the shrillest, most direct of all responses."[67] This cannot help but remind one again of Adorno's retraction of his original interdiction against post-Auschwitz poetry, where, as I discussed in chapter 1, he argues that every tortured man has the right to scream and so we should encourage poetry after and about the worst. By rejecting the interdiction against poetry and by insisting that Auschwitz be at the center of all questioning, Jabès makes a historical argument that this event takes a central place in all Western discourse. Thus, while Jabès does not represent the Holocaust with an eye toward a direct, historically accurate image, his evocations, bolstered by the occasional moment of historical description, force us to reckon with the presence of the Holocaust in our consciousness of loss, memory, forgetting, and writing.

MEMORY AND FORGETTING

Memory invented time to its own glory, without noticing that time was already the memory of eternity. —Edmond Jabès

Returning to Pierre Nora's distinction between a living, vibrant memory and an ossified, hardened history, we can see that while Jabès relies on memory to represent the Holocaust, he also strives to present, even if only occasionally, a historical scene. Rejecting the idea that memory grasps that which can be remembered, Giorgio Agamben depicts the process of remembering as a grappling with the bulk of the forgotten itself. He describes this bulk as the "incredible loss—both collective and individual—which is infinitely greater than that which can get collected in the archive of memory." And then, in terms that almost seem to be describing—remarkably accurately—the role of memory in the texts of Jabès, Agamben continues, "this bulk is not inert— it acts on us with no less strength than what we remember consciously." Thus, the work of memory has nothing to do with bringing to consciousness; rather, this bulk of the forgotten, or the remainder of the overstuffed memorial archive, "does not demand to be remembered but to *remain* within us unforgettably."[68] As against a Western, agent-centered view of history, Agamben presents history as a phenomenological way of being.

That Agamben's remainder resembles what Jabès calls the memory of death is borne out in a long yet striking passage from *Le soupçon le désert* (1978), where death exerts a force through the word:

Le passé n'est pas la mort mais la possibilité, pour la mort, de transformer un certain avenir—le sien? le nôtre?—en un temps de fiction où notre histoire, d'avoir été exhumée, se laissera récrire, au gré de la plume; immense récit qui a vaincu l'oubli mais que l'oubli avait, auparavant, confronté avec la démesure: démesure, elle-même, à l'origine de la création qu'elle fait éclater.

En ce sens, le passé de tout écrit se présente comme la mémoire de la mort; mémoire du néant qui l'empêche de mourir. Il y aurait, ainsi, un passé englouti dans le propre passé des mots par l'intermédiaire desquels la mort opère; car il ne peut y avoir de langage hors de la mort.

The past is not death, but the possibility, for death, of transforming a certain future—its? ours?—into a fictional time when our history, having been exhumed, will be left to rewrite, at the whim of the pen; vast story that has vanquished forgetting but which forgetting had, previously, confronted with the excess: excess, itself, at the origin of the creation that it had detonated. In this sense, the past of all writing presents itself like the memory of death; memory of the nothingness that it prevents from dying. There would have been, then, a past engulfed in the past of words via the intermediary through which death operates; because there cannot be language outside of death.[69]

Here, memory of death writes in much the same way as, in Agamben's formulation, the bulk of the forgotten acts on or writes us. Jabès links the past specifically to its transformative force—a transformation beyond writing, of the future. The past is here the possibility for death to transform a certain future into a fictional time when our history will have been exhumed and rewritten. The metaphorical web that includes the buried past—exhumation, buried, forgotten, buried people, ashes, the dead weight of the past speaking—cannot help but conjure up an attempted political, social, historical burial that never remained covered over. Indeed, even in texts that do not explicitly name the Holocaust, Jabès's symbolic structuring reminds us, perhaps not of *the worst* itself, but that the Holocaust exerts a force on us nonetheless, as though the repeated metaphorical and literal ashes were being written.

Like Jabès's use of the word "God," "death" is here a symbol, in this case for the bulk of the forgotten. Yet the whimsical turning and scribbling of the pen as it rewrites our history is always subject to the force of this forgotten, hence making remembering and forgetting mutually reciprocal forces in the process of self-becoming. It makes sense, then, when Jabès asks: "Et si le livre n'était que mémoire infinie d'un mot manquant?" (And if the book isn't anything but the infinite memory of a missing word?).[70] This question takes the tripartite series of Jewishness, memory, and writing, and asks if all books are nothing but the infinite memory of a missing word—the infinite memory of the remainder that can never actually be remembered but that always persists. Jabès's determination to remain within the remainder and to render the missing words by turns visible and invisible means that his evocations of the worst are beautiful, metaphorical (and/or synecdochal), but also true to the difficulty of portraying the Nazi genocide, which many survivors and war writers feel can only live within the missing word.

By evoking the Holocaust through the unwanted beauty of his sensual poetry, Jabès participates in the dialectic between beauty and the worst that I have examined in chapters 1 and 2. On the one hand, Jabès's depictions of the Nazi genocide offer us a series of complex images that strain our understanding of how the event haunts us; on the other hand, the unwanted beauty of his images challenges us to understand how poetic evocations can convey so much meaning about painful experiences. Jabès's allusive works thus strongly resonate with postwar artists who refer to the Holocaust in oblique and complicated ways. In the next chapter I take up the question of the second generation's haunting by the Holocaust—of how postmemories are transmitted and imbibed—through looking at the visual artworks of Anselm Kiefer and Christian Boltanski. Like Jabès, these artists create beautiful works that contribute to Holocaust memory even while often maintaining a loose tie to Holocaust history. As is the case with many of Jabès's poems, the references to the Holocaust in their works are often shadowy, tentative allusions to loss, nostalgia, mourning, or melancholia.

Chapter 4

AESTHETIC MOURNING:
ANSELM KIEFER, CHRISTIAN BOLTANSKI, AND
"LIGHT PULSING THROUGH ASH"

When the past is reflected in the dewy fresh "instant,"
a painful shock of rejuvenation pulls it together once more . . .
irresistibly. —Walter Benjamin

A melancholy pleasure, to be sure, but the ambiguous, diverse, complicated, sometimes funny works of the postwar German artist Anselm Kiefer and the postwar French artist Christian Boltanski arguably elicit pleasure. Indeed, their images share a poignant beauty—in the way I have been describing it throughout this book as an open-ended and diverse aesthetic—that engages questions at the center of this project about the aesthetics of Holocaust representation. By examining the role of unwanted beauty in Kiefer's and Boltanski's Holocaust art (as opposed to the writerly pleasures to be found in works by Celan, Delbo, Semprun, and Jabès), I find that visual pleasure deepens yet also complicates the process of Holocaust memory. Indeed, while much of their art is arguably beautiful, and therefore pleasurable, Kiefer's and Boltanski's works make many viewers uncomfortable. Kiefer's images disturb because they often blur the boundary between depiction and critique of Nazism and the German mythological sources that undergirded it. Because Kiefer projects a desire to mourn a lost Germany in the same breath as the loss of its citizens (and many others) in the Nazi genocide, his work exemplifies an uncomfortable cohabitation between victim and perpetrator. That is, even while creating beautiful images that allude to the Holocaust, Kiefer's work does not express a clear enough difference from the lingering strands of nostalgia for a lost Reich that continue to beset the cultural and political landscape of contemporary German discourse. Boltanski's images disturb because he collapses specific historical losses into transhistorical traumas. Because Boltanski's photo-sculptures simultaneously expand the role of the individual survivor and efface his or her individuality, because he therefore invites us to mourn loss in general and not necessarily losses in the Holocaust, his work exemplifies the postmodern tendency toward cryptic historical references that are meaningful in an emotional rather than political or historical manner. Kiefer and Boltanski thus offer nuanced reflections on the Holocaust that challenge their audiences to grapple with the effects of unwanted beauty in transforming the second and third generations of Holocaust postmemory.[1] Indeed, the emergence of the Holocaust as the most discussed and represented twentieth-century catastrophe and as the defining historical moment for the forging of Jewish identity in the 1980s was contemporaneous with Kiefer's and Boltanski's emergence as "Holocaust artists."

In my readings of Kiefer's and Boltanski's work, I am confronted with an ambivalence that is itself at the heart of this book. For, while I find many of their images beautiful and deeply moving, I am also critical of the disturbing aspects of their work. Thus aesthetic appeals confront political and historical obligations. On the one hand, because of its aesthetic pleasures, the subtle questions raised by Kiefer's and Boltanski's art encourage discussion of the Holocaust and encourage Holocaust memory; on the other hand, the political and historical ambiguities raised by their art muddies and perhaps even romanticizes memories of the Nazi genocide. One answer to this dilemma would be to blame it all on a postmodern aesthetic that glories in ambiguity and thus by nature suffers from political and historical inexactitude; but this would sidestep the larger question of Holocaust representation that these artists engage. Thus in my readings of their complicated works I cannot offer a simple answer as to how these artists treat the Holocaust; I rather follow the multivalent threads of their possible trajectories.

In addressing Kiefer and Boltanski I extend the arguments from chapter 3, on the French/Egyptian poet Edmond Jabès, about the question of historical specificity in powerful Holocaust art and literature; Kiefer and Boltanski participate in an aesthetic closely tied to the just-off-the-page notion one has in reading the poetry of Jabès, where the representation of the Shoah occurs almost through its absence. I argue that the disturbing nature of Kiefer's and Boltanski's art points toward late twentieth-century modes of Holocaust representation that use aesthetic pleasure in ways that radically depart from the unwanted beauty discussed in the first two chapters of this book. Indeed, for Celan, Delbo, and Semprun, aesthetic pleasure was an essential survival mechanism in the camps and a means of helping them come to terms with and produce beautiful narratives about their experience of the Holocaust; for

Kiefer and Boltanski, on the other hand, aesthetic pleasure functions as a means of de-emphasizing political and historical meaning. Thus, like the other examples of indirect Holocaust art examined here, Kiefer's work refers to the Holocaust through a curious combination of Nazi and Kabbalistic imagery, whereas Boltanski's refers to the Holocaust through shadowy images of its possible victims and other allusive references. Because they have both produced a stunningly varied body of work, ranging in media across painting, sculpture, clothing, actions, books, films, letters, and more, and ranging in subject matter from myths of Germania, Nazism, the Holocaust, Judaism, Hindu myths, childhood, immigration, art itself, death, and more, it is impossible to reduce Kiefer's and Boltanski's oeuvres to the category of "Holocaust art." Yet the works I focus on below, excised from a vast body of output that would take several books to treat in full, reflect on the Nazi genocide in subtle ways that deepen our understanding of the production of Holocaust memory.

This chapter is divided into two parts. In the first part I discuss Kiefer's reception and some of his fascinating Holocaust-inflected works; I then focus on four of his pieces that treat the Holocaust: two of his paintings based on Paul Celan's poem "Todesfuge": *Margarete* (1981) and *Sulamith* (1983); and two works from a series entitled *Lilith: Lilith's Daughters* (1990) and *Banner* (1990). In the second section, I discuss Boltanski's multifaceted history and focus on four of his works that treat the Holocaust in ways that divergently balance aesthetics and history, *Le Lycée Chases* (1987), *La vie impossible* (1985), *Canada* (1988), and *La maison manquante* (1990). By analyzing these diverse pieces, this chapter grapples with the transformative power of unwanted beauty for second-generation Holocaust memorialization.

"ANSELM KIEFER, where was YOUR DADDY during the WAR?"

Many commentators discuss the beauty of Kiefer's work. For example, Andreas Huyssen terms Kiefer's Lilith series "gorgeous" and notes that Kiefer's images circle around a "grand récit" in "beautiful (too beautiful, some would say) motion." Daniel Arasse finds that "Kiefer's monumental canvases [were] seen to invest the destruction of Germany with tragic beauty"; and Waldemar Januszczak finds that Kiefer's paintings are invested with a "sinister beauty."[2] As these examples make clear, the designation of beauty in the context of Kiefer's work always carries a disclaimer: the beauty is either too much, tragic, or sinister. These comments highlight the often conflicted responses that Kiefer's work produces; on the one hand, the aesthetic pleasure his pieces generate is often lauded; on the other hand, the danger in this unwanted beauty is often flagged. As I discuss below, these conflicted readings stem from the ambivalence or play at the center of Kiefer's vision.

Born in Donaueschingen, Germany, in 1945 to a Catholic family, Kiefer married in 1971, and created many paintings dedicated to his then-wife, Julia (he is now married to Renate Graf). He set up a studio in the remote village of Hornbach in the Oden Forest region, from where he produced an important series of works that reflect on the meaning of the forest in German myth and history. Kiefer was a student of the influential German artist, Joseph Beuys (1921–86), and cites him as his mentor. While Kiefer has never fit comfortably into any artistic school, he is most often considered a neo-expressionist, but can also be grouped with Jochen Gerz (whom I discuss in chapter 5), Gerhard Richter, and other postwar German artists who address the Nazi genocide. Since 1993 Kiefer has lived in Barjac, in the south of France, where he continues to work on his overarching themes of memory and the presence of the past in the present; his later work has moved from his interest in Nazism and the Jewish mystical text, the Kabbalah, into other myths and themes.[3] While Kiefer has been famously reticent about his parents' activities during the war, my correspondence with an archivist in Donaueschingen reveals that his father, who lived through the war, was in the German army during World War II and became first lieutenant and then captain.[4] Thus, Kiefer may certainly have had reason to question not only his parents' generation, but also his father's involvement with this army. Kiefer's reticence about his family, coupled with his use of Nazi imagery, has contributed to the deeply divided reception his work has received.

In the late 1960s and early 1970s, just as the German postwar generation was coming to consciousness of their parents' possible involvement in the Nazi genocide, Kiefer dressed up in costumes evoking Nazi uniforms and had himself photographed saluting in the Heil Hitler gesture. Because of this *Occupations* series, Kiefer was initially seen as "tainted" by Nazi imagery and was almost universally denounced in Germany after his first major show, the Venice Biennale of 1980 (fig. 2). Many commentators (Huyssen, Saltzman, Schjeldahl) have pointed out that while Kiefer was initially met with stony silence or outright hostility in his native Germany, he was often warmly welcomed in the rest of Europe and America.[5] As Kiefer began in the early 1980s to incorporate Jewish imagery—especially motifs from the Kabbalah—

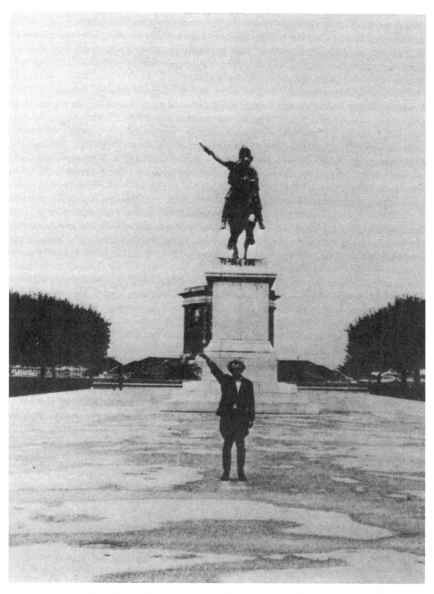

FIGURE 2. Anselm Kiefer, "Occupations" ("Besetzungen," 1969). *Interfunktionen* (Cologne) no. 12 (1975).

into his art, his paintings were bought by (largely Jewish) collectors in America and Israel and some of the vitriolic critiques gave way to reconceptualizing his work as coming to terms with the Nazi past rather than effusing nostalgia for it.[6] Thus, it was only after this (mostly) enthusiastic reception abroad that Kiefer was well received at home in Germany. Yet Kiefer's reception still sharply bifurcates between those who interpret him as a neo-Nazi glorifying the German greatness lost in the ashes of the Third Reich and those who read him as a post-Holocaust artist struggling to come to terms with the German guilt that marked his generation.[7]

An example of the ire Kiefer caused by using Nazi imagery can clearly be seen in a provocative piece created by the American artist Susan Silas. Against a black background Silas pasted letters, in varying sizes and fonts and from different newspapers, to create the effect of a ransom note bearing the following question: "Anselm Kiefer, where was your daddy during the war?" (fig. 3). This image, entitled *Ohne Titel* (1989) was featured in a group show where Kiefer's *Your Blond Hair, Margarete* (1981) was displayed (as was Boltanski's *Monument Odessa* [1991]). Silas's angry question, in the context of the show, *Burnt Whole: Contemporary Artists Reflect on the Holocaust* (Institute of Contemporary Art, Boston, 1995), represents the bitterness Kiefer caused even in America, where he was often more warmly received.[8] In discussing this piece with Silas, she told me that she made it because she distrusted Kiefer's use of Nazi imagery, she distrusted Jewish Americans' adoration of (and willingness to buy) Kiefer's art, and she found that "my gut instinct was to feel that he was exploiting the material and this suspicion of his motives increased over time. I have always felt that he lacked both genuineness and credibility."[9] Silas's piece and her comments contest the growing sense in Kiefer scholarship that he attempts to explode—rather than celebrate—fascist imagery. I love the moxie and directness of Silas's piece because it asks the question that perhaps is in the background but not expressed when we see a non-Jewish German dressed in Nazi garb and saluting in a Sieg Heil gesture. And, the discovery of where Kiefer's father was during the war makes her response piece resonate even more forcefully. Indeed, Silas's question challenges us to confront the emotionality of our own readings of Kiefer's work and to grapple with his excessive return to symbols dear to German fascism.

Because many of Kiefer's paintings are set in forests and evoke figures from German myth and history, Kiefer's forest series can be seen, along with the *Occupations* series, as engaging Nazi imagery. In a detailed explication of the meaning of the forest in this context, Simon Schama examined the

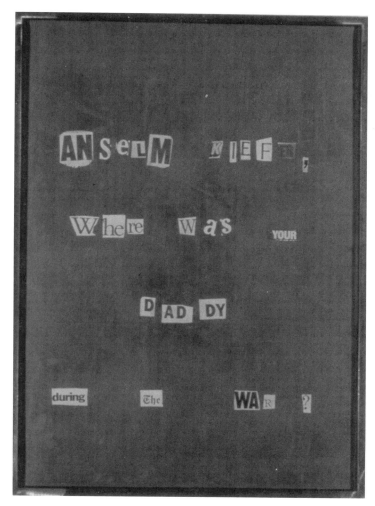

FIGURE 3. Susan Silas, *Ohne Titel* (1989). Newsprint on lead on wood, 43" × 30". Image courtesy of Susan Silas.

German myths upon which Kiefer draws. Claiming that "after 1933, forest themes invaded virtually every realm of art and politics," Schama found that the forest became indelibly associated with the Nazi regime and that anti-Semitic and naturalistic ideologies overlapped significantly.[10] Schama argues that while Kiefer is not a fascist, he may have been seduced by some of the powerful myths to which he so often alludes. Indeed, Nazi imagery and the

German myths that undergirded it are prevalent in Kiefer's work. In several paintings, for example, Kiefer painstakingly reproduces quintessential Nazi buildings, often inserting a lone palette or other incongruous symbol into the center of a room. He also created a painted/sculpted book, *Unfruchtbare Landschaften* (*Barren Landscapes* [1969]), which anticipates the powerful evocation of the terror contained in the very emptiness of former concentration camp sites that made Claude Lanzmann's film *Shoah* (1985) so powerful.[11] There are also documentary images of Nazis in Kiefer's book, *Die Überschwemmung Heidelbergs I* (*Flooding of Heidelberg I* [1969]), and a Nazi salute in a purple bubble featured in the watercolor *Jeder Mensch steht unter seiner Himmelskugel* (*Every man lives under his celestial sphere* [1970]). Equally interesting are Kiefer's burned books, linked as they are to both Nazi book burnings and to the burned remains of the Holocaust, a word that comes from the ancient Greek for "burnt whole" and that appears in Genesis 22:2, translated as "burnt offering." Kiefer's painted/sculpted books indicate that he insinuates the Nazi genocide into his work in a structural as well as content-based manner. Kiefer also created a series of "star" paintings such as *Sternen-Lager IV* (*Star-Camps IV* [1988]), which Daniel Arasse claims is Kiefer's "most direct allusion to Auschwitz to date."[12]

Resonating with *Sternen-Lager* is Kiefer's *Lichtfalle* (*Light-trap* [1999]), which was on view at the Smart Museum at the University of Chicago in 2004. *Lichtfalle* is composed of thick layers of chunky paint that could represent ashes, the cosmos, snow, or any number of non-representational phenomena; lines resembling the lines on an astrological map crisscross the painting, yet instead of indicating stars, each line leads to a number stuck to the paint. A rusty mesh metallic box containing long, sharp pieces of glass also imprinted with numbers juts out of the center of the painting. The broken glass reminds one of Kristallnacht, the night of November 9, 1938, when synagogues, Jewish homes, and businesses were smashed and burned all over Germany; yet the glass is cut rather than broken. The numbers are reminiscent of concentration camp inmates' numbers but they also seem longer than such numbers and are often combined with words. Thus *Lichtfalle* offers an example of the open-ended possibilities Kiefer's works suggest. We can read the broken glass as reminiscent of Kristallnacht but we are also discouraged by the neatness of the cut glass; we can see the resonance of the numbers with concentration camp tattoos and yet they look different. We are simultaneously invited to and thwarted from reading this painting as Holocaust art.

Another piece, *Bruch der gefäße* (*Breaking of the Vessels* [1990]), which

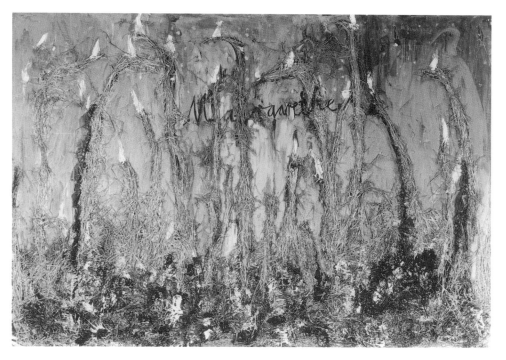

PLATE 1.
Anselm Kiefer, *Margarete* (1981). Oil and straw on canvas, 110^1/$_4$" × 149^5/$_8$".
Image courtesy of Gagosian Gallery.

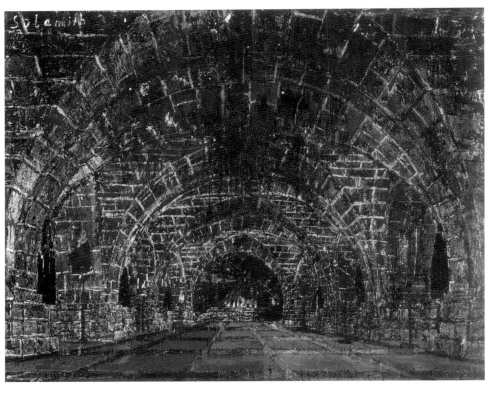

PLATE 2.
Anselm Kiefer, *Sulamith* (1983). Oil, emulsion, woodcut, shellac, acrylic, and straw on canvas, 114^1/$_8$" × 145^3/$_4$". Image courtesy of Gagosian Gallery.

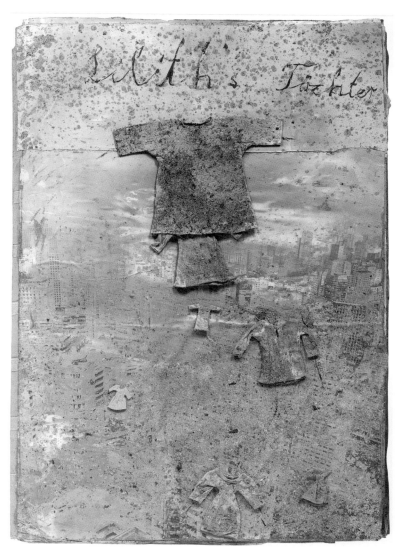

Anselm Kiefer, *Liliths Töchter* (1990). Acrylic, emulsion, and ashes on original photographs, mounted on cardboard with lead strips and burned dresses, 40⁵/₃₂" × 29¹⁵/₁₆" × 7". Image courtesy of Gagosian Gallery.

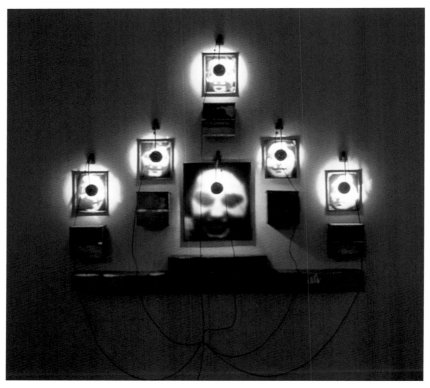

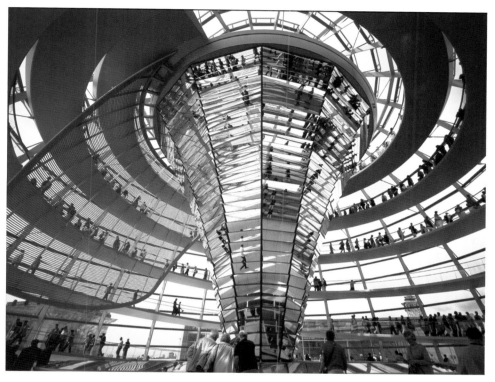

PLATE 5.
Sir Norman Foster, Reichstag, Berlin (1999). Photograph by
VIEW/Dennis Gilbert. Image courtesy of Nigel Young/Foster and Partners.

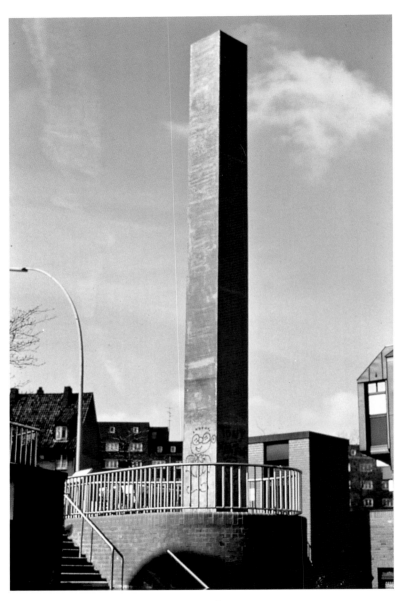

Jochen Gerz and Esther Shalev-Gerz, The Harburg Monument against
Fascism, Hamburg-Harburg (1986–1993, full column standing).
Photograph by Esther Shalev-Gerz.

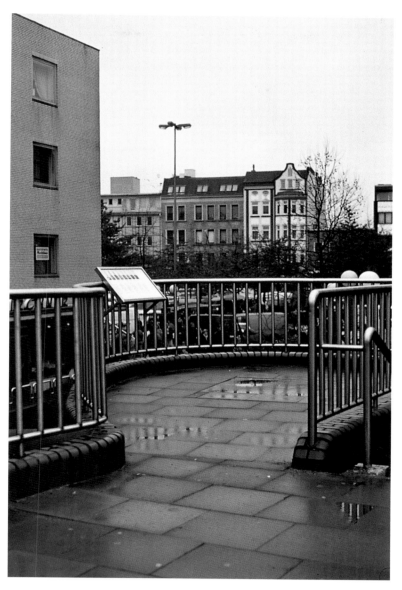

PLATE 7.
Jochen Gerz and Esther Shalev-Gerz, The Harburg Monument against
Fascism, Hamburg-Harburg, (1986–1993, just plaque, after column
was buried). Photograph by Esther Shalev-Gerz.

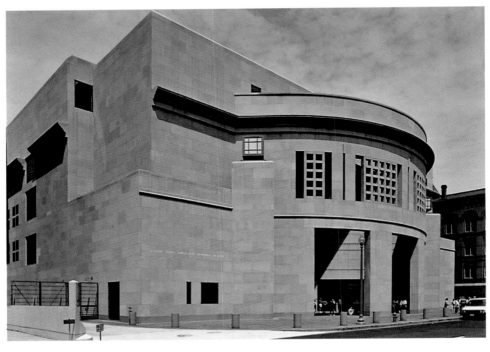

PLATE 8.
James Ingo Freed, United States Holocaust Memorial Museum entrance.
Photograph by Alan Gilbert. Courtesy of the United States Holocaust
Memorial Museum.

was on view at the Saint Louis Art Museum in 2004, features a massive bookshelf containing many leaden, misshapen books surrounded by key words from the Kabbalah. As with *Lichtfalle,* it is possible to see in this sculpture the burned, distorted remains of Jewish culture weighing down the already laden (and leaden) shelf of history. Indeed, as did *Lichtfalle,* this piece features broken glass, but here, surrounding the bookshelf, are broken shards of glass that more forcefully recall Kristallnacht. But other readings compete with the work's Holocaust resonance. While there is not enough space to address these works at length in this book, enumerating them illustrates that Kiefer has produced a vast body of texts that treat the Nazi genocide and the postwar generation's unwitting implication in it.[13] Indeed, by working on the complicated and implicated memory of the Holocaust in postwar Germany, Kiefer struggles not only with what and how to remember, with his own and his parents' generation's possible feelings of guilt, but also with how to create beautiful works that gesture toward the terror of the concentration camps. I now turn to two paintings that convey a nuanced reflection on the Holocaust through weaving together German and Jewish symbolism.

Margarete and Sulamith

In the early eighties, just at the start of the rapid increase of Holocaust imagery in the United States, Israel, and Europe, Kiefer began a series of paintings that referred to the two central and contrasting figures from Paul Celan's poem, "Todesfuge": Margarete and Sulamith.[14] As I discussed in chapter 1, "Todesfuge" is often cited as one of the most powerful representations of unwanted beauty in Holocaust art. Celan has been both harshly criticized and highly lauded for the beauty of this work, and in choosing to make several paintings and sculptures that refer to Celan, Kiefer no doubt challenges us to grapple with the beauty of his own Holocaust works.[15] The repeated refrain in Celan's poem contrasts Sulamith's ashen hair with the golden hair of Margarete, culminating in the final lines: "dein goldenes Haar Margarete / dein aschenes Haar Sulamith" (your golden hair Margarete / your ashen hair Shulamith).[16] The poem suggests that the golden hair of Margarete, the ruined German woman (from Goethe's *Faust*), survives intact, while the Jewish woman, Sulamith (from Song of Songs, 7:1), whose black hair turns ashen, not from aging but from the crematoria in the camps, will only find a home in the ash-choked sky. In Kiefer's rendering of Celan's figures, the different palettes of *Margarete* and *Sulamith* reflect the difference between the blond hair of Margarete and the initially black hair of Sulamith.[17] That Kiefer has chosen to adopt figures from one of the most famous Holocaust poems written by a Jewish survivor indicates a bold appropriation in itself; that he then reverses the range of associations between German and Jew is even bolder.

Onto the pale blue background of *Margarete* (1981) Kiefer has pasted the "golden" hair of Margarete in the form of thick straw stakes fashioned into a shape evoking a Chanukah menorah (plate 1). Thus, while the Margarete of Celan's poem glows as the golden-haired German, Kiefer transforms her into a Jewish symbol; however, the presence of nineteen lights, only some of which connect to their straw stems, disrupts the allusion to the menorah. The menorah, in contrast, has eight candles and one *shammash*, which lights the other candles. Traditionally, Jews light the menorah annually on Chanukah, the festival celebrating the biblical miracle of a small pot of oil lasting eight days instead of one, thus allowing the illumination of the temple for the entire battle against the Greco-Syrians.[18] The menorah has therefore come to symbolize the heroism of the Jewish struggle to survive. That the menorah comes wrapped in this powerful symbol of revolution can be demonstrated by the following anecdote, relayed to me by my colleague Dara Goldman: after the melting of restrictions on religious practice in Cuba, Castro decided to visit a synagogue, to which he was invited for Chanukah. To his initial question, "What is Chanukah?" the leader of the synagogue replied: "It's revolution for the Jews."[19] Thus Kiefer merges the Germanic Margarete, who survived the war by accident of birth, with the revolutionary struggles of the Jews to survive centuries of religious persecution. Through linking Margarete's hair with the menorah, Kiefer argues that Germany too will survive its destruction after Hitler's defeat.

In contrast to *Margarete,* the dark and mournful palette and mood of *Sulamith* (1983) performs the opposite conflation: whereas *Margarete* combined the German woman with the Jewish image of the menorah, the later painting merges the Jewish woman with a symbol of Nazism, Wilhelm Kreis's Funeral Hall for the Great German Soldiers (1939) (fig. 4 and plate 2). As he does in many of his other paintings, Kiefer here carefully reproduces the outlines of Nazi architecture; in this case, the painting pulls the eye back towards the altar-like piece at the center, under the heavy arches of Kreis's monumental mausoleum. And here, as in *Margarete,* we also find a menorah-like image, a seven-pointed fire. The white flames of the fire and their distinctness from each other indicate perhaps an early menorah, of the seven-

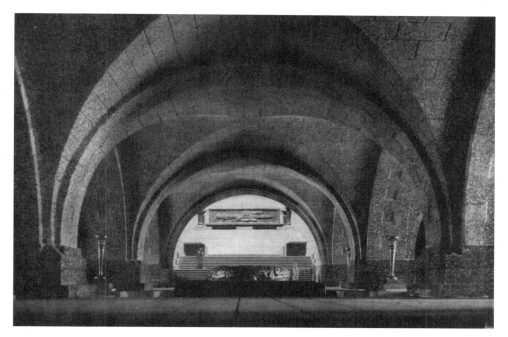

FIGURE 4. Wilhelm Kreis, *Soldatenhalle in Berlin, Beisetzungshalle der großen deutschen Soldaten*. Albert Speer, *Neue Deutshe Baukunst* (Amsterdam, Berlin, Vienna: Volk und Reich Verlag Prag, 1943).

pointed type burned from morning until evening (Exodus 27:21). But, in keeping with Kreis's Funeral Hall, the flames could also be a memorial fire. Thus Kiefer transforms the Jewish symbol of survival that Margarete inhabited into a funeral pyre for German soldiers. The aesthetic pollution (a term that I explain below and more fully in chapter 5) produced by conflating Kiefer's evocation of Sulamith from Celan's poem "Todesfuge" with a Nazi architect's mausoleum conveys the sense that the ashes of Sulamith are being interred in a Nazi space.

Kiefer thus merges a golden-haired German woman smacking of Nazi overtones with the menorah in *Margarete,* and a black-haired Jewish woman surrounded by ashes with a stark symbol of Nazism in *Sulamith*. This reversal of symbolism is deeply disturbing because the imbrication of perpetrator and victim remains an ambiguous gesture. Is Kiefer claiming that the beautiful arches of Kreis's mausoleum are an appropriate resting place for the ashes of Germany's Jewish victims? Is Kiefer trying to dislocate the too-simple divide between innocence and guilt that can mark Holocaust discourse? Does he want to reclaim the beauty of fascist architecture and save it from aesthetic dismissal because of its politics? Despite Rudi Fuchs's claim that "it would be ridiculous, of course, to assume that Kiefer in any way *likes*" Nazi architecture, one cannot help wondering when considering these paintings whether adoration or at least admiration does not drive Kiefer's repeated return to Nazi imagery.[20] And if this is the case, perhaps Kiefer is legitimately trying to wrest aesthetics from politics.

As I have noted, with much of Kiefer's work two readings seem to compete with each other. Andreas Huyssen finds that in the Sulamith painting, "Kiefer succeeds in doing for painting what Celan did for poetry more than thirty years ago." Huyssen also argues that this transformation of a Nazi space into a space for the commemoration of its victims creates an "effect that reveals fascism's genocidal telos in its own celebratory memorial spaces."[21] Huyssen thus finds that Kiefer's work exposes the violence of fascism rather than celebrating it. Peter Schjeldahl similarly argues that Kiefer reclaims fascist asethetics "from the death grip of their political uses in the Third Reich: [he offers us] comprehension of the real beauty of an Albert Speer interior, say, simultaneous[ly] with comprehension of its sinister historical significance." Schjeldahl continues that the *Margarete* and *Sulamith* series "do the supposedly impossible—make successful art of the ultimate horror."[22] In response to Schjeldahl, one might also argue that this troubling reversal equates the German war heroes too closely with the victims of the Nazi genocide. Lisa Saltzman claims that while "Kiefer's *Sulamith* indulges a certain fascination of fascism . . . it simultaneously blocks that spectatorial relationship."[23]

These readings all contend that Kiefer's work exposes something violent or sinister in fascism at the same time as it explores the seduction of fascist aesthetics. The juxtaposition of the paintings *Margarete* and *Sulamith* forces us to consider the complex implication of perpetrator, victim, artist, and viewer in creating Holocaust memory. Kiefer's art is therefore disturbing and can be frustrating even while one might be seduced by its grandeur and beauty; his work thus walks a thin line between criticism and adoration of Nazi myths.[24] Perhaps this very ambivalence is what makes Kiefer's work so enduring.

In pointing out the resonance of Kiefer's work with that of some of the postwar German figures such as the anti-Semitic and nostalgic German filmmaker Hans Jürgen Syberberg, other of Kiefer's readers have been less willing to allow that he can achieve a simultaneous exposure and exploration of fascism.[25] In *Vom Unglück und Glück der Kunst in Deutschland nach dem letzten Kriege,* Syberberg argues that due to Jewish, modernist aesthetics, beauty has been lost in postwar art. Syberberg's claim thus recalls the oft-made association of modernism with Jewishness and also the anti-Semitic rhetoric that links Jewishness with ugliness.[26] Syberberg finds that because of the deadening weight of postwar German guilt, art in Germany is boring and dull compared to the exciting mythical possibilities of prewar German culture. What Syberberg calls an "unholy alliance" (*unseliger Allianz*) between Jews and a leftist aesthetic has deadened all cultural life so that guilt kills myth and fantasy.[27] Finding that there has been a "demonization of the purely aesthetic as something tainted by fascism," Syberberg longs to "overcome the ugliness that so much postmodern society and art dwells upon."[28] Syberberg thus supports Kiefer's use of myth as a counterweight to what he sees as the guilt-ridden and dead aesthetic of postwar German art ("Bin für Anselm Kiefers Bildermythen persönlicher Visionen und Ästhetik").[29] In chapter 5 I discuss what I call "aesthetic pollution," or the fear of fascist aesthetics polluting Holocaust memorial sites. By claiming that Kiefer's work is beautiful, Syberberg assimilates the painter into his post-fascist mythical daydream of a Germany still glorious and not polluted by the modernist aesthetics he sees as being produced by German guilt. But Kiefer should not be linked too closely to Syberberg because his use of beauty does not serve a glorified Germany, but rather queries this desired use of the power of German myth. Thus, on the one hand, Kiefer invites association with a Syberbergian aesthetic, while on the other hand, his work is more complicated than a simple association with Syberberg allows.

In a speech delivered to Israel's Knesset in 1990, Kiefer claimed that his mission was to reach for an impossible reunification of a Germany split apart by the loss of its Jewish half.[30] Kiefer's desire to reincorporate Jewishness into Germanness goes a long way toward explaining the confusing nexus of fascism and Jewishness in his work; Kiefer sees himself uniting two halves of a Germany forever divided, not, in this case, by East and West (and Kiefer made these remarks on the heels of the dissolution of the Wall), but by the Nazi genocide. Thus, whereas Syberberg would clamor for a re-unified and re-glorified Germany, Kiefer finds that the divide between German and Jew has burned national glory and reduced it to ash, a literal and metaphorical staple of Kiefer's work. Ash cannot help but evoke the Holocaust, as it has become one of the most recognizable symbols of the Nazi genocide, yet the ash in Kiefer's art describes the ruin of the perpetrators as well as the victims. Kiefer evokes ashes both literally and figuratively in many of his paintings: literal ashes are often part of thick layers of paint and he also paints images of ashes into his work.[31] Thus, as do the *Margarete* and *Sulamith* paintings, *Lilith* and *Lilith's Daughters*, to which I now turn, display an uncomfortable cohabitation of perpetrator and victim.

Lilith and Her Daughters

In the early 1990s, Kiefer created several series of paintings and books under the rubric of *Lilith*. The images in these series typically include ash-covered dresses, wires, lead airplanes, and sometimes human hair and ash-covered cityscapes. While they are bleak paintings and books, their mournful beauty can carry a range of associations from war, loss of innocence, the dearth of contemporary urban living, and, indeed, the ashes of the Holocaust. In titling these series *Lilith*, Kiefer evokes a complicated figure in Jewish mythology, who has appeared in contradictory ways. The great scholar of Jewish mysticism, Gershom Scholem, reports that Lilith was the first mate of Adam and—in contrast to Eve—was made at the same time as him. However, Adam and Lilith disagreed over power in sex because Lilith was "unwilling to forgo her equality."[32] Lilith then flew off in a rage and became a demon who seduces men and strangles children at the moment of their birth. Scholem lists many versions of Lilith myths, but in almost all of them she appears as a "female demon with a woman's face, long hair, and wings" (356).

While Lilith figures often in Jewish literature as a seductive demon, no doubt because of her desired sexual equality, she has also been used by feminists as a symbol of rebellious Jewish womanhood. One of her most memorable appearances in Jewish literature is in I. L. Peretz's Yiddish poem "Monish," where she plants a young German woman who entices the precocious Monish to love amid the ruins and then forces him to swear against the name of God that he loves her above all else.[33] One of her most important feminist versions appears in the magazine *Lilith*, which first appeared in 1976 and still functions as a mixed-genre center for Jewish and feminist ideas. Combining testimonials, fiction, expository essays, art, and book reviews, *Lilith* sought to harness the sassy energy of Lilith as the first advocate for parity among men and women. In the first issue of the magazine, Judy Weinberg traced the conflicting and varied interpretations of Lilith and posed a question that resonates with the meaning of this winged demon for Kiefer's work: "Had she succeeded in her battle with Adam for equal rights, Lilith might today represent that spark of original creativity in whose image women could retrace and recreate their history. Instead history plunged her into the depths of demonhood."[34] Kiefer thus plays on this double image of Lilith and claims her as a simultaneously darkly demonic and triumphantly revolutionary symbol.

Lilith, because she is a winged creature, cannot help but recall Walter Benjamin's angel of history, to whom Kiefer refers explicitly in the title of one of his shows, "The Angel of History" (Cologne, 1992), and in of one of his works *"Der Engel der Geshichte (Mohn und Gedächtnis)"* (*The Angel of History* [*Poppy and Memory*] [1989]); this title combines Benjamin with Celan as he uses the title of the collection of Celan's poems containing "Todesfuge" after Benjamin's "angel."[35] In 1940 Benjamin famously described his angel of history thus: "This is how one pictures the angel of history. His face is turned toward the past. Where we perceive a chain of events, he sees one single catastrophe which keeps piling wreckage upon wreckage and hurls it in front of his feet."[36] The postwar resonance of this wartime image has captured the imagination of many poets, writers, artists, scholars, and others, as the density of wreckage upon wreckage is precisely what sorting through twentieth-century history feels like. Indeed, when the poet Carolyn Forché crafted a startling book of poems that reflect upon a broad sweep of twentieth-century disasters—from the Holocaust to Hiroshima to the civil war in El Salvador—she titled it *The Angel of History.* One of the most memorable images in Forché's work is the following: "Memory insists she stood there, able to go neither forward nor back, and in that / Unanimous night, time slowed, in light pulsing through ash."[37] As a meditation on Benjamin's angel of history, Forché's image of memory frozen in a "light pulsing through ash" aptly describes how Kiefer's art encourages memory. Kiefer never fails to remind us that history and memory are laden with the ash of the Nazi genocide and thus Kiefer's evocation of the angel of history in one of the Lilith series resonates with Benjamin's and Forché's depictions of the slow and difficult work of moving through the wreckage of twentieth-century history.[38] By linking Kiefer's many uses of the winged figure of Lilith to Benjamin's angel of history, and by transforming the winged palettes of his earlier work to the winged airplanes of his later pieces, one has the sense in seeing Kiefer's art—much as one had in reading Jabès's poetry—that the weight of history flies around interminably without landing in one readable space.

Kiefer is no doubt keenly aware of the vagaries of the uses and interpretations of Lilith, thus deepening his choice of this demonic/creative/rebellious Jewish figure for these series of paintings and books. Harold Bloom dramatically characterizes Kiefer's use of Lilith as identification: "Kiefer's Lilith has been redeemed by him: there is no precedent in tradition for transforming this strangler of infants, this muse of masturbation, into a darkly sympathetic figure, with whom the artist virtually identifies."[39] By claiming that Kiefer identifies with Lilith, Bloom suggests that he takes a guilty figure and redeems her into a sympathetic symbol. But by ignoring the feminist revision of Lilith into a heroic figure, Bloom misreads the fact that Kiefer refers to Lilith as demonic seducer and murderess of infants, Lilith as figure in Jewish literature, Lilith as feminist icon, and Lilith as an evocation of the angel of history, when he names his series after her.

In one book of a *Lilith* series, *Lilith's Daughters* (of which there are many versions), Kiefer superimposes burlap dresses covered in ash over a cityscape also veiled by ash. In different incarnations of the images, the cityscape emerges more or less visibly. The *Lilith's Daughters* (1990) I discuss here maintains the city as a clear but partially covered-by-ash landscape over which the familiar burlap dresses float (plate 3). The dresses evoke clothes left behind by those lost in the Holocaust as well as the Jewish ritual of mourning clothes; the cityscape covered in ash evokes the bombings of Germany at the end of the war as much as the idea that contemporary cities, contemporary lives, are covered by the ever-present memory of the Nazi genocide. By thus combining images of the Holocaust with images evoking Germany as the subject of allied bomb attacks—a confusion of victim and perpetrator—Kiefer's books and paintings offer complex reflections on the presence of the past in the present. While one way of reading *Lilith's Daughters* finds that Kiefer concerns himself with how the memory of the Holocaust persists and covers—like so much ash—all contemporary life, another interpretation finds that these mourning robes weep over the loss of German cities bombed by the Allies at the end of the war. Thus the work of mourning found in this painting is polyvalent and speaks to a multitude of losses. By simultaneously encouraging reflection on the Holocaust and on the disfigurement of Germany at the close of World War II, *Lilith's Daughters* encapsulates the problematic nature of this important artist's output, for it participates in an aesthetic encouragement of memory coupled with a political refusal of historical specificity.

I now turn to another work in the Lilith series, a sculptural painting, *Banner* (1990), that is part of the Museum of Contemporary Art (MCA) in Chicago's collection. As he constructs many of his paintings, Kiefer created *Banner* using a gray palette and dense layers of thick, bumpy paint (fig. 5). Measuring slightly more than ten feet by nine feet, this three-dimensional

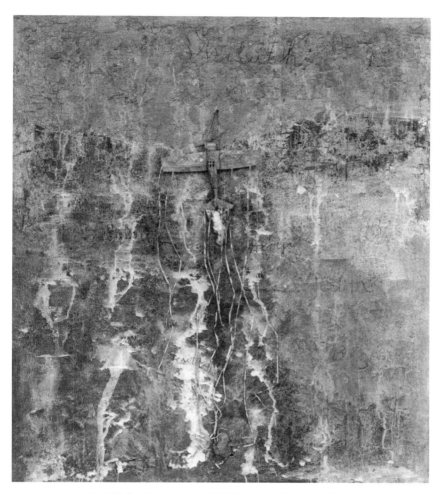

FIGURE 5. Anselm Kiefer, *Banner* (1990). Collection Museum of Contemporary Art, Chicago, gift of Camille Oliver-Hoffmann in memory of Paul W. Oliver-Hoffmann. Photograph © Museum of Contemporary Art, Chicago.

painting features a leaden airplane that dangles long lead strips, which are anchored at the bottom of the work by a rock. The plane at once evokes a military aircraft and the many winged images—such as Lilith and the angel of history—of Kiefer's other paintings. The bellicose plane evokes Germany's actions in the Second World War, yet, as I discuss below, Jewish symbolism from the Kabbalah supplies the key to the painting. Kiefer thus again combines symbols of perpetrators with victims.

Across the top of *Banner* Kiefer has written the Kabbalistic word "Atzi-luth." Scholem describes Atziluth as emanations that "occurred within 'non-temporal time,' a dimension of time which involved as yet no differentiation into past, present, and future" (103). Doreet LeVitte Harten explains that "emanation is essential to the understanding of Kiefer's works" because "it enables him to depict each of the works as a compressed and layered con-struction where each stratum is the sediment of that which succeeds it."[40] This sense of time collapsing accords well with the image of the angel of history, whose wings are caught between present and past, and who can dwell properly in neither. This time collapse also resonates with the long process of coming to terms with the past that has been at the center of Kiefer's work. For if past, present, and future collapse within the non-temporal time of Aztiluth, then Kiefer represents the angel/airplane/Lilith as functioning un-der the sign of non-temporal time.[41] One of the curators of the all-encom-passing MCA show that featured *Banner*, "Life Death Love Hate Pleasure Pain," remarks that because the plane lumbers below the handwritten word "Atziluth," this signifies that "Atziluth has not yet been achieved."[42] I read the plane's position below the word, rather, as the plane laboring under the sign of non-temporal time—as the angel of history's emplotment in a time that refuses to progress because the leaded weight of the past bears down upon it. Indeed, a lead weight that dangles from one of several streamers attached to its wings and tail thwarts the plane's progress. While the white streamers could signify the imprint of the speed of the plane in the sky, the lead weight attached to their ends radically dampens the sensation of veloc-ity. Thus, instead of viewing *Banner* as a depiction of the plane stretching toward the collapsed time of Aztiluth, I read the painting as a representation of the already-achieved collapse between an attempt to come to terms with the past and the recognition that the guilty past dwells interminably in the besmirched present.

The lead out of which Kiefer molds *Banner*'s airplane holds deep significance for the painter because lead refers to his interest in alchemy. That the alchemists failed to transform lead into gold did not stop them from making many im-portant discoveries in the process.[43] As Peter Schjeldahl puts it, alchemy evokes "at once a mystical metaphor of creativity and the folly of mumbling crackpots, who, in stinking laboratories, tried to make matter imitate an idea."[44] Thus, lead functions as an apt metaphor and material for Kiefer, not because he hopes to transform the leaden, heavy, past of Germany's guilt and German culture's demise into the light and hope of gold, but rather because he knows what the alchemists could not yet know: that the transmutation of lead into gold was impossible but that the search itself would prove meaningful and important.[45] Like wings laboring under the sign of Aztiluth, then, the leaden plane intensifies the sensation that the process of treating the painful past is more crucial than the product of that labor.

Because the alchemical tradition of speaking in code resonates with the hermeneutic processes Kiefer inspires throughout his oeuvre, one finds that reading codes is essential to understanding his work. His many images of fascist architecture, such as the Kreis memorial reproduced in *Sulamith,* for example, do not name the buildings Kiefer copies in his titles; one must know the structures to understand how closely he copies them (see fig. 4 and plate 2). As the alchemical text *Rosarium philosophorum* puts it, "Wherever we have spoken openly we have (actually) said nothing. But where we have written something in code and in pictures we have concealed the truth."[46] Thus *Banner,* by combining the alchemical symbolism of the impossible transformation of lead—in this case the lead weight of German guilt—into the gold of redemption with Kabbalistic words overshadowed by the multivalent symbol of Lilith invites us to reflect upon Germany's guilt and its Jewish victims. Like *Margarete, Sulamith,* and *Lilith's Daughters,* then, *Banner* exemplifies the problematics of the unwanted beauty of Kiefer's Holocaust art, as its allusive yet pointed encouragement toward remembering the Nazi genocide is coupled with an uncomfortable refusal to separate adequately the perpetrators from the victims.

In 1990, the contemporary artist Susan Silas, who created the provocative piece about Kiefer that I discussed at the beginning of this chapter, made another work that offers a refreshing challenge to Kiefer's art. Silas was born in the United States in 1953 to Hungarian Jewish survivor parents, and thus identifies with the role of the victim. For this later piece, Silas enlarged one of the famous photographs Margaret Bourke-White had taken at the liberation of the concentration camps to life size, cut a hole out for her head, and re-photographed the Bourke-White image in a forest with her own face inserted into the original photograph. Silas then juxtaposed her altered photograph with one of Kiefer's photographs from the series wherein he dressed in Nazi garb, *Occupations,* and titled the composite *We're Not Out of the Woods Yet* (1990) (fig. 6). By occupying the place of the victim, Silas both challenged Kiefer's appropriation of the place of the perpetrator and simultaneously

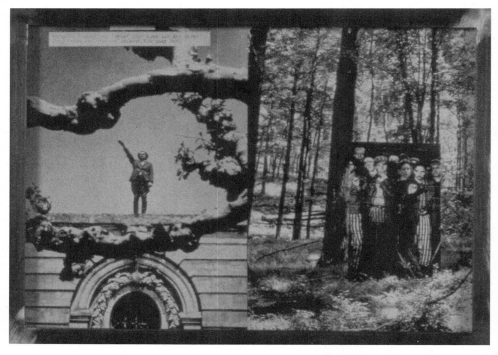

FIGURE 6. Susan Silas, *We're Not Out of the Woods Yet* (1990), 13¹/₂" × 18¹/₄". Image courtesy of Susan Silas.

invaded the space of the forest so dear to many of Kiefer's paintings made during his time in the Oden Forest region.[47] When Kiefer reproduced the Sieg Heil gesture he mocked the stance of perpetrator, whereas Silas's insertion into the concentration camp universe in a sense mocks the sacredness of victimization. Thus *We're Not Out of the Woods Yet* performs a complicated reflection on Kiefer's perpetrator stance. On the one hand, Silas occupies a morally superior position of victim and thus offers a counterweight to Kiefer's perpetrator. On the other hand, by puncturing the sacredness of concentration camp images, Silas simultaneously questions the morally superior position she inhabits. Silas's composite thus corrects the interweaving of perpetrator and victim that I have been finding in so much of Kiefer's work. For Silas does not let Kiefer's occupation of the Sieg Heil gesture stand alone; the victim side of her composite image asserts itself as a poignant commentary on how both artists are entrenched in their historically circumscribed roles as inheritors of guilt and victimization, respectively.

The past itself, as historical change continues to accelerate, has become the most surreal of subjects—making it possible, as Benjamin said, to see a new beauty in what is vanishing.
—Susan Sontag

"There is a beautiful story in Proust: A sad man whose wife has just died sees a friend going to commit suicide. They pass through a garden and he says to his friend, 'Look at these flowers, so beautiful. Look at the blue sky.' Seeing these things, the friend forgets to kill himself. He survives because he forgets. Sometimes we need to forget."[48] Thus Christian Boltanski, relaying this story from Proust in an interview in *Tate Magazine,* turns a writer frequently thought of as an important theorist of the complex turns of memory into an associate of forgetting. But the story Boltanski pulls out of Proust is as much about the aesthetic and sensual pleasures of the beautiful garden as it is about forgetting.[49] Indeed, because the beautiful garden deflects the suicide, beauty catalyzes forgetting in a positive manner. As I discussed in chapter 2, Semprun remembers Proust in order to transfigure the worst experiences. Recall that, for Semprun, the beauty of Proust's memories of gardens allowed him to transform a squalid boxcar into a manageable experience, yet when the narrator tried to return to the restful garden of Proustian memory, it was inhabited by a survivor who refused to be assimilated into the bountiful memory of the garden. In Boltanski's case, forgetting in the name of beauty amounts to a willful forgetfulness of historical specificity. I have opened with these comments on Boltanski's curious use of Proust because they illustrate my argument regarding Boltanski's art in general, that it invites us to mourn those lost in the Holocaust through powerful, beautiful images that nonetheless suffer from aestheticized forgetfulness.

Christian Boltanski, who lives and works in Paris, was born on September 6, 1944, a few days after the liberation of Paris (his middle name is consequently Liberté), to a Catholic mother and a Jewish father who had converted to Catholicism.[50] Boltanski's Jewish side shares with some French Jews a relatively recent history of immigration, for his paternal grandfather, David Boltanski, was a Jewish singer in Odessa who emigrated to Paris. In order to save their family, Boltanski's parents feigned a divorce during the war; Boltanski's father hid under the floorboards while his mother, the writer Annie Lauran, lived above.[51] Lauran's work is accordingly deeply invested in the Holocaust and in uncovering French ideas about Nazism. For example, in *La casquette d'Hitler ou le temps de l'oubli* (1974), Lauran set out to determine what had happened to the memory of the deportation of Jews in French consciousness by recording the responses of survivors and schoolchildren to a series of questions about Hitler.[52] Thus Boltanski was raised in a milieu in which the war and the Shoah figured prominently.

Throughout his career, Boltanski has pushed the limits of what constitutes art by including "actions" in his work—sometimes taking the form of walks, sometimes of letters to known and unknown people, sometimes other forms of "living art." In the early sixties he began to paint images treating the Armenian massacre, and then quickly branched out from painting into mail art, films, sculptural projects, photos, found objects, and various other media.[53] For an example of some of his more curious work, in an almost alchemically impossible search for perfection, Boltanski set out in 1969 to mold over three thousand balls of earth in order to make at least one perfect sphere; as with most of his works, the ephemeral nature of these balls of earth called into question—à la Duchamp—the permanence and meaning of art production.[54] In the mid-seventies Boltanski briefly returned to painting and created a series of images of himself in various clown guises, explaining that the "*Clowns* mark the moment in which I declared that C.B. was a false priest, and as such, was doomed."[55] He then turned to his own biography and reproduced childhood images; in fact, in interviews he confirms that he has created so many fictions about his childhood that he can no longer separate truth from fiction.[56] For example, in many interviews Boltanski repeats the dubious claim that he and his siblings slept in the same room with their parents and did not go outside unaccompanied until they were eighteen. But any story about Boltanski's childhood or biography needs to be regarded with suspicion, as Boltanski glories in disseminating conflicting information about his past.[57] These fictions of the self were endemic to the group of artists with whom he was associated, including Jean Le Gac, Sarkis, Gina Pane, and others. Another member of this group, the photographer Annette Messager, who has been Boltanski's partner for over a quarter of a century, proclaimed: "actuellement je ne sais plus très clairement si je parle de moi ou d'un de mes personnages inventés et après tout où est la différence?" (Presently, I no longer know very clearly whether I speak about myself or about one of my invented characters—and after all, what is the difference?).[58] These overlapping invented characters capture the sensation in much of Boltanski's work that we are dealing with a trickster who creates conflicting selves. Conflicting fictions of the self such as these can be read as wonderful critiques of the false certainty offered by a supposedly seamless identitary narrative, or they can be read as a childish ruse.

Indeed, perhaps because of the widely varying readings enabled by such conflicting self-presentations, and because of the emotional nature of most of Boltanski's art, critics seem either to love his work or to find it grating. Boltanski has been most well received in France, the United States, and Germany, and least well received in Britain, where some critics find his output "wearing," "dulling," "hollow," "a sham," "like a jumble sale," and "a spoof."[59] In contrast to the British readings above, some American and French critics find that Boltanski has created "an epic history of our century of war," or that his work "strums the chord of nostalgia, loss, and innocence with great effectiveness," or that his images "faire oublier l'art pour nous toucher plus profondement" (make us forget art to touch us more profoundly).[60] I hazard that many British art critics, with their sharp and cynical stance, find Boltanski's emotional work too sentimental, whereas art critics in France, the United States, and Germany may be more susceptible to reading mournful art, *especially* when it is perceived to be about the Holocaust. Nevertheless, that Boltanski has permanent pieces in such august buildings as Sir Norman Foster's Bundestag in Berlin and the Musée d'art et d'histoire du Judaisme in Paris indicates that his international reputation is well established.[61]

Boltanski's reputation has grown since the early 1980s, when he began to produce the photo-sculptures that have become his signature works. One of these works, *Monument: Les enfants de Dijon* (1985), was on display at Chicago's Museum of Contemporary Art in the fall of 2002, and, with my baby daughter asleep in my arms, I spent some time contemplating the installation and thereby experiencing the ambivalent emotions Boltanski can catalyze (fig. 7). I entered a dark and somber room and found myself confronted with many framed black-and-white photographs of children's faces. Because each face was illuminated by three small bulbs, I thought of altars to the dead, of memorial flames, of votive candles in a cathedral. From each of the three bulbs, a wire hung and thus created a jumble of electrical cords that made me think simultaneously about an electrode as a torture device and about the display of the normally behind-the-scenes mechanics of the exhibit. While I did not know the names of these children, I found myself imagining their lives, even though, because of the memorial-like setting, I imagined that they were dead. After scrutinizing each child for clues to his or her life, I sat down in the middle of the melancholy room and absorbed the crowd of images pressing down on me. After some time, I rose, examined some faces up close,

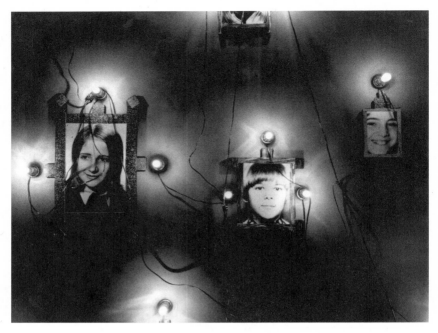

FIGURE 7. Christian Boltanski, *Monument: Les enfants de dijon* (1985). Collection Museum of Contemporary Art, Chicago, gift of the William J. Hokin Family. Photograph © Museum of Contemporary Art, Chicago. © 2004 Artists Rights Society (ARS), New York/ADAGP, Paris.

and found that they resembled my lost cousin, aunt, friend. I thought about loss. I searched the explanation boards for more details about these children, but I was offered only the barest of hints. Somehow I ignored the fact that these were French children photographed in 1973, who were probably still living and not much older than I; I found the images so mournful I wondered what had happened to them. What catastrophe had befallen these smiling children? Finally, I left the room, returned to the rest of the museum, and felt that Boltanski was indeed doing something profoundly different than the rest of the conceptual art that failed to engage me. But I didn't know who I was mourning, why I was mourning her, or if she required my tears.

Le Lycée Chases

Boltanski declares that "La photo m'intéresse parce qu'elle est ressentie comme vraie, comme preuve que l'histoire que l'on raconte est réelle, elle donne l'illusion de la réalité" (the photograph interests me because it feels true, as a proof that the story one tells is real—it gives the illusion of reality).[62] The difference between the story told by photographs and the reality they supposedly depict can be encapsulated in the case of Boltanski's installation piece, *Le Lycée Chases: Classe terminale du Lycée Chases en 1931: Castelgasse, Vienne* (1987), which was exhibited in various venues, including the New Museum of Contemporary Art, New York, and the Kunstverein für die Reinländer und Westfalen, Düsseldorf (plate 4).[63] *Le Lycée Chases* consists of a series of enlarged black-and-white photographs of faces, each with a desk lamp affixed; the wires of the lamps hang down over the faces. The room of photos has a stark quality to it that both contributes to and detracts from the melancholic scene. For on the one hand, *Le Lycée Chases* participates in the mourning tableau of Boltanski's other photo-sculptures, such as *Les enfants de Dijon,* but on the other hand, because the desk lamps so brightly illuminate each face, the exhibit offers less of the votive candle sensation of some of his other works. Rather, the lights shining into each face invite us to interrogate each image minutely.

Boltanski enlarged these faces from a 1931 photograph of a group of Jewish students at a high school in Vienna, which he had found in an important text, *Die Mazzesinsel* (1984), by the Austrian historian Ruth Beckermann, about the tragic history of Viennese Jews (translated into French as *Vienne, rue du Temple: Le quartier juif 1918–1938* in 1986) (fig. 8). Surrounding the photograph in Beckermann's book is a narrative by one of the former students about the "extraordinary school" she had attended, but this narrative does not discuss the fate of the children in the photograph.[64] The artist's book accompanying Boltanski's *Le Lycée Chases* opens with the proclamation that "Tout ce que nous savons d'eux c'est qu'ils étaient élèves au Lycée Chases à Vienne en 1931" (all that we know about them is that they were students at the Lycée Chases in Vienna in 1931).[65] Boltanski makes no claim to know the outcome of the people pictured in his installation, but he might have consulted the school in Vienna to determine their fate. Yet, as Gilbert Lascault notes, "Boltanski est un anti-historien." Boltanski echoes this evaluation when he claims that "my images have nothing to do with a particular event nor are they linked to an exact period of time."[66]

But many viewers assume that because these students attended a Jewish high school before the war, they must have perished in the Nazi genocide. For example, consider that Marianne Hirsch guesses that Boltanski's "class photo [is] of a population the majority of which certainly ended up in Hit-

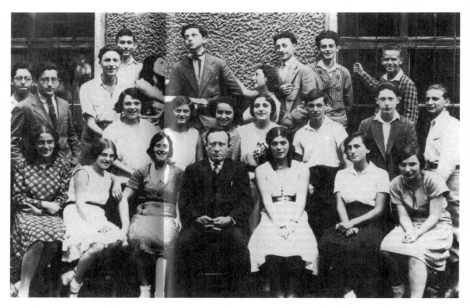

FIGURE 8. Ruth Beckermann, *Die Mazzesinsel: Juden in der Wiener Leopoldstadt 1918–1938* (Vienna: Löcker Verlag, 1984). Image courtesy of Ruth Beckermann.

ler's death camps"; Ernst van Alphen notes that "it is more than likely that most, or even all, of the represented Jewish students did not survive the Holocaust"; David Bonetti suggests that "the dark eyes look out at one as those of victims"; and Susan Gubar notes that "Boltanski uses prewar photographs of people who probably did not outlive the disaster."[67] Yet Lynn Gumpert reports that after these images were exhibited in New York in 1989, a survivor, Debora Preschel, wrote to Boltanski explaining that the name of the school was in fact "Chajes" (named after Rabbi Chajes) and not "Chases," and that most of the students in Beckermann's photograph survived. Originally named in 1919 for Rabbi Zwi-Perez Chajes, an educational reformer, the Zwi-Perez-Chajes-Realgymnasium, which served as an assembly point for Jews who were transported to the camps from 1939 to 1941, was reestablished in 1980 and is currently a functioning secondary school.[68] Thus, whereas one reads the images in Boltanski's piece as mournful and tragic, one could rather read the images, and indeed the story of the Chajes school, as one of persistence and survival.

I spoke to Debora Preschel, the survivor who had written to Boltanski, and she confirmed that she had been surprised to see Boltanski's exhibition.[69]

Another survivor, Leo Glückselig, who sadly passed away in the summer of 2003, just days before I attempted to telephone him, had supplied the original photograph that Beckermann used in *Die Mazzesinsel.* Glückselig is the young man at the center of the photo, in the back row, framed by the two women looking up at him (indeed it seems that he got into trouble for misbehaving during the taking of this photo). In the fall of 2004 I spoke to his daughter, Nina Glückselig, who told me that her father had been "shocked" to see Boltanski's exhibit in New York and that he had eventually arranged a conversation with Boltanski about this piece.[70] Nina recommended that I speak to a great friend of Leo's, Janet Gerson.

During a long phone conversation with me in January 2005, Janet reported that, in 1989, Leo was looking through *New York* magazine, and that, seeing an exhibition by Boltanski that included images of a Viennese Jewish high school, he rushed out to see the exhibit. At the installation he was confronted with "ghostlike, tall, shadowy images," which, slowly, he began to recognize. With an uncanny sensation he realized: "that's me, there's my cousin Richard, these are my friends." He felt as though he were looking at himself as if he were dead, yet he experienced a series of complicated emotions because, as Boltanski is keenly aware, one's younger self is in a sense dead. In response to *Le Lycée Chases* Leo internally protested, "but we're not all dead, but we're not all dead," and he was left grappling with an experience deeply reminiscent of the moment I cited in chapter 1 where a very much alive Charlotte Delbo witnessed her name pronounced among a list of the dead. After seeing *Le Lycée Chases,* Leo very much wanted to meet with Boltanski; he consequently wrote a letter to the artist that was exhibited at the New York Public Library in a show entitled *Christian Boltanski: Books, Prints, Printed Matter Ephemera* (1992).[71] It was at this exhibit that Boltanski and Glückselig met. While there is no formal record of their meeting, Janet tells me that Boltanski was "impressed, shocked, and pleased" to meet Leo, and that he seemed slightly in awe of the elder Viennese survivor.[72] Thus, whereas we are encouraged to read the images in *Le Lycée Chases* mournfully, survivors themselves report a complex series of responses, from shock to understanding, when confronted with these shadowy images of their youthful selves.

The *Lycée Chases* episode is paradigmatic of the interest and dismay Boltanski's art causes. On the one hand, his photo-sculptures, evoking loss, mourning, and melancholia, seem to be powerful examples of Holocaust art. On the other hand, his photo-sculptures evoke the Holocaust in radically anti-historical ways that challenge viewers' investments in finding the

Holocaust in many forms of commemorative art. Like Edmond Jabès's shadowy allusions to the Shoah (which I discussed in chapter 3), then, Boltanski's work meditates on our interpretative strategies as much as on his desire to portray or treat the Nazi genocide. That Hirsch, van Alphen, Bonetti, Gubar, and no doubt many other viewers of Boltanski's *Le Lycée Chases* assume that these are images of victims when they are in fact images of survivors means that we read Boltanski's photographs as mournful when they can rather be read triumphantly. But what, exactly, is at stake in this difference between the living and the dead? Between celebration and mourning? As I mentioned above, Delbo was stunned to find that at a ceremony commemorating French war victims, her name was called out among the dead. She responded by feeling that because a part of her had died at Auschwitz, this assessment was both right and wrong. Yet while Boltanski freely admits that he did not know the fate of the Chajes schoolchildren, the comments cited above make it clear that viewers respond to *Le Lycée Chases* as though it depicted the dead. In other words, what are we being invited to mourn? Is Boltanski merely conjuring up Holocaust sentimentality to emotionally engage his viewers?

Judging by his comments in countless interviews, Boltanski would no doubt argue that even though these Viennese high school children survived the war, their young selves nonetheless "died" and the images should righfully be read mournfully. Boltanski would no doubt agree with Susan Sontag's assessment that "Photographs state the innocence, the vulnerability of lives heading toward their own destruction, and this link between photography and death haunts all photographs of people."[73] While the fact that most viewers read the people in *Le Lycée Chases* as dead when they survived the war may not diminish the emotional power of Boltanski's images, this difference between celebration and mourning does call into question Boltanski's conflation of history and aesthetics.[74]

While Hirsch was understandably moved (as was I) by the mournful power of *Le Lycée Chases'* images, she remained suspicious of the general lack of historical grounding Boltanski demonstrates and wondered whether works such as *Le Lycée Chases* "risk too radical a disconnection from their source and thus the possibility of further manipulation and appropriation, [producing] too decontextualized and ungrounded a form of looking."[75] This is precisely the risk that viewers must struggle with in interpreting Boltanski's art. Much like Jabès's allusive poetry, or the ambivalent clothes of Kiefer's *Lilith's Daughters* series, Boltanski's photo-sculptures only sometimes refer directly to the Holocaust, yet they always seem to evoke the Nazi genocide even when the images have been enlarged and otherwise manipulated so that they are de-historicized. Despite their historical ungrounding, Boltanski's photo-sculptures are nonetheless meaningful and nuanced productions of Holocaust memory.

La vie impossible

Boltanski's artist's book, *La vie impossible de Christian Boltanski* (1985; this was also the title of one of Boltanski's short films, made in 1968), offers contradictory comments on the artist, thus heightening the impression that he is a creature of ambiguity, mystery, illusion, and deceit. The book collects impressions of Boltanski by one hundred unnamed authors (all or some of whom are possibly Boltanski himself), who each contributed a sentence or two (printed in French, German, and English) about his characteristics, work, and life. A translucent page combining photographs, fragments of letters, sketches, identity cards, and other detritus of daily life accompanies each entry. Images from Boltanski's works are often juxtaposed with mementos from his own life, thereby creating the curious impression that he shares memories with the often anonymous figures who populate his haunting photo-sculptures. Because all epistles are cut so that one can see only a portion of them on the page, and because many of the fragments included feel unimportant, the overall effect is that Boltanski's book represents the confusions of memory itself. By always being incomplete and by juxtaposing historical documents with images from his works—of unnamed people who are often de-historicized—Boltanski mirrors the fragmentary, messy, and contradictory nature of memory. This postmodern memoir thus exemplifies the aesthetic dissolution of the subject. Perhaps this explains the impossibility of the "vie" (life) of the title, as the book's infinite twists of memory disallow the creation of a smooth narrative out of a conflicted life.

I am particularly interested in *La vie impossible* because bubbling underneath the cacophony of memories we find a reflection on Jewishness and the Holocaust. Among the comments in *La vie* one finds such anti-Semitic remarks as, "He was a wise guy with his don't touch attitude, his poor little frightened Jew look, he knew how to play his cards well I tell you," or "I remember him as a somewhat dirty little boy with black frizzy hair and an old navy blue coat, we didn't have much contact with him, we all called him the little rabbi."[76] Boltanski evinces an uncomfortable and fluctuating relationship to his Jewishness, which perhaps explains why he demonstrates his Jewishness through anti-Semitic language rather than through more positive views. Boltanski has often noted that he feels both drawn to and alienated from his Jewish background. For example, in an interview with Delphine Renard in 1984 he claimed that

> *Dans la culture juive, je suis attiré par le fait de dire à la fois la chose et son contraire, ou cette façon de répondre à une question par une autre question et constamment tourner en dérision la chose que l'on fait.... J'imagine que mes rapports ambigus avec la peinture et mon utilisation de la photographie sont liés à cette conscience juive, si tant est que j'en aie une.... De toute façon, cela demeure très flou chez moi; je n'ai aucune culture juive.*[77]

In Jewish culture, I'm attracted by the possibility of saying one thing and its opposite at the same time, or this way of responding to a question with another question and constantly mocking what one has done.... I imagine that my ambiguous relationship to painting and my use of photography are tied to this Jewish consciousness, insofar as I have one.... This remains very fluid with me; I don't have a Jewish culture.

In another interview Boltanski announces his estrangement from Jewish culture by noting that "I know nothing about Jewish culture and religion; I've almost never been to a synagogue."[78] These kinds of fluctuating self-representations fit, of course, within what Boltanski here—perhaps somewhat tongue-in-cheekedly—terms "Jewish consciousness," with its stereotypical self-mockery and contradiction. As I discussed in chapter 3, Edmond Jabès was also very taken with Judaism's ability to contain contradictions, but here Boltanski evinces a lack of interest in the substance of Jewish culture, whereas Jabès, especially later in life, became very knowledgeable about Judaism.

In addition to its conflicted references to Jewishness, *La vie impossible* is also littered with allusions to the Holocaust. For example, Yad Vashem, the Holocaust memorial, museum, and library in Israel, is mentioned, and in a fragment of a letter one can make out the words "witness of the Holocaust." Finally, one comment reads, "He didn't admit it until later, but as early as 1970 I told him that the Holocaust and in a more general way his relationship to Judaism played a major role in his work [and] a work like 'François C's Clothes' bears a direct relationship to the image of a pile of clothes in the concentration camps."[79]

It is interesting that this commentator finds a "direct relationship" between the tidily folded clothes of *Les habits de François C* (fig. 9) and the Holocaust; as I discuss below, the jumbles of clothes that Boltanski uses in *Canada* can

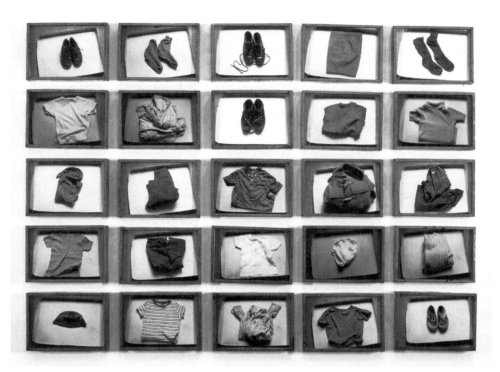

FIGURE 9. Christian Boltanski, *Les habits de François C* (1972).
Image courtesy of Fonds national d'art contemporain, Ministère de la culture, Paris.
© 2004 Artists Rights Society (ARS), New York/ADAGP, Paris.

clearly be seen in this light, but I find different resonances in *François C*. That Boltanski "didn't admit it [the effect of the Shoah] until later" is both true and not true in terms of Boltanski's own assessment of the role of the Holocaust in his work. The ambiguity of, and fluctuations in Boltanski's understanding of the Holocaust content of his art speaks to the ambiguous possibilities of reading much of his work as Holocaust art while it also speaks to other moments of loss. While in the mid-eighties (when *La vie* was first published) Boltanski was willing to admit that the Holocaust was an important theme for him, in the late eighties and early nineties Boltanski issued a series of vociferous rejections of the image of himself as a Holocaust artist. By the late nineties Boltanski was indeed "admitting" the importance of the Holocaust in his work, often with the caveat that his approach to the Holocaust is always indirect. There is a curious inversion between the years when

Boltanski was most avidly rejecting the idea that his work is centrally about the Holocaust and the Holocaust art that he created during this time. The two Holocaust works I discuss below, *Canada* and *Missing House,* were made in 1988 and 1990, and the most stringent denials that his work relates to the Holocaust were uttered between 1989 and 1993. In another curious inversion, one of his most forceful statements embracing his association as a Holocaust artist came in 1995 in the context of a show in New York that is in fact only at a very great stretch "Holocaust art" at all but was nevertheless almost always read by critics as "Holocaust art." This perhaps speaks volumes about the larger context of Holocaust imagery and how prevalent it has become. Nonetheless, charting the twists and turns of Boltanski's understanding of the relationship of his work to the Shoah highlights the deeply ambivalent intentions of the artist and sheds light on how allusive art that could have been read in many ways came to be understood as "Holocaust art."

In an interview conducted in 1985, Boltanski claimed that his early work, which treated the Armenian massacre, stemmed from his feeling of isolation after World War II, when "anti-Semitism was still strong in France . . . [and he wanted] no doubt to deal indirectly with the massacre of the Jews."[80] Echoing the above statement, Boltanski told Elisabeth Lebovici the following year (1986) that "Je pense . . . qu'une des sources de mon activité vient de ma découverte des camps de concentration" (I think . . . that one of the sources of my activity comes from my discovery of the concentration camps).[81] Boltanski then (1989) powerfully rejected the stance taken in these statements from the mid-eighties, and claimed that his work was not to be understood in relation to the Holocaust at all: "I have never used images that came from the camps, it would be impossible for me, it would be something too shameful to use, too sacred. My work is not about the camps, it is after the camps."[82] In another context, in 1993, Boltanski echoed the sense that the Holocaust is too "sacred" to treat: "Les gens me disent aussi que je travaille sur l'Holocauste, ça me rend furieux. C'est une chose trop sacrée, qui n'est pas touchable. Je n'ai jamais travaillé directement sur l'Holocauste. Je travaille après" (People also tell me that I work on the Holocaust, and that makes me furious. It's something too sacred, that cannot be touched. I have never worked directly on the Holocaust. I work afterwards).[83] In these statements, Boltanski expresses the sentiment prevalent in much discourse on Holocaust representation, that direct images from the camps are sacrilegious because they disrupt the graceful silence the event demands. Thus, Boltanski's fluctuating understanding is historically in keeping with trends in Holocaust discourse, for, as

I discussed in the introduction, it was in the early 1990s that the most stringent calls for oblique representations were accepted as aesthetic dictates for Holocaust representation.

In the mid-nineties, Boltanski seems to have capitulated and, rather than being furious that his art is read as referring to the Holocaust, he embraced these kinds of readings: "It [the Holocaust] was always present and unsaid. . . . Now I've started to say it aloud."[84] In the following year, 1996, Boltanski assessed the importance of the Holocaust to his work:

> I was born at the end of the war. My mother was a Christian, and my father, who was Jewish, had been hunted by the Nazis. Most of my parents' friends were survivors of the Holocaust, and even though I have never talked directly about the *Shoah,* those years of horror are undoubtedly, in one way or another, always present in my work. I became interested, for example, in the notion of guilt. Have we all got it in us to be murderers?[85]

And again, in 1998, "la connaissance de la Shoah a été très marquante dans mes anées d'apprentissage, et même si je n'ai jamais voulu parler directement de ce drame dans mon travail, il est central" (knowledge of the Shoah was very marked during my apprenticeship, and even if I never wanted to speak directly about this drama in my work, it is central).[86] Because Boltanski suggests here that indirect allusions to the Shoah are not sacrilegious in the way that direct representations are, he recalls Lyotard's argument, discussed in the introduction to this book, that the Holocaust will be forgotten if remembered too directly. Yet while Boltanski began to admit the Holocaust as a central presence in his work, he often produced art that was only distantly about the Holocaust.

A glance at critical responses to Boltanski's 1995 multi-part exhibit in New York, "Lost: New York Projects," commissioned by the Public Art Fund, indicates that even when the explicit context, content, and aims of Boltanski's work do not seem to refer to the Holocaust, they are read as "Holocaust art." The New York exhibit recycled, with one exception, work Boltanski had done before. "Dispersion," at the Church of the Intercession in Harlem, featuring a ton (literally) of used clothes for sale in two-dollar bags marked with the exhibition details, reprised the previous year's exhibit in Barcelona and the same year's exhibit at Whitechapel in London (1995); "Inventory," at the New York Historical Society, re-used the concept of cataloging one person's ordinary objects, which Boltanski had been doing for almost a quarter of a century; "Lost Property," at Grand Central Terminal, recalled the collection and display of lost objects that Boltanski had exhibited in Tokyo and other places.[87] The fourth installation was something new for Boltanski. "What They Remember," an audio exhibit at the Eldridge Street Synagogue on the Lower East Side, which replayed interviews Leslie Cahmi had done with Chinese and Jewish children who were asked about the immigration stories of their parents and grandparents, was, to my knowledge, the first time audio was the centerpiece of Boltanski's art.[88] "What They Remember" also seems the most personal, most narrative, and one of the most evocative pieces Boltanski has done.[89]

These four installations were almost universally read by art critics as referring to the Holocaust: "The dresses, pants, sweaters, and baby items are piled into small pyramids that read like funeral mounds, instantly transporting us to Nazi Germany."[90] Referring to "a heap of gloves piled as if in a mass grave" in "Lost Property," one critic quotes Boltanski, "'For me, lost gloves are very sad,' said Mr. Boltanski, who often refers to the Holocaust in his work."[91] Another critic finds that "'Lost Property' . . . most clearly evokes the Holocaust."[92] Another: "Now, increasingly, he has turned to a more specific issue—the Holocaust. Whether in the objects on display in Grand Central—suitcases, bags and toys reminiscent of those left behind by victims at Nazi death camps—or a mountain of second hand clothing . . . similar in image, if not in function, to the piles of clothing found in concentration camps."[93] As these critical statements attest, viewers are quick to find the Holocaust in conceptual art projects, even when the ordinary urban context would seem to dissuade such a reading. Thus, while Boltanski's description of his work as Holocaust art has been contradictory, his evocative images contribute to Holocaust art by catalyzing Holocaust memory, even as they challenge our desire to read the Holocaust into mourning tableaux.

Apart from this 1995 exhibit in New York, an intensification of direct Holocaust imagery in Boltanski's work since the mid-nineties corresponds with the growth of Holocaust imagery in contemporary culture. While *Canada* and *La maison manquante,* which I discuss below, treat the Holocaust more explicitly, Boltanski also created other pieces, not as often commented upon in the critical literature, about the Nazi genocide. Although space constraints do not permit me to treat them in full, I catalog a few of these pieces here to demonstrate the variety and fascinating nature of these little-known works. In 1993 (the same year he was made "furious" by critics claiming him as a Holocaust artist), Boltanski pasted up images of German resistance fighters executed by the Nazis on the walls of the *Haus der Kunst* in Munich. In the same year Boltanski literalized the metaphor of pulling ghosts out of the closet by bringing to light secreted Nazi artworks and other items acquired during the Third Reich and previously hidden in the recesses of a German museum. This exhibit, *Hinter verschlossenen Türen* (Behind Closed Doors), consisted of a series of mini-displays of these hidden artworks, thereby forcing viewers to confront the cultural remains of the Third Reich. In the following year, 1994, Boltanski and some helpers set up a table in the train station in Köln where they displayed and distributed thousands of reproductions of Red Cross posters originally printed after the war and designed to reunite missing German children with their parents.[94] Boltanski has also created an installation, *Réflexion,* that meditates on the work of the artist and Holocaust victim, Charlotte Salomon.[95] There has thus been a sharp intensification of Boltanski's engagement with the Holocaust, including a clothing installation, to which I now turn.

Canada

In a moving essay about inheriting a jacket worn and loved by his late friend (and mine), Allon White, Peter Stallybrass explains that "If I wore the jacket, Allon wore me. He was there in the wrinkles of the elbows, wrinkles that in the technical jargon of sewing are called 'memory'; he was there in the stains at the very bottom of the jacket; he was there in the smell of the armpits. Above all he was there in the smell." Stallybrass then deepens the discussion of the memory contained in clothes by asserting that "cloth *is* a kind of memory."[96] Boltanski explores the idea of cloth as memory in many of his installation pieces (such as "Dispersion," mentioned above) where the memories contained in clothes are encouraged to circulate, even though the identity of the wearers remains hidden. Noting that "Clothing reminds you of the person who was in it. . . . It is a hollow image of the person, a negative," Boltanski echoes Stallybrass's assessment of cloth as linked to memory; yet, in his works using clothing, we never know whose hollow image we witness.[97] Like Kiefer, Boltanski admired Beuys, suggesting that the two younger artists' shared interest in clothes perhaps refers to Beuys, whose *Felt Suit* (1970) used an empty suit as an evocation of lost presence (fig. 10).[98] Hanging on its own, the empty felt suit looks lifeless and slightly misshapen. Although Beuys wore a version of it in an anti-Vietnam war performance piece, the suit does not contain traces of a particular past in the way that the jacket described by Stallybrass does; rather, the suit evokes absence in general without invoking a historically specific past.[99] In Boltanski's clothing exhibits, he combines the sensation of the powerful individual presences being called up by the smell,

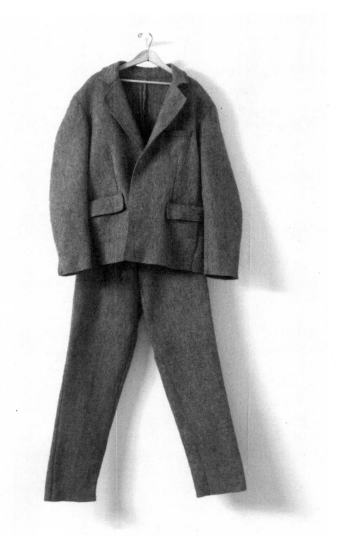

FIGURE 10. Joseph Beuys, *Filzanzug (Felt Suit)* (1970).
Collection Museum of Contemporary Art, Chicago, gift of Dr. Paul and
Dorie Sternberg. Photograph © Museum of Contemporary Art, Chi-
cago. © 2004 Artists Rights Society (ARS), New York/VG Bild-Kunst,
Bonn.

the stain, the worn look of clothes, with the more abstract, generic concept of loss conjured up by Beuys in *Felt Suit*. Kiefer has also used clothing extensively in his works. Whereas in the series *Lilith's Daughters,* which I discussed earlier, Kiefer juxtaposed ash and simple clothing over cityscapes, he also created several installations using clothing as exhibits in glass cases, or on beheaded mannequins. These clothing pieces have a very different tone than Boltanski's installations—they are much colder, more abstract, and less visceral. Thus, as I discuss below, Boltanski's jumbles of clothing, crowded into his installation pieces, conjure up an image of the lost crowd, whereas Kiefer's clothing reflects individual loss—or perhaps more accurately the loss of the individual as the absence of the person is present in the empty shell of the cloth.

For a 1988 installation at the Ydessa Hendeles Foundation in Toronto, Boltanski created *Canada,* a vast collection of over six thousand pieces of clothing covering the walls of a large room (Ydessa Hendeles declined to allow me to reproduce an image of this installation). The clothes are pressed in together, tacked to the wall from floor to ceiling, in a multicolored jumble of mixed fabric, style, and vintage. While the clothes themselves do not directly indicate the Nazi genocide—they were clearly crafted long after the war and are mostly cheap, colorful items—their crowding in together and sheer profusion seem to indicate so many ghosts or the presence of things absent. The term "Canada" refers to the depot where the Nazis stored clothing and other items taken from Jews murdered in the camps. Raul Hilberg insists throughout his groundbreaking history of the Final Solution that a central part of the Nazi genocide was the kind of verbal masking that would turn murder into "treated appropriately"; however, Hilberg also extends his analysis of verbal masking to the victims as well. He finds that the victims created obfuscatory vocabulary: "A crematorium was called a 'bakery,' a man who could no longer work—and who was therefore destined for a gas chamber—was designated a 'Moslem,' and the depot holding the belongings of the gassed was named 'Canada.'" And Hilberg reports that "On January 23 [1945] the SS set fire to barracks full of clothing in the 'Canada' section.... When the Soviets moved in, twenty-nine of thirty-five storerooms had been burned down. In six of the remaining ones, the liberators found part of the camp's legacy: 368,820 men's suits, 836,255 women's coats and dresses, 5,525 pairs of women's shoes, 13,964 carpets, large quantities of children's clothes...."[100] While Boltanski's six thousand pieces of clothing cannot compare to the obscene numbers Hilberg cites here, by choosing this title for his willy-nilly collection of garments, Boltanski clearly refers to the euphemistic use of "Canada" to designate the storage depots in the concentration camps.

Boltanski makes the Holocaust connection explicit when he again echoes Stallybrass's description of the materiality of clothing: "Second-hand clothes speak about someone who was here but is no longer here. The smell and the creases have remained, but not the person. Pieces with clothes are more difficult, *Canada* for example, where one thinks of the Holocaust."[101] Here the viewer is being invited to mourn the loss of the wearers of these clothes even though the wearers are most likely still alive, just missing these particular clothes. Thus, as was the case in *Le Lycée Chases,* we are asked to grieve for the living, but under a suggestive Holocaust rubric that weaves this event into reflections on loss.[102]

Writing in the *Nation* after seeing a Boltanski exhibit of clothing very similar to *Canada,* Arthur Danto claims that lost clothes become "a piece of Holocaust art, and if so then perhaps the only convincing example I have encountered of a genre I would have thought impossible but now recognize as merely terribly difficult." As Danto describes these clothes, they are "clothing that has somehow survived its wearers, been left behind by vanished kids. Left behind and then improvised into a memorial to their wearers, the garments are made somehow self-metaphorical and almost unendurably poignant."[103] Danto here points to how, even while using cheap eighties clothing, the "unendurable poignancy" of the clothes reminds us of the Holocaust. Danto holds up Boltanski's use of clothing as breaking through the impossible constraints on creating Holocaust art, even though there is no actual, historical Holocaust content to this installation.

This sensation of a reference to the Holocaust with only scant pointers is what Ernst van Alphen terms a "Holocaust-effect." In speaking of Boltanski's *Les habits de François C* (1972; see fig. 9), van Alphen claims: "The Holocaust-effect is created once more. Not only do we wonder who and where the owner of the clothes is, but we also inevitably think of the warehouses in the death camps, where all the belongings of the inmates were stored."[104] Neither Boltanski nor Kiefer have to use actual clothes from the Holocaust or actual images of children who perished in order for their work to be interpreted as Holocaust art. Like Jabès, then, these artists reflect as much on the way their viewers and readers have come to see the Holocaust in melancholy images as they themselves produce "Holocaust art."[105] However, as I discuss below, a curious inversion between historical specificity and aesthetic and emotional effect takes place in some of Boltanski's work, meaning, paradoxically, that his more historically accurate works are often less meaningful and evocative than his allusive, "Holocaust-effect" works.

La maison manquante

The historical confusions produced by *Le Lycée Chases'* images and *Canada's* collection of clothing are missing from *La maison manquante* (*Missing House*, 1990), wherein Boltanski had his research assistants find out the names, birthdates, and professions of the people who lived in an apartment house in Berlin that was destroyed during the war (fig. 11). He then affixed a simple plaque bearing a small amount of information about each of the former inhabitants to the remaining walls of the surrounding building. An introductory board explained to viewers the meaning of these cryptic names, and Boltanski expanded on the information given in the plaques by creating a series of glass cases, exhibited elsewhere in the city, that included other documents relating to each person. John Czaplicka claims that *Missing House* is "a work of history as well as a work of art."[106] Yet its historical specificity sharply differentiates it from some of Boltanski's other work, such as *Le Lycée Chases,* where, without this, viewers were nonetheless deeply moved. *Missing House* took Boltanski's work in another direction, which almost seems a correction of the radical unspecificity of some of his earlier work. Curiously, though, *Missing House* is also de-aestheticized and less evocative than the photo-sculptures. While I agree with Czaplicka about the historical contribution of *Missing House,* I disagree with his assessment that the work has a "strong aesthetic component."[107] The photo-sculptures such as *Dijon* and *Lycée Chases* are beautiful, meditative, and poignant, while *Missing House* feels colder and less personal. Ironically, *Le Lycée Chases* confronts the viewer with a face that, while lacking in clarity due to enlargement and reproduction, nonetheless engenders a series of speculations about that person. The plaques of *Missing House,* in contrast, do not contain images, merely a few details. Furthermore, due to the location of many plaques, they are rendered literally illegible because the viewer, standing on the street, cannot read the ones that are several stories high. Thus, while the historically empty image of the survivor portrayed as a victim of the earlier work becomes the historically full depiction of actual names and dates and professions of victims of the Nazi genocide in the later work, the focus of Boltanski's energy has shifted from the aesthetic to the historical in ways that ironically diminish the impact of his art.

This dimunition recalls the effect of the mostly negatively received installations of phone books that Boltanski exhibited early in the first decade of

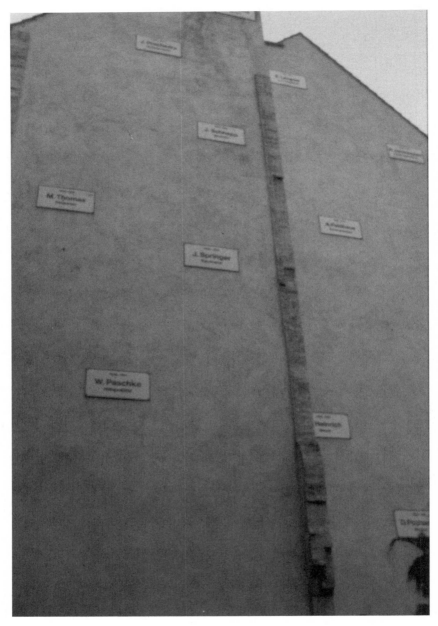

FIGURE 11. Christian Boltanski, *La maison manquante* (1991).
Photograph by Stephen Feinstein, Director, Center for Holocaust and Genocide
Studies, University of Minnesota. © 2004 Artists Rights Society (ARS), New York/
ADAGP, Paris.

the twenty-first century. Richard Dorment notes that "names in themselves just don't have the resonance that photographs or articles of clothing do. Any work by Boltanski represents a conjuring trick, a magical transformation of ordinary elements into works of art that haunt the imagination. Here, the setting is perfect, the idea promising, only the magic just doesn't work."[108] One might say the same thing for *Missing House,* where the balance between aesthetics and history means the latter is more accurate and the former less compelling. In discussing Boltanski's work, Adam Gopnik notes that "Part of his discovery involves a fact about photography: we can look at people's faces in photographs, and particularly in enlarged photographs, with a kind of intensity and intimacy that in life we normally reserve only for extreme emotional states."[109] The lack of photographs in *Missing House* disallows this kind of intense and intimate contemplation, yet Boltanski went to great lengths to pay homage to historical accuracy, thus demonstrating the slippery dilemmas of aesthetics vs. history.

೧ ೧ ೧

Boltanski's and Kiefer's images have encouraged me to try to grapple with some of the questions that frame this book: how do we balance aesthetics and history, how do we understand the unwanted beauty of much Holocaust art, and is there something indecent or unethical about this beauty? I contend that Kiefer's and Boltanski's evocative and often very difficult works address these questions by finding that the resonance and richness that makes something beautiful is a condition of possibility for attempting to see the Nazi genocide. As Jorge Semprun puts it in *Literature or Life* when discussing the reactions of two women to seeing Buchenwald immediately after the war, "J'ignore si elles ont compris, mais pour ce qui est de voir, elles auront vu" (161) (I don't know if they understood, but as far as seeing goes, they saw, 120). By arguing here that Kiefer provocatively conflates symbols of victimization with symbols of Nazism, and that Boltanski invites us to mourn in an (often) historically decontextualized way, I have also tried to show how Kiefer and Boltanski paradoxically contribute to Holocaust memory. While I agree with many survivors who argue that nonwitnesses cannot hope to understand the experience of the camps, and while one cannot help recalling Primo Levi's famous claim (cited in chapter 2) that the true witnesses to the Holocaust are those who perished and thus cannot testify to that which they witnessed, historical accounts and artistic renderings such as Kiefer's and Boltanski's, which force us to question the presence of the Holocaust in the postmemories of successive postwar generations, together create Holocaust remembrance. As I mentioned in the introduction, Ernst van Alphen, in his study of Holocaust art, admitted that "Whereas the education I received failed to make the Holocaust a meaningful event for me, Holocaust art and literature finally succeeded in calling my attention to this apocalyptic moment in human history."[110] Effects such as that on van Alphen encourage me to find in these evocative and allusive Holocaust artists a pedagogical hope. This pedagogical question is particularly pressing in the case of Holocaust memorial sites, and it is to them that I turn in the final chapter. Whereas some historical and documentary sources may not capture the imagination of successive generations of Holocaust rememberers, beautiful, evocative images and sites might trigger an emotional response that can enliven Holocaust memory.

Chapter 5

AESTHETIC POLLUTION:
PETER EISENMAN, JOCHEN GERZ AND
ESTHER SHALEV-GERZ, JAMES INGO FREED,
AND "NAZI CONTAMINATION"

Designs that are vast only by their dimensions, are always
the sign of a common and low imagination. —Edmund Burke

"Too fascistic," "Speer-like monumentality," "identified with the architecture
favoured by Hitler," "Nazi contamination"—this concluding chapter demonstrates that the fear that commemorative sites dedicated to the Holocaust
have been aesthetically polluted by fascist monumentality has forced the
architects and designers of some sites to diminish the emotional and political impact of many monuments, museums, and memorials by altering their
original designs so that they are not perceived as "fascist."[1] I close this book
with this brief examination of commemorative sites in order to offer final
case studies of the problem that unwanted beauty in Holocaust representation poses. For the fear of fascist aesthetics is also a fear of beauty, a fear of
reprising the terrible uses to which aesthetics where put during the Third
Reich.[2] By developing the concept of "aesthetic pollution" I indicate the
prevalent idea that commemorative sites dedicated to the Holocaust must
not be monumental because in replicating the monumentality of fascist
architecture they would reproduce the politics of fascism, hence polluting
their aesthetic composition with traces of unacceptable political histories.
This fear of aesthetic pollution is so prevalent that many designs for commemorative sites are deemed inappropriate for remembering the Holocaust
because they echo fascist monumentality.

For example, consider these statements in articles covering the reconstruction of the center of Berlin: "As for any hint of monumentalism, it is quickly—
and often glibly—equated with the plans of Hitler's architect, Albert Speer,
for the grandiose capital of the 1,000-year Reich." And, "So onerous has been

the burden of the Nazi past that anything even vaguely hinting at fascist architecture has been strenuously shunned throughout the rebuilding of Berlin."[3] And Rolf Goebel argues that Berlin's postwar architectural planners "sought to use radically new beginnings and ahistorical styles for the redemptive absolution of the German people from the political disasters before 1945."[4] Thus, as Berlin's city planners and architects try to reconstruct the confused aesthetic of the city, they are haunted by the fear of aesthetic pollution.[5] What underlies this fear is not often made clear, but I suspect it has to do with the vague sense that certain architectural forms carry within them the implied violence of the politics with which they are loosely—and often erroneously—associated.[6]

In response to these fears of recreating fascist aesthetics, many designers have opted to create counter- or anti-monumental forms that utilize fresh aesthetic choices, sometimes at the cost of their larger cultural function of encouraging remembering. Indeed, when the paradoxical question of how remembering (or forgetting) is enabled by Holocaust commemorative sites is driven by the fear of aesthetic pollution, this fear distorts the larger project of memorializing the Shoah. Before discussing the political, ethical, and historical implications of aesthetic pollution in the creation of three commemorative spaces dedicated to the Holocaust, I examine the development of the counter-monumental aesthetic and the distribution of so-called fascist architectural aesthetics across a range of not-necessarily monumental forms. I then explore how the fear of aesthetic pollution influenced Peter Eisenman and Richard Serra's Memorial to the Murdered Jews of Europe (in Berlin), Jochen Gerz and Esther Shalev-Gerz's Monument against Fascism (in Harburg-Hamburg), and James Ingo Freed's United States Holocaust Memorial Museum (in Washington, D.C.). Among the many proliferating Holocaust commemorative sites that would have been interesting for this discussion, I have limited this chapter to these three because they offer particularly fruitful examples of the problem that aesthetic pollution poses for designers and architects.[7] I then examine the implications of the very idea of aesthetic pollution and its relationship to the racial engineering practiced by the Nazi regime. The chapter ends with some concluding remarks to this book. The threat that the fear of aesthetic pollution poses for artists attempting to represent the Nazi genocide, and the assumption that this particular genocide requires a new aesthetic form, together characterize some of the most trenchant concerns over Holocaust representation today.

Because aesthetic forms used by the Nazi regime are seen as dangerous, and because post-fascist architecture has struggled to shy away from the colossal, monumental forms often used by fascist architects, the fear of aesthetic pollution has radically altered the outcome of plans for Holocaust commemorative sites. But if one succumbs to the facile argument that monumentalism is a priori fascistic, then one would have to review the monumental forms that inhabit our cityscapes; clearly not all monumental forms are specific to fascism. For example, the monumentality of Friedrich St. Florian's plan for the controversial National World War II Memorial in Washington, D.C., was often discussed in negative terms; as Paul Goldberger notes, many critics "fretted about Albert Speer and Fascist Architecture."[8] And St. Florian sagely responds to these critiques: "The most nonsensical of it all is [the claim] that our architecture is gigantic, that it is monumental—and the reference was made to Nazi and Fascist architecture. . . . It has been said that our two arches, the memorial arches we call them, are very tall. The Arc de Triomphe in Paris is 164 feet tall, and our memorial arches are 43 feet tall."[9] St. Florian's point is well taken, as many other monumental works constructed before and after the war are not considered "fascist." St. Florian has certainly not succumbed to the wave of counter-monumentalism that has absorbed many of his radical contemporaries, who, wary of fascist forms of monument-making, have tended to employ a more interactive and less "monumental" architecture meant to enable individual and cultural mourning and remembering. A special edition of *Harvard Design Magazine* devoted to monuments and memorials captures this feeling of entanglement in the past: "it is impossible to write about monuments now without skepticism." Or, put another way, in "this debunking age, a monument is just as likely to be a colossal melting popsicle . . . as a bronze likeness of the commander of the latest localized war."[10] Thus, most monuments have become "counter-monuments" or "anti-monuments." James Young describes the rise of counter-monumentalism in Germany as growing out of a "deep mistrust of monumental forms in light of their systematic exploitation by the Nazis," yet while the goals of counter-monumentalism are commendable, the assumed relationship between fascist architecture and monumentality that underlies the counter-monumental movement is complicated by the history of fascist architecture.[11] For, as Barbara Miller Lane, Brian Ladd, and Michael Wise demonstrate, much fascist architecture was not aesthetically true to the monumentality that has come to stand in as a shorthand for the architecture of the Nazi era. The fear of aesthetic pollution therefore rests in large part on an ahistorical understanding of the relationship between monumentalism and fascism.

Brian Ladd reports that the monumental plans Hitler and architect Albert Speer hatched were not original and had been desired as early as 1840.[12] According to Barbara Miller Lane, the leaders of the Nazi party never agreed on what architectural styles to adopt, and much Nazi architectural aesthetic theory was "sympathetic to the work of the radical architects." While Hitler favored monumental architecture, many of the designs he approved of (some of which he helped draft) were clearly in "debt to the radicals of the twenties."[13] Thus, the fascist architecture that we might imagine as monolithically monumental draws not only on diverse styles but is also influenced by the radical artists whom the Nazis purged. Nazi architecture was thus itself polluted by elements the regime wished to excise. Indeed, Ladd reminds us that "National Socialist architecture did not take a single form: industrial buildings continued to display glass, steel, and concrete in typically modernist fashion."[14] What we often rather quickly refer to as "fascist architecture" sometimes employed the modernist aesthetics that are generally taken to be its polar opposite. As Michael Wise argues in *Capital Dilemma,* the congruence of ideology with architecture can be extremely difficult to pin down. We assume, for example, that the transparency and endless glass of Sir Norman Foster's new Reichstag symbolizes an anti-fascistic, democratic access to power (plate 5). Nonetheless, Wise reports that Mussolini's architect used transparent forms to symbolize that "fascism is a glass house into which everyone can peer."[15] In short, while the new Reichstag is lauded as a symbol of democracy, the same forms that Foster used in the Reichstag were attractive to some fascist architects.

As Lane argues, because the Nazi regime "constantly stressed the ideological significance of Nazi architecture, . . . [it] achieved unprecedented political significance in the Nazi state."[16] This conflation of the political with the architectural is exactly what Walter Benjamin meant when he observed, as I discussed in the introduction, that the manipulation of aesthetics for political ends would become the hallmark of the Nazi regime: "The logical result of Fascism is the introduction of aesthetics into political life."[17] This prescient phrase has become famous because it captures the diabolical side of aesthetics when applied to politics. Citing Marinetti, who claimed that "war is beautiful," Benjamin pinpointed how the murderous choices of the Nazi regime could be understood as aesthetic. On this reading the glory-mongering orchestration of mass rallies as state-adoring performance pieces and the choices Speer would have made for the Thousand Year Reich's architectural landscapes are not merely aesthetic—or, rather, they are aesthetic if understood in Benjamin's more powerful sense of it. Indeed, Benjamin also argued that "all efforts to render politics aesthetic culminate in one thing: war."[18] Thus Benjamin makes the stakes for the aesthetification of politics extremely high.

We might wonder whether, if Benjamin had lived long enough to survive the Nazi genocide, he would have gone as far as Jean-Luc Nancy and Philippe Lacoue-Labarthe, who expanded his conclusion about war to argue that because the entire mechanism of the Third Reich was devoted to the aesthetic improvement of the German state, the Final Solution was an aesthetic solution. Through citing Nazi propaganda minister Joseph Goebbels, who claims that "Politics, too, is an art, if not the highest and most all-embracing there is," Lacoue-Labarthe suggests that "'l'esthétisation de la politique' faisait bien, essentiellement, le programme du national-socialisme. Ou son projet" ("the aesthetification of politics" essentially made up the program of National Socialism. Or its project).[19] This radical extension of Benjamin's argument makes a powerful move toward understanding the mechanisms underlying the Third Reich. That historians have still not settled the argument about the causes of the Holocaust, whether intentional, structural, or a combination of the two, underscores the importance of Lacoue-Labarthe's and Nancy's claims because he has essentially dispensed with these arguments by claiming that the decisions that led to the Holocaust were *aesthetic*.[20] While Lacoue-Labarthe and Nancy expand this argument further in *Le mythe nazi* (1991), finding that the Final Solution was an aesthetic solution, I stop short of accepting the full implications of their claim while nonetheless maintaining that examining the historical problem aesthetically deepens our understanding of how the Holocaust occurred. Indeed, Benjamin's claim and Lacoue-Labarthe and Nancy's elaboration of his important revelation enable us to understand why the very category of the aesthetic has itself been seen as tainted by fascism. But we must separate aesthetics from its particular uses by the Nazis, and indeed, by extension, from the post-fascist use of aesthetics by figures such as Syberberg, whom I discussed in chapter 4. For the realm of aesthetics, like the particular category of "fascist aesthetics," cannot be delimited to one political or historical moment. The unwanted beauty in the worst that this book has examined is very different than the beauty desired by the Nazi regime.

Returning to Benjamin, in addition to discussing the logical result of fascism, Benjamin also predicted that communism's response to the aesthetification of politics would be "politicizing art."[21] What is at stake in the fear of aesthetic pollution is precisely the feared politicization of art that so crippled the aesthetic practices of communist-era artistic production. By conflating aesthetic choices such as abstract and deeply context-based phenomena like glass, height, monumentality—or any of the other forms discussed above—with political concepts such as fascism and democracy, contemporary critics who cry out against so-called fascist architectural forms in effect reproduce what Benjamin locates as the communist impulse to politicize art. Some sixty years after Benjamin's proclamations, it is clear that neither the aesthetification of politics nor the politicization of art are tenable means of cultural production; art suffers under both fascism and communism, whether from aestheticizing politics or politicizing aesthetics. The commemorative sites produced within democracies, then, are not politicized in the same way as under totalitarian regimes. For an example of this one need only imagine the Mall in Washington, D.C., where monumental forms flourish and are not generally criticized—except perhaps the World War II memorial mentioned above—for echoing fascist architecture. Nonetheless, the point of recalling Benjamin's claims is to notice how assessments that discount commemorative sites based on perceived fascistic aesthetic elements perform a similar displacement of the political onto art that Benjamin feared in totalitarian regimes.

THREE APPROACHES TO HOLOCAUST COMMEMORATIVE SITES

By constructing a series of buildings that question place even while they must, of necessity, embody it, the work of the architect Peter Eisenman, whose Memorial to the Murdered Jews of Europe (fig. 12) occupies a significant space in the center of Berlin, has made material the Derridean questioning of the metaphysics of presence.[22] Eisenman's interest in deconstruction demonstrates that while he has been charged with creating a memorial designed specifically to commemorate the murdered Jews of Europe, he employs forms that have been generated through a series of reflections on place and placelessness in postmodern life, and he is *not* therefore forging an aesthetics specific to the Holocaust. Thus, while, as I discussed in the introduction, one strand of the debate over Holocaust representation insists on a *specific* aes-

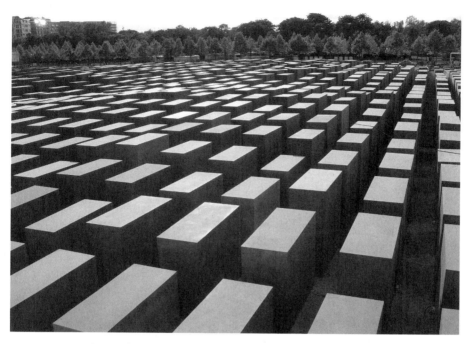

FIGURE 12. Peter Eisenman, Memorial to the Murdered Jews of Europe in Berlin (model). Image courtesy of Eisenman Architects.

thetic for the Holocaust, the architect whose design was chosen for one of the most politically charged memorials in the world recycles aesthetic forms derived from the poststructural theory that critics such as Elaine Marks see as similar to fascism.[23] Likewise, Michael Naumann claimed that Eisenman's original design seemed to have a "Speer-like monumentality," and he opposed the model for the memorial, arguing that it is "reminiscent of the monumental architecture of the Third Reich architect Albert Speer."[24] To combat this charge of the aesthetic pollution of the memorial by Speerism, Eisenman redesigned the memorial, which initially featured four thousand jagged stone pillars of varying height (some up to twenty feet) covering a huge field near the Brandenburg gate.[25] Originally the pillars were to be tilted to suggest the possibility that they might topple; once inside the field of pillars, there was no guarantee that one would be able to get out. By planning it to be anti-touristic and even dangerous, Eisenman and his original co-designer, Richard Serra meant to suggest a labyrinthine fear of entrapment, even though the pillars would not compose, strictly speaking, a labyrinth; once one ventured a certain distance in, the view to the outside would have completely disappeared, so one could wander for a very long time before finding a way out. In 1998 Serra decided not to continue working on the memorial, although his influence is clearly visible in the original design.[26] In the original conception of the memorial, Eisenman and Serra relied heavily upon the former's interpretation of deconstruction's relationship to place. In a conversation with Derrida, Eisenman noted: "PE: The site of the labyrinth is the site of the destruction of the narrative; the breakdown of the continuous story . . . the site of erasure. . . . The labyrinth is the only architectural metaphor for discontinuity and 'no place.' JD: The labyrinth is structured by the hope of getting out. PE: The hope of reaching a conclusion, yes. . . . The labyrinth, architecturally, is the nearest thing to a non-narrative, non-linear, non anthropocentric condition."[27] Eisenman links the idea of the labyrinth to an anti-narrative structure and to a symbol of placelessness that has more to do with the postmodern condition than with the Holocaust. As Young reports, the Berlin memorial's use of non-narrative form was both applauded and criticized by his fellow commissioners. Many critics felt that without a narrative the stories of the victims would be muffled by the vague abstractions of conceptual design. Eisenman was thus encouraged to scale down the labyrinthine fear of loss of place, to shorten the pillars so that viewers would be able to see the surrounding city, and to add an accompanying documentation center that would supply the narrative that the pillars on their own denied.[28] The memorial, then, was criticized for lacking specificity, and for not creating a new aesthetic capable of representing the Holocaust.

In an interesting twist on the concept of aesthetic pollution that I am developing here, construction on the Memorial to the Murdered Jews of Europe was briefly halted because the corporation Degussa, which was supplying "anti-graffiti material" for the memorial, had manufactured Zyclone B during the war. When this was uncovered, a huge controversy erupted in Berlin and globally over guilt and the present's relationship to the past. According to Cynthia Davidson at Eisenman's office, "Peter [Eisenman] argued that to forgive does not mean to forget, and he and those who agreed with him 'won' the debate."[29] The memorial opened on May 10, 2005, in coordination with the sixtieth anniversary of the armistice. While on the one hand the shape of the memorial was seen as polluted aesthetically by its early monumentalism, the materials used to create it were seen as polluted by a manufacturer's involvement in the creation of deadly materials during the war.

Eisenman's (and Serra's) initial solution to the paradox of Holocaust representation relied on empathy because their idea was to *produce fear* in order to induce a visceral understanding in the viewer. That this empathic-fear aesthetic is not "original" to Holocaust representation can be further demonstrated by looking at some of Eisenman's earlier works, notably the Nunotani Office Building (Tokyo, 1992) and the Alteka Office Building (proposed for Tokyo, 1991) (figs. 13 and 14).[30] Like the Memorial to the Murdered Jews of Europe, both buildings elicit a sensation of the imminent possibility of toppling, and both strive to produce in the user of the space a sense of empathy for victims of earthquakes, bombs, and other forces of destruction. The outer appearance of these earlier works conveys the sense that were one to blow wolf-like on the outside the whole house would tumble down. Yet this sense of imminent destruction functions as a metaphor for the dislocation of place that characterizes postmodern business practices, which decentralize workers to such an extent that most interactions can happen via cyberspace rather than geographical space. The aesthetic production of fear

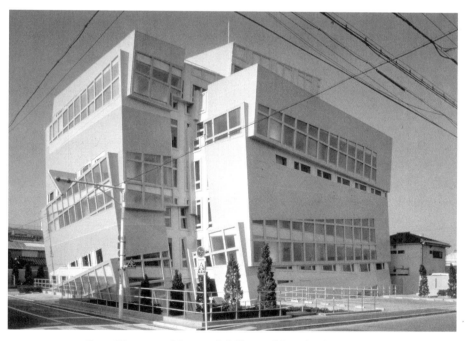

FIGURE 13. Peter Eisenman, Nunotani Office Building (Tokyo, 1992). Image courtesy of Eisenman Architects.

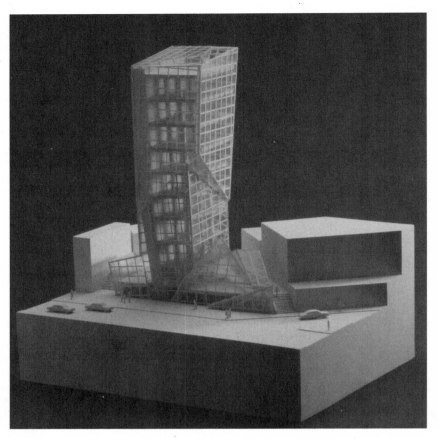

FIGURE 14. Peter Eisenman, Alteka Office Building (model, Tokyo).
Image courtesy of Eisenman Architects.

through empathic memory of destructive trauma turns out to have been a well-trodden architectural feature. Eisenman has therefore taken a formal architectural and historical idea and recycled it for a Holocaust memorial, thus indicating that aesthetic forms cannot be attached to single political histories. According to the fear of aesthetic pollution that drives much Holocaust representation, Eisenman should have come up with an aesthetic uniquely appropriate to the unique event of the Holocaust, but as I have shown here, his appropriation of other aesthetic forms has nonetheless produced an interesting and effective commemorative site.[31]

A Holocaust monument that takes a very different approach than Eisenman and Serra's is Jochen Gerz and Esther Shalev-Gerz's Monument against Fascism (plates 6 and 7). This sculpture is counter-monumental because it actively disrupts monumental form by literally being buried over time. By adhering to counter-monumentalism, Young argues, the Gerzs ward off the danger of replicating fascist aesthetics: "the didactic logic of monuments, their demagogical rigidity, recalled too closely traits they associated with fascism itself."[32] They created a monument that, while initially monumental, erases itself and therefore its claims to monumentality. Erected in 1986 in Harburg, a suburb of Hamburg, the Monument against Fascism was a colossal square lead column that was designed to be written on by locals and tourists and then sunk into the ground in intervals of a few meters at a time. Eventually, the monument sunk completely, and merely left (in 1993) a plaque reminding the viewer that it lies buried on this spot. As Young notes: "As if in mocking homage to national forebears who planned the Holocaust as a self-consuming set of events—that is, intended to destroy all traces of itself, all memory of its victims—the Gerzs have designed a self-consuming memorial that leaves behind only the rememberer and the memory of a memorial."[33] The Gerzs' counter-monument, then, aims to prevent the erasure of Judaism from German consciousness by turning the effort, the work of memory, away from the structure and back to the tourist. Despite Young's praise, it seems that the Gerzs' paradoxical "solution" to the replication of fascist architecture creates a form whose anti-monumentality eradicates the memory site. Thus the fear of aesthetic pollution compromises the excellent aims of their monument.

Like other counter-monuments, the Gerzs' Monument against Fascism was designed to make viewers aware of their responsibility to remember, to turn the work of remembering back onto the viewer. As Jochen Gerz phrases it: "The monument takes no sides. It is completely indifferent, so much so that one can't even get emotional. People want to deal with this theme in ways that bring peace and reconciliation. . . . People seem to find it unbearable that the monument does not fulfil this function."[34] Gerz's oeuvre is dedicated to the confusion of viewer and viewed, yet in creating an openly interpretable interactive piece against fascism, he and Shalev-Gerz could not have predicted that some tourists would use the monument as a place to draw swastikas and express other anti-Semitic or racist sentiments (as happened frequently during the years when the monument was visible, 1986–93). In fighting against monumental form and inviting viewer participation, the Gerzs unwittingly offered a site of pro-fascist venting. They also, of course, offered a site of anti-fascist expression and insisted that viewers take part in creating local memories of the fascist era and the Holocaust. By subverting monumental form, which the creators feared because of its supposed aesthetic pollution, the Gerzs' counter-monument asks significant aesthetic questions, but at the same time it functions on a paralyzing reversal because the monument exists invisibly, underground. Thus, this monument, clever and wonderful as it is, does not escape being changed by fear of aesthetic pollution.

Like Eisenman and Serra's and the Gerzs' designs, the original plans for the United States Holocaust Memorial Museum (USHMM) were thought to be too fascistic because it was too monumental (plate 8). The museum's final architect, James Ingo Freed, was then called in to take over and reduce its fascist aura. The original plan was so fascistic that "You could not escape identifying it with the architecture favoured by Hitler. It seemed to be more a memorial to the perpetrators of the crime, not the victims."[35] Edward Linenthal, in his study of the debates around the creation of the USHMM, echoes this assessment when he reports that some commissioners argued that Karl Kaufman's earlier model "looked more like a monument to the perpetrators than to the victims." Linenthal further notes that one critic described it as "'neo-classicism worthy of Albert Speer.'"[36] To combat this fear of aesthetic pollution, Freed's solution was to replicate the aesthetics of the camps while transforming that grim aesthetic into a demonstration of postmodern architecture's ability to use light, shape, and diverse materials to help the USHMM meld into and mimic the surrounding environment of the Mall while asserting its difference from it. Adrian Dannatt, whose views I discussed in the introduction, interprets the convergence of the evocation of the camps with the use of the surrounding memorial environment as symbols for how the "Holocaust is both part of the twentieth century and an unbridgeable dislocation within it."[37] Indeed, while the USHMM is architecturally, symbolically, and historically very different from the monuments among which it resides, Freed has nonetheless opened up a dialogue between the capital's more traditional monuments and the USHMM. For example, he combined the brick of the neighboring Auditor's Building with the limestone of the Bureau of Engraving and Printing while also shaping the peaked roofs of the interior, designed to look like concentration camp watchtowers, to align with the Washington Monument. Thus the bricks we associate with Auschwitz and other camps are also in conversation with the Auditor's Building while the "camp towers" talk to the Washington Monument.

Like Eisenman, Freed had to accommodate his original design to the needs of local city councils—in this case the Fine Arts Council—that forced him to remove the invocation of danger from the original design. Due to the council's pressure, Freed changed his original, more daring and jagged design so that the new façade suggests "not suffering but redemption."[38] This, I think, overstates the case, yet there is a way in which the grand pedagogical designs of the museum meant that this type of "scaling down" was necessary in order for it to fulfill its mission. As Freed puts it, "The public process is one of sandpapering away irregularities, to the extent that the building loses some of its bite." Freed goes on to admit that he lost many battles with the Fine Arts Council; for example, he notes, "In an earlier version, the Fifteenth Street entry had a large steel plate projecting above, creating a real sense of discomfort. This was another battle that I lost."[39] Thus, as was the case for Eisenman's original plan for a series of jagged labyrinthine stones, Freed had to smooth out the plans for the museum in order to attenuate the empathic association of danger that he originally envisioned. Freed reports that he has been struck by the concatenation of horror and beauty in the scenes of death camps themselves: "It was always incomprehensible to me why the places where the most atrocious things happened were so often the most beautiful places. The Germans had a sort of purist aesthetic sensibility." But he also worried a great deal about making the USHMM too beautiful: "The danger always existed of making the images too heroic, too monumental, too beautiful."[40] In designing the USHMM, Freed nonetheless reproduced much of the beauty of the worst places and created—despite this "danger"—a beautiful memorial space.

The quest for an aesthetics appropriate to the Holocaust, and the contortions that the fear of replicating fascist architecture force on the forms of Holocaust monuments, memorials, and museums, mistakes the way in which, while linked, aesthetic forms need to be seen on their own terms and not as patterns that may be readily reduced to their prior histories. Indeed, there are no "innocent" aesthetic forms. But there are also no inherently guilty aesthetic forms. In agreement with Saul Friedländer's view, cited in the introduction to this book, that there is only a crisis of representation insofar as the Holocaust is an event that seems hard for historians, survivors, literary theorists, trauma theorists, and architects to understand, I argue that the project of Holocaust representation is, after all, an ethical, pedagogical, aesthetic, and political project of working through the past in order to incorporate that past into our understanding of the present and the future. Thus, by moving beyond the fear of aesthetic pollution, we might produce commemorative sites whose forms will defy the conflation of political with artistic histories.

I have argued here that the connection between particular aesthetic choices and particular ideologies cannot be maintained and that therefore commemorative sites to the Nazi genocide should maintain their pedagogical aims over and above fears of aesthetic pollution. In "Monumental Seduction," Andreas Huyssen makes a seductive argument about the need to historicize the very concept of monumentality: "Once we focus on the historical specificity of monumentality, I could well imagine arriving at a conclusion that the identification of monumentalism with fascism . . . [is] itself a historical text rather than [a] universal condition or metahistorical norm."[41] Indeed, as Mussolini's architects' and Sir Norman Foster's use of transparency to demonstrate fascism and democracy, respectively, illustrates, and as Lane's, Ladd's, and Wise's arguments that Nazi architecture was not necessarily monumental and was sometimes influenced by modernism indicate, the conflation of monumentalism with fascism may prove to have been a passing response to our fears about the meaning of contemporary aesthetic choices.

AESTHETICS AND PURITY

By choosing the term "pollution" to designate the fear that fascist aesthetics may taint designs for monuments, memorials, or museums, I evoke the ritualistic and religious connotations implicit in commemorative sites. Aesthetic pollution also points toward the way Nazi national identity was based on purity. In her influential study of purity and pollution, Mary Douglas contends that all cultures maintain deeply subtle and often contradictory boundaries delimiting the pure from the polluted, the holy from the unclean.[42] In keeping with these findings, the fear of being tainted by fascist architecture is understandably more astringent when it is a question of remembering the Holocaust, which by extension implies remembering Nazism. On the one hand, the fear of aesthetic pollution naturally haunts attempts to remember the Holocaust; on the other hand, the fact that cultural critics argue for a "pure," unused aesthetic vis-à-vis representations of the Nazi genocide indicates a ritualistic idea of the Holocaust that separates it from the rest of Western history, as if it were a religious meta-event outside history. Thus, the fear of the aesthetic pollution of commemorative sites indicates an understanding of the Nazi genocide as in excess of history, rather than a deeply shameful element that nonetheless needs to be recognized as part of our history.

The fear of aesthetic pollution also belies a model of contamination that is itself reminiscent of fascist ideology. As Omer Bartov observes of the Nazi regime, the "nation's collective identity" relied on "purging it of everything that polluted and undermined it."[43] Further, Brian Ladd links Hitler's architectural goals explicitly with his racist goals: "the creative [architectural] work in which Hitler took such pride was built on the obliteration of cities, communities, and entire peoples—'races,' in Nazi terminology."[44] This echoes Zygmunt Bauman's much-cited contention that the driving force behind the extermination was the need to garden—to weed out undesirable elements in the building of the new, pure, German Reich. Bauman's argument about the intense connection between social engineering and extermination along racial lines is equally apt for describing the architectural shaping of the Reich: "Racism comes into its own only in the context of a design of the perfect society and intention to implement the design through planned and consistent effort."[45] While by "design" in this context Bauman does not refer explicitly to the sweeping architectural designs that were to have made on the new German state a mark so powerful that even the ruins would be as beautiful as those of Rome, we can apply his argument to architectural goals, for a close connection prevails between the desire for a largely monumental landscape during the Nazi regime and the need for its architecture to represent the purified empire of a single race. The feared pollution of the Aryan race by the contamination of the Jews was thus reinforced in the architectural goals Speer and Hitler worked hard to attain. The postwar inversion making the contaminating element not Jews or "Jewish" modernist aesthetics but the taint of Nazi aesthetics indicates a similar structure of fearing aesthetic pollution at the hands of alien elements—whether fascist or Jewish. This is of course not to say that accusations of replicating fascist architecture are themselves simply fascist; modes of contamination are extremely flexible and ever-changing. Arguing that both fascism and anti-fascism function through the desire to weed out polluting elements in no way collapses the two ideologies. Rather, it heightens a plea to reconsider the knee-jerk cry of "fascism" when considering an aesthetic paradigm with so many mutations and contradictions, and when the monumental itself inhabits an equally complex and contradictory series of aesthetic values.

CONCLUDING REMARKS

In responding to Adorno's argument about the disastrous link between modernity and the Holocaust (which I discussed in chapter 1), Andreas Huyssen notes that "Without memory, without reading the traces of the past, there can be no recognition of difference (Adorno called it 'nonidentity'), no tolerance for the rich complexities and instabilities of personal and cultural, political and national identities." In this formulation, the complexity of memory saves us from the perilous "fantasies of omnipotence and superiority that haunt Western modernity."[46] In other words, the failure to appreciate otherness that characterized both fascism and totalitarianism can be rectified in some small measure by embracing the Gordian knots of memory and difference. The characters in *Unwanted Beauty* are all keenly aware of the intersections of memory and difference, and have used the vagaries of their striated lives to convey this awareness and thus to ward off the dangers of forgetting outlined by Adorno.

Indeed, many of the artists and writers discussed in this book are leading (or have led) diasporic, hyphenated lives in which multiple languages and homes exert powerful cultural and political influences, therefore pressing diffuse and often receding horizons on their imaginations. Some of the artists and writers in this book are Jewish, some are half Jewish, and some are not Jewish. As we have seen, different markers regarding gender, ethnicity, nation, and religion influence the literary, visual, or architectural representation of the Holocaust, and at times intersect with Jewish aesthetics and Jewish religious texts. While the experience of diaspora, for example, is often considered quintessentially Jewish, and while figures such as Edmond Jabès are supremely conscious of this connection, others who meditate on exile and diaspora, such as Jorge Semprun, embrace the sense of diaspora employed by many multicultural thinkers as a general scattering from a real or imagined homeland. Thus, whether it takes the form of Jewish diasporic meditations or other understandings of the complexity of the shifting postwar landscape, a sense of displacement often enriches these works' exceptional beauty and descriptive power. In this sense, the works discussed herein have not only helped us to look back on the shattered past with fresh eyes but also to think more critically about the current moment, when diasporas multiply daily.

The designation of something as "beautiful" will remain subjective and undecidable. On one hand, an aesthetics of the sublime or the monumental can often smack of fascism; German fascism's manipulation of the aesthetics of the sublime, the beautiful, and the monumental has certainly haunted many of the artists and critics discussed in this book. On the other hand, to return to one of the points I raised in the introduction, I have shown that even if we gain an "illicit pleasure" (in Irving Howe's phrase) from the unwanted beauty of some Holocaust works, that does not mean that we have emphatically refused understanding or that we have not attempted to glean meaningful lessons from the past. Rather, I have argued that memory is transformed by beauty and that beauty—even though unwanted—allows us to approach diverse painful pasts in deeper ways.

To offer an analytic structure for understanding the transformative power of beauty, I have designated five categories. "Aesthetic survival" (chapter 1) refers to the use of beauty both within horrific situations and the creation of beautiful work after experiencing trauma in order to continue to survive. When Charlotte Delbo traded bread for drama and recited plays at Auschwitz, she used beauty as a survival mechanism; when she devoted her life to creating beautiful works that treated her experience during the war, she literally survived through aesthetic pleasure. "Aesthetic memory" (chapter 2) refers to how theories of memory themselves become significant parts of the art of re-telling traumatic narratives. When Jorge Semprun incorporated Proust's philosophy of memory into his meta-narratives about the process of remembering his experience at Buchenwald, he created an aesthetics of memory that helped nonwitnesses understand the extreme difficulty of living with and portraying traumatic history. The first two chapters of this book, then, are designed to counter the demonization of beauty in Holocaust literature by examining, from the vantage point of the witness, the rich and complex use of beauty in surviving and remembering trauma.

"Aesthetic allusion" (chapter 3) refers to allusive gestures toward traumatic events that, in their obliqueness, open up those events to other historical moments. When the poet Edmond Jabès can turn a meditation on the burning book simultaneously into an examination of the Holocaust and of the poststructural concern with the power of writing, his allusive aesthetic forces us to confront how postmemories of the Holocaust influence us. Yet these allusions also risk historical slippage that can sometimes compromise the effects of such poetry. "Aesthetic mourning" (chapter 4) refers to works that mourn losses from traumatic histories in beautiful ways that expand our understanding of the events themselves. When Anselm Kiefer and Christian Boltanski aestheticize mourning, they participate in a mode of Holocaust art that, like aesthetic allusions, takes a broad sweep of historical traumas and mourns them together. At its best, aesthetic mourning encourages us to think critically about the Holocaust and other difficult histories; at its worst it risks slipping into a denuded mode of memory production that is ahistorical and unmoored. The third and fourth chapters of this book, then, working from the vantage point of the second generation of nonwitnesses, examine the use of beauty in post-memories and discover both effective and ungrounded forms of conveying the past.

"Aesthetic pollution" (chapter 5) refers to the fear that certain histories have stained entire aesthetic categories and made them therefore unusable. When monument, memorial, and museum makers are concerned that their work is "too fascistic," they are afraid that the aesthetics of fascism has polluted contemporary aesthetics. In addition, they may not take into account the aesthetic contradictions within fascism itself. In response to the fear of aesthetic pollution, many makers of commemorative sites have adopted a counter-monumental aesthetic that can sometimes undermine the memorial projects on which they embark. The final chapter, then, moves the discussion of the demonization of beauty into the realm of fascism and questions whether we need to give in to a fear that too quickly conflates aesthetics and politics.

These five categories of the use of aesthetics are not neat; they bleed into one another in contradictory, confusing, and sometimes expressively useful ways. Nonetheless, these categories offer models for thinking about the uses of unwanted beauty in constructing historical understanding. They also foreground the need to be vigilant about the fragile border between deepening our understanding and exploiting our emotions. For there is indeed a fine line between the unwanted beauty I have been analyzing and the aestheticization of horror that is so pervasive in popular culture today. This is what Susan Sontag, in an examination of the photographs from the Abu Ghraib prison scandals of Iraqi detainees being tortured by American soldiers, calls "an easy delight" in violence. Sontag continues, "America has become a country in which the fantasies and the practice of violence are seen as good entertainment, fun."[47] Any aesthetic appeal of the images to which Sontag refers is not what I mean by unwanted beauty. Indeed, I hope that I have shown that the beautiful in the way I have been describing it prevents the exploitation of "easy delight" by remaining uneasy, complicated, and difficult. Moreover, I hope that these five aesthetic categories will be useful outside of Holocaust literature and art. For two examples of unwanted beauty that do not offer "easy delight," consider the following.

As I was finishing this book, a political artist and friend, Richard Kammler, showed me Michael Light's *100 Suns,* a collection of sumptuous photographs of nuclear tests performed in the United States during the era of above-ground nuclear testing, from 1945 to 1962. As I perused these images of immensely dangerous materials, I realized that it was their beauty that conveyed the horror of nuclear catastrophe. Light clearly hoped the photographs would caution us against any future use of nuclear weapons, thus closing his book with the argument that "Photographs only tell us about the surface of things, and how they look. It exists. It happened. It is happening. May no further nuclear detonation photographs be made, ever."[48] Light aestheticized nuclear testing in order to drive home his cautionary message. In other words, he took negatives of nuclear tests that, presented in a smaller, simpler format, would not be nearly as beautiful, and magnified them, massaged them, and transformed them into gorgeous images that present each unfolding cloud as gently as a Turner painting.

By producing beautiful images that mourn the losses to the environment and to many participants' well-being incurred through the deadly use of nuclear testing, Light has offered a perfect example of aesthetic mourning (in the best sense). Like the artistic renderings of trauma addressed in this book, Light's images caution us—in this case never to turn to nuclear materials again. He has thus used the beauty of his images for an explicitly political purpose. While we may not want images of nuclear blasts to be beautiful, their unwanted beauty is what works on us, what effects change, what discourages us from accepting the normalization of nuclear war.

Another example of the beauty of trauma used to deepen understanding can be seen in Christian Frei's film *War Photographer*. Documenting the work of James Nachtwey, a brilliant photographer who has dedicated his life to producing beautiful images that convey the horror of war, Frei's film speaks to the aesthetics of trauma in powerful ways. In one pivotal scene, Nachtwey and a photographic technician work on an image of a young child in war-torn Kosovo. The image features a close-up of a boy's near-bald head and distressed eyes while the ravages of war scatter behind him. The technician presents different versions of the image to Nachtwey, who instructs him how to make the photograph as effective as possible, how to "see more of the forms of the destruction." Nachtwey also expresses concerns about getting "more out of the sky" and thus tries to contrast the peace of the natural world with the violence of human-made destruction. They alter the image repeatedly until it is just right, until it is beautiful. As Nachtwey and the technician work on the photograph, a voice-over comments that Nachtwey possesses the "precision of a war surgeon," but that he would reject this characterization and find that it portrayed him as "cold-hearted."[49] Thus, obsessive striving toward beauty risks being read as "cold" rather than as an impassioned manipulation of the beautiful for larger political aims.

This episode in *War Photographer*, coupled with Michael Light's *100 Suns*, speaks to how beauty is often very much wanted by the writers and artists who produce art about traumatic history. It is the critics of these pictures who may not want their beauty. As Nachtwey strives at an aesthetic level to make the destruction more visible, he creates an image whose beauty will arrest the viewer, and then, at the moment of stilled watching, prompt the viewer to consider the depth of the destruction in Kosovo. The resonance between Light's and Nachtwey's photographs and the beautiful literary texts and multimedia images and spaces I have discussed here indicates that the arguments in my book about the place of unwanted beauty in the representation of mass violence and its inevitable trauma are applicable to other histories where violence, memory, trauma, and aesthetics cross.

The line between an effective unwanted beauty and an exploitative use of aesthetics as described by Sontag will always be as hard to determine as the designation "beautiful" in the first place. Yet it has been a goal of this book to make a place for the beautiful within the representation of traumatic events so that we might make concrete use of the lessons to be learned from beautiful works. It is the beautiful itself—in the complex and open-ended definition I have been using throughout—that has come to be seen as "polluted" when representing traumatic histories. I have tried to ameliorate its image, to allow the flux of the beautiful to teach us about the past, and to offer the hope that these works will deepen our understanding of our endless capacity both to create suffering and to heal wounds.

As one final example, I close with a survivor's reflections on unwanted beauty. For fifteen years after the war, from roughly 1945 to 1960, Jorge Semprun willfully refused to think through his time in Buchenwald, the concentration camp where he had been interned from 1944 to 1945. He began to write about his memories first in *Le grand voyage* (1963) and then in another text, *L'écriture ou la vie* (1994). Semprun wonders how, alongside the strange, fleeting memories he involuntarily experienced, he would also feel a strange happiness at the memories' rare moments of ghostly visitation:

Parfois, certes, une douleur aiguë, brève, m'avait traversé le coeur. Un instant de souffrance mêlée de nostalgie. D'étrange bonheur, qui sait? Comment dire cette absurdité, le bonheur insolite de ce souvenir? (311)

Sometimes, it's true, I felt a pang in my heart. An instant of anguish tinged with nostalgia, with a strange joy—who knows? How can I describe that absurdity, the uncanny happiness of that memory? (241)

The unwanted happiness when painful memory seeps through a willed amnesia is an instance of the paradoxical mix of pleasure and pain that the works discussed in *Unwanted Beauty* have uncovered. Semprun wonders how the two poles—pain and pleasure, forgetting and remembering, nostalgia and horror—can coexist, and, like Paul Celan, Charlotte Delbo, Edmond Jabès, Anselm Kiefer, Christian Boltanski, Peter Eisenman, Jochen Gerz and Esther Shalev-Gerz, and James Ingo Freed, is unafraid to explore these strange contradictions.

Thus, at the close of *L'écriture ou la vie,* Semprun portrays the experience of visiting Buchenwald in 1992, when he was deeply moved by one of the monuments erected at the camp. As he stood reflecting about the difference between past and present, he thought about beauty:

Le monde s'offrait à moi dans le mystère rayonnant d'une obscure clarté lunaire. J'ai dû m'arrêter, pour reprendre mon souffle. Mon coeur battait très fort. Je me souviendrai toute ma vie de ce bonheur insensé, m'étais-je dit. De cette beauté nocturne. (396)

The world lay spread out before me in the luminous mystery of a darkling lunar clarity. I had to stop, to catch my breath. My heart was pounding. All my life, I thought, I'll remember this insane happiness. This nocturnal beauty. (310)

Note: Throughout the book, where no translator is given, translations are my own. Full references are given at the first occurrence only; subsequent brief references are given as author, abbreviated title, and page number in footnote; subsequent frequent references are noted with page numbers within the text.

INTRODUCTION

1. Timothy Taylor, imagining Edward Saroyan's thoughts in *Ararat: The Shooting Script* (New York: Newmarket Press, 2002), 134.

2. Irving Howe, "Writing and the Holocaust," in *Writing and the Holocaust,* ed. Berel Lang (New York: Holmes and Meier, 1988), 175–99, 181.

3. Howe, "Writing and the Holocaust," 178. Michael Rothberg's "After Adorno: Culture in the Wake of Catastrophe" in *Traumatic Realism: The Demands of Holocaust Representation* (Minneapolis: University of Minnesota Press, 2000) offers a helpful contexualization of Adorno's maxim.

4. Aharon Appelfeld, "After the Holocaust," in Lang, *Writing and the Holocaust,* 83–92, 89.

5. Aharon Appelfeld, *Beyond Despair* (New York: Fromm International, 1994), xiv.

6. Susan Gubar, *Poetry after Auschwitz: Remembering What One Never Knew* (Bloomington: Indiana University Press, 2003); Norman Kleeblatt, ed., *Mirroring Evil: Nazi Imagery/Recent Art* (New York and New Brunswick, N.J.: Jewish Museum/ Rutgers University Press, 2002); Shelly Hornstein, Laura Levitt, and Laurence Silberstein, eds., *Impossible Images: Contemporary Art after the Holocaust* (New York: New York University Press, 2003).

7. Saul Friedländer, ed., *Probing the Limits of Representation: Nazism and the "Final Solution"* (Cambridge: Harvard University Press, 1992), 2. See also Berel Lang, *Holocaust Representation: Art within the Limits of History and Ethics* (Baltimore: Johns Hopkins University Press, 2000).

8. Hayden White, "Historical Emplotment and the Problem of Truth," in Friedländer, ed., *Probing the Limits,* 52.

9. For questions of uniqueness see Alan S. Rosenbaum, ed., *Is the Holocaust Unique? Perspectives on Comparative Genocide* (Boulder, Col.: Westview Press, 1998); Steven Katz, *The Holocaust in Historical Context* (New York: Oxford University Press, 1994); and Berel Lang, *The Future of the Holocaust: Between History and Memory* (Ithaca,

N.Y.: Cornell University Press, 1999); for proponents of a unique aesthetic approach see, among others, Jean-François Lyotard, *Heidegger et les "juifs"* (Paris: Galilée, 1988); and Lawrence Langer, *Holocaust Testimonies: The Ruins of Memory* (New Haven, Conn.: Yale University Press, 1991).

10. Elie Wiesel, *From the Kingdom of Memory* (New York: Summit Books, 1990), 168.

11. Ibid., 14–15.

12. Lawrence Langer, *Admitting the Holocaust: Collected Essays* (New York: Oxford University Press, 1995), 93. See also Jean Améry, *At the Mind's Limits: Contemplations by a Survivor on Auschwitz and Its Realities*, trans. Sidney Rosenfeld and Stella P. Rosenfeld (New York: Schocken, 1986).

13. Adrian Dannatt, *The United States Holocaust Memorial Museum: James Ingo Freed* (London: Phaidon, 1995), 4.

14. Jean-François Lyotard, *Heidegger and "the jews,"* trans. Andreas Michel and Mark Roberts (Minneapolis: University of Minnesota Press, 1990), 26. For an analysis of Lyotard's text see Dominick LaCapra, *Representing the Holocaust: History, Theory, Trauma* (Ithaca, N.Y.: Cornell University Press, 1994).

15. Geoffrey H. Hartman, *The Longest Shadow: In the Aftermath of the Holocaust* (Bloomington: Indiana University Press, 1996), 129.

16. James Young, *At Memory's Edge: After-Images of the Holocaust in Contemporary Art and Architecture* (New Haven, Conn.: Yale University Press, 2000), 194, 199.

17. Alexander Gottlieb Baumgarten, *Reflections on Poetry* [1735] (London: Cambridge University Press, 1954), 78.

18. Immanuel Kant, *Critique of Pure Reason* [1781], trans. Norman Kemp Smith (New York: St. Martin's Press, 1965), 66. Here Kant refers to Baumgarten's *Aesthetica* (1750).

19. Edmund Burke, *A Philosophical Enquiry into the Origin of Our Ideas of the Sublime and the Beautiful* [1757] (Oxford: Oxford University Press, 1990), 36.

20. For Burke's influence on Kant see Paul Crowther, *The Kantian Sublime: From Morality to Art* (Oxford: Clarendon Press, 1989), and Jean-François Lyotard, *Lessons on the Analytic of the Sublime* (Stanford, Calif.: Stanford University Press, 1994); on Lyotard see Hugh J. Silverman, ed., *Lyotard: Philosophy, Politics, and the Sublime* (New York: Routledge, 2002).

21. Immanuel Kant, *Critique of Judgment* [1790], trans. Werner S. Pluhar (Indianapolis: Hackett Publishing, 1987), 115.

22. Barbara Claire Freeman argues for an interesting disruption of these categories in *The Feminine Sublime: Gender and Excess in Women's Fiction* (Berkeley: University of California Press, 1995).

23. Immanuel Kant, *Observations on the Feeling of the Beautiful and Sublime* [1763], trans. John T. Goldthwait (Berkeley: University of California Press, 1991), 47–48.

24. Kant, *Critique of Judgment*, 135.

25. Among the vast literature on the sublime see Jean-François Lyotard, *The Postmodern Condition: A Report on Knowledge* [1979], trans. Geoff Bennington and Brian Massumi (Minneapolis: University of Minnesota Press, 1997); *On the Sublime: Mark Rothko, Yves Klein, James Turrell* (Berlin: Deutsche Guggenheim, 2001); Frances Ferguson, *Solitude and the Sublime: Romanticism and the Aesthetics of Individuation* (New York: Routledge, 1992); Neil Hertz, *The End of the Line: Essays on Psychoanalysis and the Sublime* (New York: Columbia University Press, 1985); and Slavoj Žižek, *The Sublime Object of Ideology* (London: Verso, 1989).

26. Paul Crowther, ed., *The Contemporary Sublime: Sensibilities of Transcendence and Shock* (London: Art and Design Profile no. 40, 1995), 7.

27. See Crowther, *Kantian Sublime.*

28. My use of "ordinary people" here is meant to echo the phrase as used in Christopher Browning's *Ordinary Men: Reserve Police Battalion 101 and the Final Solution in Poland* (New York: HarperPerennial, 1992), and in Daniel Jonah Goldhagen's *Hitler's Willing Executioners: Ordinary Germans and the Holocaust* (New York: Vintage Books, 1997).

29. Margaret Olin, *The Nation without Art: Examining Modern Discourses on Jewish Art* (Lincoln: University of Nebraska Press, 2001), 192. For two more works on Jewish art see Matthew Baigell, *Jewish-American Artists and the Holocaust* (New Brunswick, N.J.: Rutgers University Press, 1997), and *Jewish Artists in New York: The Holocaust Years* (New Brunswick, N.J.: Rutgers University Press, 2002).

30. Robert Rosenblum, "The Abstract Sublime," *Art News* 59:10 (February 1961): 38–58.

31. Neal Benezra, "The Misadventures of Beauty," in Neal Benezra and Olga Viso, *Regarding Beauty: A View of the Late Twentieth Century* (Washington, D.C.: Smithsonian, 1999), 21.

32. Walter Benjamin, *Illuminations: Essays and Reflections,* trans. Harry Zohn (New York: Schocken Books, 1969), 241.

33. Barnett Newman, "The Sublime Is Now" [1948], repr. in *Barnett Newman: Selected Writings and Interviews,* ed. John P. O'Neill (Berkeley: University of California Press, 1990), 170–73, 172.

34. Benezra, "Misadventures of Beauty," 29–36.

35. See Hal Foster, ed., *The Anti-Aesthetic: Essays on Postmodern Culture* (Port Townsend, Wash.: Bay Press, 1983); Brian Wallis, ed., *Art after Modernism: Rethinking Representation* (New York: New Museum of Contemporary Art/David R. Godine, 1984).

36. Alexander Nehamas, "An Essay on Beauty and Judgment," *Threepenny Review* 80 (Winter 2000): 4–7, 4; Craig Lambert, "The Stirring of Sleeping Beauty," *Harvard Magazine* (September–October 1999): 46–53, 46.

37. Peter Schjeldahl, "Beauty Is Back," *New York Times Magazine,* September 29, 1996; Lambert, "Stirring of Sleeping Beauty," 46; Dennis Donoghue, *Speaking of*

Beauty (New Haven, Conn.: Yale University Press, 2003), 8; Liliane Weissberg, "In Plain Sight," *Visual Culture and the Holocaust,* ed. Barbie Zelizer (New Brunswick, N.J.: Rutgers University Press, 2001), 13–27, 13.

38. For another example see the *New York Times Book Review* article on Denis Donoghue's *Speaking of Beauty,* which begins, "Beauty is apparently back as a topic of academic discussion" (September 14, 2003: 12).

39. Wendy Steiner, *The Scandal of Pleasure: Art in an Age of Fundamentalism* (Chicago: University of Chicago Press, 1995), 211.

40. Elaine Scarry, *On Beauty and Being Just* (Princeton, N.J.: Princeton University Press, 1999), 31.

41. Ernst van Alphen, *Caught by History: Holocaust Effects in Contemporary Art, Literature, and Theory* (Stanford, Calif.: Stanford University Press, 1997), 3.

42. Jorge Semprun, *L'écriture ou la vie* (Paris: Gallimard, 1994), 167; *Literature or Life,* trans. Linda Coverdale (New York: Penguin, 1997), 125. Hereafter original and translation cited in the text.

43. Craig Owens, "The Allegorical Impulse: Toward a Theory of Postmodernism," in Wallis, *Art after Modernism,* 209.

44. Marianne Hirsch, "Post-Memory and Exile," *Exile and Creativity: Signposts, Travelers, Outsiders, Backward Glances,* ed. Susan Ruth Suleiman (Durham, N.C.: Duke University Press, 1998), 418–46.

45. David Mickenberg, Corine Granof, Peter Hayes, eds., *The Last Expression: Art and Auschwitz* (Evanston, Ill.: Northwestern University Press, 2003). See also Janet Blatter and Sybil Milton, *Art of the Holocaust* (New York: Rutledge Press, 1981).

CHAPTER 1: AESTHETIC SURVIVAL

1. Lawrence Langer tells this story in his introduction to the translation of Delbo's *Auschwitz et après, Auschwitz and After,* trans. Rosette C. Lamont (New Haven, Conn.: Yale University Press, 1995), xviii.

2. Gary Weissman, *Fantasies of Witnessing: Postwar Efforts to Experience the Holocaust* (Ithaca, N.Y.: Cornell University Press, 2004).

3. Georges Perec, "Robert Antelme ou la vérité de la littérature," in *Robert Antelme: Textes inédits sur "L'espèce humaine," essais et témoignages* (Paris: Gallimard, 1996), 173–90.

4. Theodor Adorno, "Cultural Criticism and Society," *Prisms,* trans. Samuel and Shierry Weber (Cambridge: MIT Press, 1990), 34, written in 1949 and originally published as "Kulturkritik und Gesellschaft" in *Soziologische Forschung in unserer Zeit* (1951).

5. Theodor Adorno, "Commitment," *Notes to Literature, vol. 2,* trans. Shierry Weber Nicholsen (New York: Columbia University Press, 1992): 76–94, 88. Adorno made this statement in "Engagement oder künstlerische Autonomie," a talk on Radio Bremen, March 28, 1962, which was published in *Die Neue Rundschau* 73:1 (1962) and then reprinted in *Noten zur Literatur* in 1965.

6. Theodor Adorno, *Negative Dialectics* [1966], trans. E. B. Ashton (New York: Continuum, 1973), 362.

7. Ibid., 362–63.

8. Lisa Saltzman, *Anselm Kiefer and Art after Auschwitz* (New York: Cambridge University Press, 1999), 19; Amy Colin, *Paul Celan: Holograms of Darkness* (Bloomington: Indiana University Press, 1991), xvii; Sidra Dekoven Ezrahi, "The Grave in the Air," in Friedländer, ed., *Probing the Limits*, 259–76, 260; Ulrich Baer, *Remnants of Song: Trauma and the Experience of Modernity in Charles Baudelaire and Paul Celan* (Stanford, Calif.: Stanford University Press, 2000), 335.

9. Critical commentary discussed by Amir Eshel, "Flowers of Memory, Flowers of History: Paul Celan and Historical Time," University of California, Berkeley, February 26, 1999. See also Eshel's "Aporias of Time: A Rhetorical Figure in the Poetry of Jewish Authors after the Shoah," *The Conscience of Humankind: Literature and Traumatic Experiences,* ed. Elrud Ibsch (Amsterdam: Rodopi, 2000), 25–36.

10. On the poem's musical structure see Karl S. Weimar, "Paul Celan's 'Todesfuge': Translation and Interpretation," *PMLA* 89 (1974): 85–96; Gérard Raulet, "Engagement et utopie dans le lyrisme allemand contemporain," *Études Germaniques* 36:2 (April–June 1981): 176–87; Leonard Olschner, "Fugal Provocation in Paul Celan's 'Todesfuge' and 'Engführung,'" *German Life and Letters* 43:1 (October 1989): 79–89; Lars Ellstrom, "Paul Celan's 'Todesfuge': A Title and a Poem," *Yearbook of Interdisciplinary Studies in the Fine Arts* 1 (1989): 125–53.

11. John Simon, "Death Fugues: The Poems of Paul Celan," *New Criterion* 14:9 (May 1996): 28–38, 30.

12. John Felstiner, *Paul Celan: Poet, Survivor, Jew* (New Haven, Conn.: Yale University Press, 1985), 23, 28.

13. Aharon Appelfeld, "Buried Homeland," *New Yorker,* November 23, 1998: 48–61, 51. Appelfeld reports that Bukovina belonged to the Hapsburg Empire from 1774 until 1918, when it was transferred to Romania. Matti Bunzl notes that "By becoming culturally German, the Jews of Czernowitz had emerged as the bearers of modernity" ("Schiller in the Shtetl: Karl Emil Franzos and the Cultural Colonization of Eastern Jewry," paper delivered at the Meeting of the American Anthropological Association, San Francisco, November 15–19, 2000).

14. See Marianne Hirsch and Leo Spitzer, "'We Would Not Have Come without You': Generations of Nostalgia," *American Imago* 59:3 (2002): 253–76.

15. Appelfeld, "Buried Homeland," 50.

16. See Israel Chalfen's detailed description of the occupation in *Paul Celan: A Biography of His Youth* (New York: Persea Books, 1991).

17. Some Celan scholars claim that his father was also shot, but in any case neither parent returned from the camps.

18. See Colin, *Paul Celan*, xiv; and Chalfen, *Paul Celan,* 147.

19. Simon, "Death Fugues," 30.

20. Chalfen, *Paul Celan,* 169.

21. See *Paul Celan/Nelly Sachs: Briefwechsel,* ed. Barbara Wiedmann (Frankfurt: Suhrkamp, 1993).

22. Simon, "Death Fugues," 31. For a reading of the correspondence between Celan and his wife, see Julia Kristeva, "Paul Celan: Celanie, la douleur du corps nomade," *Magazine littéraire* 400 (July–August 2001): 52–56.

23. For an examination of exile and language in Celan see Alexis Nouss, "La Demeure de la lettre (L'être juif dans la poésie de Celan)," special issue of *Études Littéraires* entitled *L'ethnicité fictive: Judéité et littérature* 29:3–4 (Winter 1997): 107–20; see also Michel Deguy, "Paul Celan, 1990," *Les temps modernes* 529–30 (August–September 1990): 2–14. While agreeing that Celan can be considered a "Holocaust poet," Emery George is careful to note that the poet was also concerned with the Vietnam War, the Spanish Civil War, and other tragedies. See Emery George, "Language and the Holocaust: Reflections on the Poetry of Paul Celan," *Michigan Quarterly Review* 36:3 (Summer 1997): 475–83.

24. Conversation with Daniel Boyarin, April 25, 2002.

25. Simon, "Death Fugues," 31–32.

26. See Jacques Derrida, *Schibboleth. Pour Paul Celan* (Paris: Galilée, 1986), trans. Joshua Wilner in *Midrash and Literature,* Geoffrey Hartman and Sanford Budick ed. (New Haven, Conn.: Yale University Press, 1986); Philippe Lacoue-Labarthe, *La poésie comme expérience* (Paris: Christian Bourgois, 1986); Rochelle Tobias, "The Ground Gives Way: Intimations of the Sacred in Celan's 'Gespräch im Gebirg,'" *MLN* 114:3 (1999): 567–89; for a critique of Derrida's and Lacoue-Labarthe's readings of Celan see Mark M. Anderson, "The 'Impossibility of Poetry': Celan and Heidegger in France," *New German Critique* 53 (Spring–Summer 1991): 3–18. For Celan's response to his visit to Heidegger see his poem "Todtnauberg." Felstiner reports that Celan read Jabès's *Le livre des questions* in 1967 and reacted strongly to it (see Felstiner, *Paul Celan,* 233).

27. Françoise Meltzer, *Hot Property: The Stakes and Claims of Literary Originality* (Chicago: University of Chicago Press, 1994), 60. Among the vast literature on Heidegger's Nazism see Jacques Derrida, *Of Spirit: Heidegger and the Question,* trans. Geoffrey Bennington and Rachel Bowlby (Chicago: Chicago University Press, 1989), and Philippe Lacoue-Labarthe, *Heidegger, Art, and Politics,* trans. Chris Turner (Oxford: Basil Blackwell, 1990).

28. "Engführung" is Celan's other famous Holocaust poem and is analyzed by Peter Szondi in *Celan Studies,* trans. Susan Bernofsky with Harvey Mendelsohn (Stanford, Calif.: Stanford University Press, 2003). For a discussion of Jené's illustration see Weimar, "Paul Celan's 'Todesfuge,'" 91, and Mona Sandqvist, "Alchemy and Interart," in *Interart Poetics: Essays on the Interrelations of the Arts and Media,* ed. Ulla-Britta Langerroth, Hans Lund, and Erik Hedling (Amsterdam: Rudopi, 1997), 269–82. On date of composition see Felstiner, *Paul Celan,* 27.

29. Paul Auster, "The Poetry of Exile," *Studies in Twentieth Century Literature, Special Issue on Paul Celan* 8:1 (Fall 1983): 101–10, 103, 105.

30. Paul Celan, *Paul Celan: Poems, A Bilingual Edition* trans. Michael Hamburger (Manchester, U.K.: Carcanet New Press Limited, 1980), 50–53.

31. Aharon Appelfeld claims that the milk also represents the Holocaust in "After the Holocaust," in Lang, *Writing and the Holocaust,* 83–92, 90. There has been much speculation about the source of Celan's phrase "Schwarze Milch"; Celan was implicated in a devastating (for him) charge of plagiarism due to the fact that this phrase echoed that of the poet Yvan Goll. The phrase also echoes a poem of Rose Ausländer's. For discussion of the mostly discounted plagiarism charge see Meltzer, *Hot Property,* and Felstiner, *Paul Celan.*

32. Chalfen, *Paul Celan,* 54.

33. John Felstiner's translation is considerably less sensual: "he shouts scrape your strings darker you'll rise then as smoke to the sky / you'll have a grave then in the clouds there you won't lie too cramped" (*Paul Celan,* 31).

34. Leonard L. Duroche, "Paul Celan's 'Todesfuge': A New Interpretation," *MLN* 82 (1967): 472–77, 477.

35. Shoshana Felman and Dori Laub, *Testimony: Crises of Witnessing in Literature, Psychoanalysis, and History* (New York: Routledge, 1992), 31.

36. Letter to Peter Jokostra, March 4, 1959, quoted in Felstiner, *Paul Celan,* 149.

37. Günter Blöcker in *Der Tagesspiegel,* October 11, 1959, quoted in Felstiner, *Paul Celan,* 148.

38. Felstiner, *Paul Celan,* 26–30.

39. Baer, *Remnants of Song,* 178. See also Werner Hamacher, "The Second of Inversion: Movements of a Figure through Celan's Poetry," *Yale French Studies: The Lesson of Paul de Man* 69 (1985): 276–311; and Alain Suied, "Paul Celan: Poet of the Shoah," *New Literary History* 30:1 (1999): 217–19.

40. Jonathan Skolnik, "Kaddish for Spinoza: Memory and Modernity in Celan and Heine," *New German Critique* 77 (Spring–Summer 1999): 169–86, 179.

41. Quoted in J. M. Coetzee, "In the Midst of Losses" *New York Review of Books* 48:11 (July 5, 2001): 4–8, 5. For an examination of Celan's use of German see Martin Rumscheidt, "Poetry, Theology, and Ethics: A Study in Paul Celan," *Between Ethics and Aesthetics: Crossing the Boundaries,* ed. Dorota Glowacka and Stephen Boos (Albany: Sate University of New York Press, 2002): 117–29; Dennis J. Schmidt, "Black Milk and Blue: Celan and Heidegger on Pain and Language," and Christopher Fynsk, "The Realities at Stake in a Poem: Celan's Bremen and Darmstadt Addresses," both in Aris Fioretos, ed., *Wordtraces: Readings of Paul Celan* (Baltimore: Johns Hopkins University Press, 1994): 110–29; 159–84; and Hartman, *Longest Shadow,* 161ff.

42. Theodor Adorno, *Aesthetic Theory* [1970], trans. C. Lenhardt (London: Routledge and Kegan Paul, 1984), 109, 179, 444.

43. Zsuzsanna Osváth, "Radnóti, Celan, and Aesthetic Shifts in Central European

Holocaust Poetry," *Comparative Central European Culture,* ed. Steven Tötösy de Zepetnek (West Lafayette, Ind.: Purdue University Press, 2002), 51–69, 67; see also Paul Celan, *Last Poems,* trans. Katherine Washburn (San Francisco: North Point Press, 1986).

44. Felman and Laub, *Testimony,* 37.

45. Meltzer, *Hot Property,* 49.

46. Hamburger's translation in Celan, *Poems,* 268–69.

47. Colin, *Paul Celan,* 46.

48. Both Lawrence Langer and Rosette Lamont's introductions to the translations of *Auschwitz et après* and *La mémoire et les jours,* respectively, stress this mission. I use "over there," both as a translation of Delbo's repeated use of "là-bas" to designate the camps and also, following David Grossman's *See Under: Love,* trans. Betsy Rosenberg (London: Jonathan Cape, 1989), in which survivors living in Israel describe the camps and/or the old world using this term.

49. Charlotte Delbo, *La mémoire et les jours* (Paris: Berg International, 1985), 9 (my translation; Bott's introduction is not included in Lamont's translation); *Days and Memory,* trans. Rosette Lamont (Marlboro, Vt.: Marlboro Press, 1990). Hereafter, original and translation cited in the text.

50. Delbo describes this in her entry on herself in her *Le convoi du 24 janvier* (Paris: Éditions de Minuit, 1965), 100–102.

51. For an analysis of Delbo's plays see Rosette C. Lamont, "Charlotte Delbo's Frozen Friezes," *L'Esprit Créateur* 19:2 (Summer 1979): 65–74; Claude Schumacher, ed., *Staging the Holocaust: The Shoah in Drama and Performance* (New York: Cambridge University Press, 1998). For discussions of Delbo's bonds with other women see Ethel Tolansky and Nicole Thatcher, "Testimony and Vision: Poetic Responses to Concentration Camp Experience," *Romance Studies* 30 (Autumn 1997): 59–72; and Nicole Thatcher, *A Literary Analysis of Charlotte Delbo's Concentration Camp Re-Presentation* (Lewiston, N.Y.: Edwin Mellen Press, 2000).

52. There is a growing body of research about gender and the Holocaust. See, for example, S. Lilian Kremer, *Women's Holocaust Writing: Memory and Imagination* (Lincoln: University of Nebraska Press, 1999); S. L. Wisenberg, *Holocaust Girls: History, Memory, and Other Obsessions* (Lincoln: University of Nebraska Press, 2002); Dalia Ofer and Lenore J. Weitzman, eds., *Women in the Holocaust* (New Haven, Conn.: Yale University Press, 1998); *Signs: Journal of Women in Culture and Society, Feminism and Cultural Memory,* special issue edited by Marianne Hirsch and Valerie Smith, 28:1 (2002); Miriam Cooke and Angela Woollacot, eds., *Gendering War Talk* (Princeton, N.J.: Princeton University Press, 1993).

53. Sylviane Gresh, *Les veilleuses: Le 3 février 1995, 320 commédiennes lisent Charlotte Delbo-Auschwitz N° 31 661 à l'initiative de la compagnie Bagages de Sables* (Solignac, France: Le Bruit des Autres, 1997), 23.

54. Letter from Louis Jouvet to Delbo, July 29, 1940, at the Bibliothèque Nationale, Arsenal, Paris, LJMu52; LJMu106.

55. See Lawrence Langer's introduction to the translation of Delbo's *Auschwitz et après* and his earlier version of the introduction, "From Sight to Insight: The Legacy of Charlotte Delbo," *Contemporary French Civilization* 18:1 (Winter–Spring 1994): 64–71; and Nicole Thatcher, "Charlotte Delbo's Voice: The Conscious and Unconscious Determinations of a Woman Writer," *L'Esprit Créateur* 40:2 (Summer 2000): 41–51.

56. Charlotte Delbo, *Auschwitz et Après II, Une Connaissance Inutile* (Paris: Éditions de Minuit, 1970), 125. Translation is from *Auschwitz and After,* 188.

57. Delbo, *Auschwitz et Après II,* 125; Delbo, *Auschwitz and After,* 188.

58. Letter from Delbo to Louis Jouvet, July 29, 1940, at the Bibliothèque Nationale, Arsenal, Paris, LJMu52; LJMu106.

59. Like Carolyn Forché's powerful book of poems, *The Angel of History* (New York: HarperPerennial, 1994) then, Delbo's text moves across different twentieth-century catastrophes in order to highlight both the connections and the differences among historically grounded moments of trauma.

60. Sigmund Freud, *Beyond the Pleasure Principle* [1920], trans. James Strachey (New York: Bantam, 1959), 51.

61. For analyses that treat Delbo's modes of figuration, see Renée A. Kingcaid, "Charlotte Delbo's *Auschwitz et après:* The Struggle for Signification," *French Forum* 9:1 (January 1984): 98–109; Nathan Bracher, "Histoire, ironie et interprétation chez Charlotte Delbo: une écriture d'Auschwitz," *French Forum* 19:1 (January 1994): 81–93; Nathan Bracher, "Faces d'histoire, figures de violence: métaphore et métonymie chez Charlotte Delbo," *Zeitschrift für Französische sprache und literatur* 102:3 (1992): 252–62; and Lea Fridman Hamaoui, "Art and Testimony: The Representation of Historical Horror in Literary Works by Piotr Rawicz and Charlotte Delbo," *Cardozo Studies in Law and Literature* 3:2 (Fall 1991): 243–59.

62. Langer, introduction to Delbo, *Auschwitz and After,* xiv. See also Michael Rothberg's chapter, "Unbearable Witness: Charlotte Delbo's Traumatic Timescapes," in *Traumatic Realism.*

63. On the connection with Hesiod see Edmund White, *Marcel Proust* (New York: Penguin, 1999), 57.

64. Charlotte Delbo, *Spectres, mes compagnons* [1972] (Paris: Berg International, 1995), 15. Rosette Lamont translated parts of *Spectres* in the *Massachusetts Review* 12:1 (Winter 1971): 10–30, and 14:2 (Spring 1973): 310–15.

65. The literature on Proust is formidably large, but some of the works I have consulted are Antoine Compagnon, *La Troisième république des lettres, de Flaubert à Proust* (Paris: Seuil, 1983); Margaret E. Gray, *Postmodern Proust* (Philadelphia: University of Pennsylvania Press, 1992); Gérard Genette, "Proust et le langage indirect,"

Figures II (Paris: Seuil, 1969); Vincent Descombes, *Proust: Philosophie du roman* (Paris: Minuit, 1987); Julia Kristeva, *Proust and the Sense of Time,* trans. Stephen Bann (New York: Columbia University Press, 1993); Clive Bell, *Proust* (New York: Harcourt, Brace and Company, 1929); Joyce N. Megay, *Bergson et Proust: Essai de mise au point de la question de l'influence de Bergson sur Proust* (Paris: Librairie Philosophique J. Vrin, 1976); Elisabeth Ladenson, *Proust's Lesbianism* (Ithaca, N.Y.: Cornell University Press, 1999); Jean-François Chevrier, *Proust et la photographie* (Paris: Editions de l'Etoile, 1982); Lawrence Schehr, "Rachel, quand du Seigneur," *L'Esprit Créateur* 37:4 (Winter 1997): 83–93; Gilles Deleuze, *Proust et les signes* (Presses Universitaires de France, 1964).

66. Adorno, *Notes to Literature,* 316.

67. Marcel Proust, *À la recherche du temps perdu, Du côté de chez Swann* (1909; Paris: Gallimard, 1987), 6. Hereafter cited in the text.

68. Marcel Proust, *À la recherche du temps perdu, Le temps retrouvé* (1927; Paris: Gallimard: 1987), 177–78.

69. Marcel Proust, *In Search of Lost Time,* trans. C. K. Scott Moncrieff and Terence Kilmartin, revised by D. J. Enright (New York: Modern Library, 1992), 63–64. Translation slightly modified; hereafter if a translation other than my own is given, I refer to this (Moncrieff and Kilmartin) translation.

CHAPTER 2: AESTHETIC MEMORY

1. Gérard de Cortanze, *Le Madrid de Jorge Semprun,* with photographs by Antonin Borgeaud (Saint-Amand-Montrond: Éditions du Chêne—Hachette Livre, 1997), 16.

2. Françoise Nicoladzé, *La deuxième vie de Jorge Semprun: Une écriture tressée aux spirales de l'histoire* (Castelnau-Le-Nez: Éditions Climats, 1997), 97.

3. Semprun details this acrimonious break in one of the texts he published in Spanish, *Autobiografía de Federico Sánchez* (Barcelona: Editorial Planeta, 1978).

4. Semprun discusses these films in interviews in Dan Georgakas and Lenny Rubenstein, *The Cineaste Interviews: On the Art and Politics of the Cinema* (Chicago: Lake View Press, 1983), 265–81; and Christian Salé, *Les scénaristes au travail* (Lausanne: 5 Continents/Hatier, 1981), 103–14.

5. Isabelle de Courtivron, "A Book That Can't Be Written," *Washington Post Book World,* March 16, 1997: X06.

6. For an examination of Spanish writers writing in French see Jean Tena "Trois Ecrivains Espagnols D'Expression Française: Michel del Castillo, Augustin Gomez-Arcos, Jorge Semprun," *Images et Influences de l'Espagne dans la France Contemporaine,* ed. Jean Sagnes (Ville de Béziers: Presses Universitaires de Perpignan, 1994), 55–69.

7. For a reading that I think mistakenly places *Le grand voyage* under the genre of travel literature see Sally M. Silk "Writing the Holocaust/Writing Travel: The Space

of Representation in Jorge Semprun's *Le grand voyage*," *Clio: A Journal of Literature, History, and the Philosophy of History* 22:1 (Fall 1992): 53–65.

8. For an analysis of time in Semprun see Lawrence Langer, "Of Time and Atrocity," *The Holocaust and the Literary Imagination* (New Haven, Conn.: Yale University Press, 1975).

9. Jorge Semprun, *L'écriture ou la vie*, 336; Semprun, *Literature or Life*, 262. This invention is discussed in Ofelia Farrán, "'Cuanto más escribo, más me queda por decir': Memory, Trauma, and Writing in the Work of Jorge Semprún," *MLN* 116:2 (March 2001): 266–94.

10. Lawrence Langer discusses this nexus of living and dying in "Pursuit of Death in Holocaust Narrative," *Partisan Review* 68:3 (Summer 2001): 379–95.

11. Jorge Semprun, *Le grand voyage* (Paris: Gallimard, 1963), 215; *The Long Voyage*, trans. Richard Seaver (New York: Penguin, 1997), 216. Hereafter original and translation cited in the text. For an analysis of doubling in Semprun see Nicoladzé, *Dieuxième vie*, 65–94.

12. Robert Antelme, *L'espèce humaine* (Paris: Gallimard, 1957), 114; *The Human Race*, trans. Jeffrey Haight and Annie Mahler (Evanston, Ill.: Marlboro Press/Northwestern, 1992), 109. Hereafter original and translation cited in the text.

13. Appelfeld, *Beyond Despair*, 70.

14. Ann Smock, "Disastrous Responsibility," *L'Esprit Créateur* 24:3 (Fall 1984): 5–20, 19.

15. Sarah Kofman, *Paroles Suffoquées* (Paris: Éditions Galilée, 1987), 15–16.

16. Susan Rubin Suleiman, "Historical Trauma and Literary Testimony: Writing and Repetition in the Buchenwald Memoirs of Jorge Semprun," *Journal of Romance Studies* 4:2 (Summer 2004): 1–19; 11.

17. For an analysis of Proust in Semprun see Kathleen M. Vernon, "The Trauma of History/The History of Trauma: Plotting Memory in Jorge Semprun," *Cine-Lit 3: Essays on Hispanic Film and Fiction* (1997): 157–67; Péter Egri, *Survie et réinterprétation de la forme Proustienne, Proust-Déry-Semprun* (Debrecen: Studia Romanica, 1969). For a very different analysis of Proust's role in *Le grand voyage* see Sally M. Silk, "The Dialogical Traveler: A Reading of Semprun's *Le grand voyage*," *Studies in Twentieth Century Literature* 14:2 (Summer 1990): 223–40. For an introduction to Semprun in the context of Holocaust literature see Naomi Diamant, "The Boundaries of Holocaust Literature: The Emergence of a Canon," diss., Columbia University, 1992.

18. Martin Jay, *Cultural Semantics: Keywords of Our Time* (Amherst: University of Massachusetts Press, 1998), 160.

19. While the English translator, Richard Seaver, has chosen to italicize the title of Proust's volume, Semprun does not. Therefore, there is an ambiguity in the original between whether the narrator reconstructs Proust's text, *Swann's Way*, or rather the pathway along which Proust's narrator wanders.

20. Proust, *Le temps retrouvé*, 351; *Time Regained,* trans. Andreas Mayor and Terence Kilmartin (New York: Modern Library, 1993), 529. Hereafter original and translation cited in the text.

21. Ruth R. Wisse, "The Individual from the Ashes: Hitler and the Genre of the Holocaust Memoir," *Weekly Standard* (April 21, 1997): 29–35, 31.

22. Jorge Semprun and Elie Wiesel, *Se taire est impossible* (Paris: Éditions mille et une nuits, 1995), 7, 12.

23. Primo Levi discusses the musulman in *Survival in Auschwitz and the Reawakening: Two Memoirs,* trans. Stuart Woolf (New York: Summit Books, 1986); Giorgio Agamben discusses the musulman via Levi and Améry in *Remnants of Auschwitz: The Witness and the Archive,* trans. Daniel Heller-Roazen (New York: Zone Books, 1999).

24. Delbo, *Auschwitz et après I, Aucun de nous ne reviendra,* 147; *Auschwitz and After,* 92.

25. Robert Boyers, "Remembrance of Things to Come," *Times Literary Supplement* 4206 (November 11, 1983): 1253.

26. Samuel Beckett, *Proust* (London: Chatto and Windus, 1931), 29.

27. Maurice Blanchot, *Le livre à venir* (Paris: Gallimard, 1959), 22; *The Book to Come,* trans. Charlotte Mandell (Stanford, Calif.: Stanford University Press, 2003), 12–13.

28. Newspaper articles cited in Alexandra Przyrembel, "Ilse Koch, the 'Kommandeuse of Buchenwald,'" *German History: The Journal of the German History Society* 19:3 (2001): 369–99, 389; Susannah Heschel brought this film to my attention via her paper, "The Grey Zone: Feminist Historiography of the Holocaust," delivered at the Association for Jewish Studies Conference, December 19, 2004.

29. Claudia Koonz, *Mothers in the Fatherland: Women, the Family, and Nazi Politics* (New York: St. Martin's Press, 1981), 404.

30. Przyrembel, "Ilse Koch," 384.

31. Primo Levi, *The Drowned and the Saved,* trans. Raymond Rosenthal (London: Abacus, 1990), 63–64.

32. David Carroll, "The Limits of Representation and the Right to Fiction: Shame, Literature, and the Memory of the Shoah," *L'Esprit Créateur* 34:4 (Winter 1999): 68–79, 77.

33. Tony Judt discusses this in "The Reliving of Death: Jorge Semprun and the Effort to Tell the Untellable Truth," *Times Literary Supplement* 4952 (February 17, 1998): 10.

34. Cathy Caruth, *Unclaimed Experience: Trauma, Narrative, and History* (Baltimore: Johns Hopkins University Press, 1996), 4.

CHAPTER 3: AESTHETIC ALLUSION

Note: The quotation in the chapter title is from Carolyn Forché, *The Angel of History* (see 181n59), 69; epigraph to the section titled Memory and Forgetting is from

Jabès's *Desire for a Beginning Dread of One Single End,* trans. Rosmarie Waldrop (New York: Granary Books, 2001), 44.

1. Hirsch, "Post-Memory and Exile."

2. Pierre Nora, *Realms of Memory: The Construction of the French Past,* trans. Arthur Goldhammer (New York: Columbia University Press, 1996), 3. I use the word "fascinating" to evoke Susan Sontag's famous essay "Fascinating Fascism," in *Under the Sign of Saturn* (New York: Vintage Books, 1981).

3. Edmond Jabès, *Le livre du partage* (Paris: Gallimard, 1987), 66.

4. Jabès quoted in Didier Cahen, "Écrire sa vie," *Portrait(s) d'Edmond Jabès,* ed. Steven Jaron (Paris: Bibliothèque nationale de France, 1999), 32.

5. Kerwin Lee Klein, "On the Emergence of *Memory* in Historical Discourse," *Representations* 69 (Winter 2000): 127–49, 136, 145, 141. Description of Klein's argument from Thomas Laqueur's introduction to this issue, 3.

6. For a detailed study of Jabès's use of the word "Auschwitz" see Albert Mingelgrün, "Edmond Jabès et Auschwitz," *Les Lettres romanes* (1995): 113–20.

7. As Richard Stamelman, in a chapter on Jabès, remarks: "In the last century . . . confidence in the indelibility of the written word has waned. Modern poets no longer look at the poem as an unchanging, ineffaceable monument of feeling and perception; it has lost the presence it was once able to articulate." *Lost Beyond Telling: Representations of Death and Absence in Modern French Poetry* (Ithaca, N.Y.: Cornell University Press, 1990), 223.

8. Mary Ann Caws, "Questioning the Question," *The Sin of the Book: Edmond Jabès,* ed. Eric Gould (Lincoln: University of Nebraska Press, 1985), 171. See also Caws's article "Edmond Jabès: Sill and Sand," *L'Esprit Créateur* 32:2 (Summer 1992): 11–18.

9. Zohreh Sullivan, *Exiled Memories: Stories of Iranian Diaspora* (Philadelphia: Temple University Press, 2001), 268.

10. Caryn Aviv and David Shneer, *New Jews: The End of the Jewish Diaspora* (New York: New York University Press, 2005), 18.

11. Rosmarie Waldrop, *Lavish Absence: Recalling and Rereading Edmond Jabès* (Middletown, Conn.: Wesleyan University Press, 2002), 57–58.

12. Ezrahi, "Grave in the Air," 276.

13. Biographical information is from Edmond Jabès, *Du désert au livre: Entretiens avec Marcel Cohen* (Paris: Pierre Belfond, 1980), 46–54. Also see Daniel Lançon, *Jabès, l'Égyptian* (Paris: Jean-Michel Place, 1998). For a detailed study of the Egyptian diaspora, see Joel Beinin, *The Dispersion of Egyptian Jewry: Culture, Politics, and the Formation of a Modern Diaspora* (University of California Press, 1998).

14. Jabès, *Du désert,* 22.

15. Ibid., 25, 26.

16. Edmond Jabès, *Le soupçon le désert* (Paris: Gallimard, 1978), 85. For a reading

of Jabès's relationship to God, see Beth Hawkins, *Reluctant Theologians: Franz Kafka, Paul Celan, Edmond Jabès* (New York: Fordham University Press, 2003).

17. In remarking on Jabès, Fanny Howe notes: "This is not even a speaking for the abyss. This is worse. The mind is empty, a helpless mechanism on the lookout for words which will, seemingly, arrive by chance." Howe, "The Contemporary Logos," *Code of Signals: Recent Writings in Poetics,* ed. Michael Palmer (Berkeley: North Atlantic Books, 1983), 47–55.

18. Jabès, *Du désert,* 87.

19. Arthur A. Cohen, "Some Observations about Literature and Theology," *Prooftexts* 7:2 (1987): 107–21, 109.

20. Jabès, *Soupçon,* 57.

21. Jean-Paul Sartre, *Réflexions sur la question juive* [1946] (Paris: Gallimard, 1954), 167, original emphasis. For a detailed account of the vagaries of Jewish self-presentation, see Sander Gilman, *Jewish Self-Hatred: Anti-Semitism and the Hidden Language of the Jews* (Baltimore: Johns Hopkins University Press, 1986).

22. Edmond Jabès, "My Itinerary," trans. Rosmarie Waldrop, *Studies in Twentieth Century Literature* 12:1 (1987): 3–12, 4.

23. Sigmund Freud, "Mourning and Melancholia," *The Standard Edition of the Complete Psychological Works of Sigmund Freud,* 14, trans. James Strachey (1915; London: Hogarth Press and the Insititute of Psychoanalysis, 1957).

24. Rachel Whiteread, interview in *Art Now: Interviews with Modern Artists* (London: Continuum, 2002): 46–59, 56. See also *Rachel Whiteread: Transient Spaces* (Berlin: Deutsche Guggenheim, 2001; New York: Harry Abrams, 2001).

25. Michael Kimmelman, "Behind Sealed Doors, Opening Up the Past," *New York Times,* October 30, 2000: B1.

26. James Young, *Memory's Edge,* 113. For an examination of Whiteread's monument in the context of the history of Viennese Jews, see Matti Bunzl, *Symptoms of Modernity: Jews and Queers in Late-Twentieth-Century Vienna* (Berkeley: University of California Press, 2004).

27. Saul Friedländer, *Nazi Germany and the Jews. Volume 1: The Years of Persecution* (New York: Harper Collins, 1997), 100–101, emphasis added. Geoffrey Hartman also discusses this figure in *The Longest Shadow,* 78ff.

28. Jabès, *Partage,* 97.

29. Edmond Jabès, *Le livre du dialogue* (Paris: Gallimard, 1984), 66.

30. Jabès, *Dialogue,* 69. See also Edmond Jabès, "The Key," trans. Rosmarie Waldrop, *Midrash and Literature,* Hartman and Budick, eds., 349–60.

31. Edmond Jabès, *Le parcours* (Paris: Gallimard, 1985), 81.

32. Jabès, *Partage,* 106.

33. Ibid., 100.

34. Ibid., 19.

35. Jabès, *Dialogue,* 81.

36. For another example of an attempt to disconnect historical Jews from figurative Jews see Lyotard, *Heidegger et les "juifs."* For a classic text on Jewishness and memory see Yosef Hayim Yerushalmi, *Zakhor: Jewish History and Jewish Memory* (Seattle: University of Washington Press, 1982).

37. Waldrop, *Lavish Absence,* 115.

38. Jacques Derrida, "Edmond Jabès et la question du livre," *L'écriture et la différence* (Paris: Éditions du Seuil, 1967), 112.

39. Ibid.

40. For an interesting analysis of Derrida's relationship to Judaism that notices the ways "Derrida's constructions evoke Judaic echoes and kabbalistic meditations," see Shira Wolosky, "Derrida, Jabès, Levinas: Sign-Theory as Ethical Discourse," *Prooftexts* 2:3 (1982): 283–302, 290.

41. Waldrop, *Lavish Absence,* 82.

42. Jabès, "My Itinerary," 5.

43. Susan Handelman, "'Torments of an Ancient Word': Edmond Jabès and the Rabbinic Tradition," in Gould, *Sin of the Book,* 56.

44. Ibid.

45. Gershom Scholem is one notable exception to this rule. See his *Kabbalah* (New York: Dorset Press, 1987) and *The Messianic Idea in Judaism,* trans. Michael Meyer (New York: Schocken Books, 1971).

46. Handelman, "'Torments,'" 56, 59.

47. For other analyses of the connection between the Talmud and poststructuralism, see Daniel Boyarin, *Intertextuality and the Reading of Midrash* (Bloomington: Indiana University Press, 1990), Susan Handelman, *The Slayers of Moses: The Emergence of Rabbinic Interpretation in Modern Literary Theory* (Albany: State University of New York Press, 1982), and Elaine Marks, "Cendres juives: Jews Writing in French 'After Auschwitz,'" *Auschwitz and After: Race, Culture, and "the Jewish Question" in France,* ed. Lawrence D. Kritzman (New York: Routledge, 1995).

48. Handelman, "'Torments,'" 83.

49. Ibid., 81.

50. Derrida, "Edmond Jabès," 102, emphasis added.

51. See Peter Novick, *The Holocaust in American Life* (New York: Houghton Mifflin, 1999).

52. Jabès, *Partage,* 121.

53. Hillel Seidman, *Tog Buch fun Varshever Geto* (New York: Duenom-Ayrem, 1947), 13–14.

54. For an analysis of these two characters see Warren F. Motte Jr., "Questioning Jabès," *French Forum* 11:1 (January 1986): 83–94.

55. This has been discussed by Primo Levi in *The Drowned and the Saved* and addressed by Giorgio Agamben in a lecture given at the University of California, Berkeley, "What Does It Mean to Bear Witness?" October 21, 1999.

56. Waldrop, *Lavish Absence*, 69.

57. Jabès, "My Itinerary," 6, emphasis added. See also Jabes, *Du désert*, 92–93.

58. Jabès, *Du désert*, 93.

59. Jabès, *Parcours*, 43.

60. Ibid.

61. Berel Lang, "Writing-the-Holocaust: Jabès and the Measure of History," in Gould, *Sin of the Book*, 198.

62. See Rosenbaum, ed., *Is the Holocaust Unique?*

63. Lang, "Writing," 206.

64. Eric Gould, "Introduction," *Sin of the Book*, xiii, xv.

65. Ibid., xv.

66. Ibid., xvii.

67. Ibid., xvii.

68. Giorgio Agamben's seminar at the University of California, Berkeley, "The Time That Is Left," October 15, 1999.

69. Jabès, *Soupçon*, 95–96.

70. Jabès, *Partage*, 36.

CHAPTER 4: AESTHETIC MOURNING

1. Hirsch, "Post-Memory and Exile."

2. Andreas Huyssen, "Kiefer in Berlin," *October* 62 (Fall 1992): 85–101, 91, 92; Daniel Arasse, *Anselm Kiefer,* trans. Mary Whittall (New York: Harry N. Abrams, 2001), 36; Waldemar Januszczak, "Masoleums of Black Guilt," *Manchester Guardian Weekly,* June 5, 1983: 20.

3. In 2000, for example, Kiefer produced works relating to his 1993 travels to China and focusing on Mao Zedong; see Thomas McEvilley, *Anselm Kiefer: Let a Thousand Flowers Bloom* (London: Anthony d'Offay, 2000).

4. After the war, Kiefer's father was a professor at the Institut für Kunstpädagogik der Universität Frankfurt, and his mother was a teacher at the Handelsschule in Donaueschingen. Many thanks to Amy Blau for facilitating my correspondence with the Donaueschingen archives, and thanks to the archivist, Ernst Zimmerman, for his prompt response to our queries.

5. Andreas Huyssen, "Anselm Kiefer: The Terror of History, the Temptation of Myth," *October* 48 (Spring 1989): 25–45, and "Kiefer in Berlin"; Lisa Saltzman, *Anselm Kiefer and Art after Auschwitz;* Peter Schjeldahl, "Our Kiefer," *Art in America* 76:3 (March 1998): 116–27.

6. Interestingly, Kiefer's works sell for considerably higher prices than Boltanski's. For a smug look at the cost of Kiefer's paintings, see Roberta Smith, "Anselm Kiefer, Émigré, in Two-Part Installation," *New York Times,* May 7, 1993: C30; Anthony Thorncroft notes that Kiefer's *Die Sefiroth* sold for £300,000 ("Modern Artists

Are Tops," *Financial Times* [London], July 3, 1987: 19); Paul Taylor also mentions the high price of Kiefer's work in "Painter of the Apocalypse: Anselm Kiefer has gained international fame with provocative works that recall Germany's nightmarish past," *New York Times*, October 16, 1988: SM 48–49, 80, 102–3; Charles Bremmer notes that contemporary French works, including Boltanski's, have hardly ever sold for more than £32,500, or one-tenth of the price of Kiefer's *Die Sefiroth* ("French Artists Left Out of the World Picture," *Times* [London], June 13, 2001). While Boltanski and Kiefer are rarely compared at length, Arthur Danto mentions them together in *Encounters and Reflections: Art in the Historical Present* (New York: Farrar, Straus and Giroux, 1990), 260; for more press that mentions Boltanski and Kiefer together, see Christine Temin, "Superb, Disturbing 'Two Artists Painting the Holocaust'" (on Arnold Trachtman and Susan Erony), *Boston Globe*, October 7, 1992: 74; Necee Reglis, "There's Plenty to Lure Art Lovers to Southern France," *Boston Globe*, March 10, 2002: M7; Leslie Camhi, "Peering Under the Skin of Monsters," *New York Times*, March 17, 2002, sec. 2: 36; Alan Riding, "Art in Germany Crosses the Borders," *New York Times*, December 2, 1999: E1; Mary Sherman, "Trachtman Offers Take on Holocaust," *Boston Herald*, May 16, 1999: 051. Kiefer had been represented by Marian Goodman but has now moved to Gagosian Gallery. For some of the details of his break with Goodman, see Peter Schjeldahl, "Dealership: How Marian Goodman Quietly Changed the Contemporary-Art Market," *New Yorker*, February 2, 2004: 36–41.

7. Adorno uses the phrase *Aufarbeitung* (coming to terms) to denote the important postwar German concept of treating the guilty past; "What Does Coming to Terms with the Past Mean?" *Bitburg in Moral and Political Perspective*, ed. Geoffrey Hartman (Bloomington: Indiana University Press, 1986), 114–29. On Kiefer's reception, see Donald Kuspit, "Flak from the 'Radicals': The American Case against Current German Painting," in Wallis, *Art after Modernism*.

8. For a review of *Burnt Whole*, see Mary Sherman, "Pain and Suffering; Artists Touched by the Holocaust Create Images More Powerful and Poignant Than Words Alone Could Express," *Boston Herald*, January 27, 1995: SO2; Christine Temin, "Hell Is in the Details," *Boston Globe*, January 25, 1995: 57. See also the exhibition catalog *Burnt Whole: Contemporary Artists Reflect on the Holocaust* (Washington, D.C.: Washington Project for the Arts, 1994). Note that the title of Silas's piece in the *Burnt Whole* catalog is given as "*Dear Mr. Kiefer* (1994)" but Silas told me that this was a mistake and the correct title and date are *Ohne Titel* (1989).

9. Conversation with Susan Silas, August 4, 2003.

10. Simon Schama, *Landscape and Memory* (London: HarperCollins, 1995), 118.

11. On Holocaust landscapes see Ulrich Baer, *Spectral Evidence: The Photography of Trauma* (Cambridge, Mass.: MIT Press, 2002) and W. G. Sebald's novel *Austerlitz*, trans. Anthea Bell (New York: Modern Library, 2001). In comparing Kiefer to Richard

Long, Herman Rapaport notes that Kiefer's "empty charred landscapes . . . remind us of how alien earth is to the human and the extent to which the land is restored to beauty in the absence of human *Dasein*." Rapaport, "Brushed Path, Slate Line, Stone Circle: On Martin Heidegger, Richard Long, and Jacques Derrida," *Deconstruction and the Visual Arts: Art, Media, Architecture,* eds. Peter Brunette and David Wills (New York: Cambridge University Press, 1994), 166. For an exploration of Kiefer's books see Adriani Götz, ed., *The Books of Anselm Kiefer, 1969–1990,* trans., Bruni Mayor (New York: George Braziller, 1991).

12. Arasse, *Anselm Kiefer,* 150; for an analysis of Kiefer's Star paintings see Katharina Schmidt, "Cosmos and Star Paintings," *Anselm Kiefer: The Seven Heavenly Palaces, 1973–2001* (Ostfildern-Ruit, Germany: Hatje Cantz, 2001).

13. As Daniel Arasse phrases it, "What Kiefer does is not so much a work *of* memory as a work *on* memory" (Arasse, *Anselm Kiefer,* 74).

14. In addition to a series of paintings about Margarete and Sulamith, Kiefer also made the sculpture *Poppy and Memory* (1989), which refers to Celan's eponymous book of poems, published in 1952 and containing "Todesfuge." In another poem from Celan's *Poppy and Memory,* "Aspen Tree," about the death of his mother, who was exterminated during the war, Celan evokes the image of lead (a substance important to Kiefer in an abstract way, and important to Celan in the literal, brutal lead bullet that killed his mother) in the line, "My mother's heart was ripped by lead" (Meiner Mutter Herz war wund von Blei). Paul Celan, *Paul Celan: Poems,* 32–33.

15. Cordula Meier argues that a commonality binds Kiefer and Celan's "discovery and hiding of both historical and collective consciousness" (das Auf- und Verdecken von sowohl historischem als auch kollektivem Bewußtstein) (*Anselm Kiefer: Die Rückkehr des Mythos in der Kunst* [Essn: verlag Die Blaue Eule, 1992], 200). Many thanks to Amy Blau for finding and translating this passage.

16. Celan, *Poems,* 52/53.

17. In discussing Kiefer's use of hair in another work, Armin Zweite notes that hair "might easily evoke the shaving of heads in the concentration camps" but that it also evokes "human beauty," "sexual fantasies," and "revulsion." This disturbing link between the concentration camp image of human remains, in the form of hair, and the sensual image of hair is encapsulated in *Margarete.* Anselm Kiefer and Armin Zweite, *Anselm Kiefer: The High Priestess* (London: Thames and Hudson/Anthony d'Offay Gallery, 1989), 13: Book 97, unpaginated.

18. Philip Birnbaum, *Encyclopedia of Jewish Concepts* (New York: Hebrew Publishing Company, 1979), 226–30.

19. Dara Goldman, a professor in the Spanish Department at the University of Illinois, relayed this story to me after a research trip to Cuba in the summer of 2003; Adele Dworin, of the newly remodeled Patronato synagogue in Havana, told the story to Dara.

20. Rudi Fuchs, "[. . .]," in *Anselm Kiefer* (Düsseldorf: Städtische Kunsthalle/Paris: Musée d'Art Moderne de la Ville de Paris/Jerusalem: Israel Museum, 1984), 8.

21. Huyssen, "Terror," 40, 43; for other readings of the Margarete and Sulamith paintings see Rafael López-Pedraza, *Anselm Kiefer: The Psychology of "After the Catastrophe"* (New York: George Braziller, 1996), and Städtische Kunsthalle, *Anselm Kiefer*, 130.

22. Schjeldahl, "Our Kiefer," 123, 121.

23. Saltzman, *Anselm Kiefer*, 31; for a very different reading of Kiefer's use of architecture see Schmidt, "Archaic Architectures," *Anselm Kiefer: The Seven Heavenly Palaces*.

24. Matthew Biro finds that "Kiefer's works simultaneously support both left-wing and fascist readings" (*Anselm Kiefer and the Philosophy of Martin Heidegger* [New York: Cambridge University Press, 1998], 92).

25. Saltzman refers to Syberberg (18); and Suzanne Pagé, in discussing a show of Kiefer's in Paris, notes that "Kiefer's work has a point in common with Syberberg's" because of their joint "lifting away of taboo and repression," "Apropos the 'Unknown Painter.' . . ." in Städtische Kunsthalle, *Anselm Kiefer*, 18.

26. See Gilman, *Jewish Self-Hatred*.

27. Hans Jürgen Syberberg, *Vom Unglück und Glück der Kunst in Deutschland nach dem letzten Kriege* (München: Matthes and Seitz, 1990), 14. Many thanks to Matti Bunzl for translating several passages from Syberberg's work. For commentary on Syberberg's controversial film, *Hitler: A Film from Germany*, see Susan Sontag, "Syberberg's Hitler" in *Saturn*, and Anton Kaes, *From Hitler to Heimat: The Return of History as Film* (Cambridge, Mass.: Harvard University Press, 1989).

28. Hans Jürgen Syberberg, "Germany's Heart: The Modern Taboo," *New Perspectives Quarterly* 10:1 (Winter 1993): 20–25, 23.

29. Syberberg, *Vom Unglück*, 17; Syberberg and Kiefer are often noted together as artists who explore German myth; see, for example, Bazon Brock, "The End of the Avant-Garde? And So the End of Tradition: Notes on the Present 'Kulturkampf' in West Germany," *Art Forum* 19:10 (Summer 1981): 62–67.

30. Anselm Kiefer, "Das Grenzenlose Licht des Ain Soph," *Das Plateau: Die Zeitschrift im Radius-verlag*, October 3, 1990: 45. Thanks to Amy Blau for finding and translating this short speech. According to Mark Rosenthal, it was Kiefer's 1983 visit to Israel that sparked his interest in Kabbalah. See Mark Rosenthal, *Anselm Kiefer* (Chicago: Art Institute of Chicago/Philadelphia Museum of Art, 1987), 160 n. 66.

31. Wim Beeren asks of Kiefer's work, "Was a German identity to be found? Had the roots been burnt? Could ashes render the land fertile?" (*Anselm Kiefer: Bilder 1986–1980: Stedelijk Museum Amsterdam, 20.12.1986–8.2.1987* [Amsterdam: Stedelijk Museum, 1987], 7).

32. Gershom Scholem, *Kabbalah*, 357; hereafter cited in the text.

33. Ruth Wisse, ed., *The I. L. Peretz Reader* (New Haven, Conn.: Yale University Press, 2002).

34. Judy Weinberg, "Lilith Sources," *Lilith* 1:1 (Fall 1976): 38.

35. Boltanski also uses angels in a series of images from his group of works entitled *Leçons des ténèbres*. Christian Boltanski, *Leçons des Ténèbres* (München: Kunstverein/Gotteswinter, 1986).

36. Benjamin, "Theses on the Philosophy of History," *Illuminations,* 257.

37. Forché, *Angel,* 55.

38. Kiefer has been described as "not a history painter," and has claimed that "I see history as synchronous. . . . When you go to them, most things are already formulated" (Zweite, *High Priestess,* 67, 98); Rudi Fuchs echoes this by asserting that Kiefer is "not . . . a historical painter," (*"[. . .],"* in Städtische Kunsthalle, *Anselm Kiefer,* 12).

39. Harold Bloom, introduction to Anselm Kiefer, *Merkaba* (New York: Gagosian Gallery, 2002), 26.

40. Doreet LeVitte Harten, "Canticle for a God Unknown," *Anselm Kiefer: Lilith* (New York: Marian Goodman Gallery, 1991), 11.

41. Interestingly, the iconography of *Banner* and that of *Lilith's Daughters* are combined in Kiefer's *Jason,* an exhibit at the Douglas Hyde Gallery shown in Dublin in 1990; see *Jason* (Dublin: Douglas Hyde Gallery, 1990).

42. Lynne Warren's comments in Elizabeth A. T. Smith, Alison Pearlman, Julie Rodrigues Widholm, *Life Death Love Hate Pleasure Pain* (Chicago: Museum of Contemporary Art, 2002), 214.

43. Hal Foster, in his study of Surrealist aesthetics notes that the Surrealists were also interested in alchemy; see *Compulsive Beauty* (Cambridge, Mass.: MIT Press, 1993); for a study of alchemy in Kiefer see Michele Louise Czernik, "Alchemical Symbolism in the Art of Anselm Kiefer," M.A. thesis, Northern Illinois University, 1999; some critics have also compared Beuys to an alchemist: see Stuart Morgan, "Joseph Beuys: Camera as Eavesdropper in New British Television Documentary," *Artscribe International* (January–February 1988): 53.

44. Schjeldahl, "Our Kiefer," 121; interestingly, Arthur Danto dismisses Kiefer as a "crackpot" who has produced a "sustained visual lament for a shattered *Vaterland*" (*Nation,* January 2, 1989, repr. in *Encounters and Reflections,* 238); Gudrun Inboden also discusses Kiefer's use of lead; see "Exodus from Historical Time," *Anselm Kiefer* (Cologne: Galerie Paul Maenz, 1986), 13. Many other commentators note the alchemical references in Kiefer's works; for example, Germano Celant notes that, in one of his paintings, Kiefer achieves an "alchemic reconciliation between painting and photography" (Massimo Cacciari and Germano Celant, *Anselm Kiefer* [Milan: Charta, 1997], 18), and John Hallmark Neff finds that "Like an alchemist, he [Kiefer] posits lead as the low end of a metaphor for spiritual transformation" ("Reading

Kiefer," Anselm Kiefer, *Bruch und Einung* [New York: Marian Goodman Gallery, 1987], 9).

45. See Keith Thomas, *Religion and the Decline of Magic* (New York: Oxford University Press, 1971); Charles B. Schmitt and Quentin Skinner, eds., *The Cambridge History of Renaissance Philosophy* (New York: Cambridge University Press, 1988); Betty Jo Teeter Dobbs and Margaret C. Jacob, *Newton and the Culture of Newtonism* (New Jersey: Humanities Press, 1995).

46. Cited in Alexander Roob, *The Hermetic Museum: Alchemy and Mysticism* (Köln: Taschen, 1997). Joseph Beuys, whom Kiefer refers to as his mentor, was also interested in alchemy and produced two images, reproduced in Roob, referring to alchemical texts.

47. Dora Apel discusses this work of Silas's in *Memory Effects: The Holocaust and the Art of Secondary Witnessing* (New Brunswick, N.J.: Rutgers University Press, 2002).

48. Cited in "Studio Christian Boltanski," *Tate Magazine* 2, http://www.tate.org. uk/magazine/issue2/boltanski.htm. References to Proust abound in Boltanski's own comments and those of others. In one interview Boltanski claimed "I'm a little like Proust" (Stuart Morgan, "Little Christians," interview with Christian Boltanski, *Artscribe International* [November–December 1988]: 46–49, 49), and in another he drew parallels between Proust's magic lantern and his own literal and figurative projections: "Dans les premières pages de *La recherche du temps perdu,* Proust parle d'une lanterne magique qui projette sur les rideaux l'histoire de Brabant et de Lancelot; et il raconte que la poignée de la porte devient un cavalier. . . . Les projections que j'ai faites jadis viennent en partie de là: je projetais de petits objets sur des formes en relief" (In the first pages of *In Search of Lost Time,* Proust speaks of a magic lantern that projects the stories of Brabant and Lancelot on his curtains; and he recounts that the handle of the door became a cavalier. . . . The projections that I make come in part from that: I project small objects on forms in relief) (Delphine Renard, "Entretien avec Christian Boltanski," *Boltanski* [Paris: Musée national d'art moderne au Centre Georges Pompidou, 1984], 83). In *La vie impossible,* one of Boltanski's statements reads: "C'était un artiste très français, un peu trop littéraire dans la tradition proustienne" (He was a very French artist, a bit too literary in the Proustian tradition) (Boltanski, *La vie impossible* [Köln: Anhaltische Gemäldegalerie Dessau, Verlag der Buchhandlung Walther König, 2001], unpaginated, translation in original), and Didier Semin notes: "Outre sa dette envers Breton, Boltanski se réclame volontiers (et à la fois) de Proust et de Kafka; nulle insolence dans cette revendication prestigieuse." (Notwithstanding his debt to Breton, Boltanski readily invokes [and at the same time] Proust and Kafka; there is no insolence intended by this prestigious claim) ("Procédure d'inventaire," *Christian Boltanski, Daniel Buren, Gilbert and George, Jannis Kounellis, Sol LeWitt,*

Richard Long, Mario Merz [Bordeaux: capcMusée d'art contemporain, 1990], 47); Gloria Moure notes that "When he formalises, he plainly reveals his Proustian preferences and his almost fetishistic weaknesses" (Gloria Moure, *Christian Boltanski: Advent and Other Times* [Barcelona: Ediciones Polígrafa/Centro Galego de Arte Contempránea], 31).

49. In an interview, Boltanski perhaps playfully confided, "I think that aesthetics means nothing. There is no such thing as a beautiful or non-beautiful thing. There is art that works and art that doesn't. . . . I don't believe in aesthetics, but then I don't think anybody does" (Didier Semin, Tamar Garb, and Donald Kuspit, *Christian Boltanski* [London: Phaidon, 1997], 34). Klaus Honnef adds, in referring to Boltanski's photos, that "Ainsi la réaction du monde de l'art aux photos de Boltanski est-elle celle du rejet. Car d'autres notions du beau prédominent depuis longtemps dans l'art, . . . Si esthétique il y a, c'est l'esthétique de la laideur qui triomphe" (Because other notions of beauty have predominated for a long time in art, the art world rejects Boltanski's photographs. . . . If the aesthetic is there, it's the aesthetic of ugliness that triumphs) ("Les images du bonheur," in Musée national d'art moderne, *Boltanski,* 97).

50. Many commentators claim Boltanski was born the "very day" of Paris's liberation, but de Gaulle's triumphant march was twelve days earlier, on August 25, 1944.

51. Donald Kuspit argues that Boltanski's "gloom" is the gloom of the search for the father; "Christian Boltanski's Art of Gloom," *Signs of Psyche in Modern and Postmodern Art* (New York: Cambridge University Press, 1993), 257.

52. Annie Lauran, *La casquette d'Hitler ou le temps de l'oubli* (Paris: Les Éditeurs Français Réunis, 1974); Boltanski has illustrated another of her works, *Quatre histoires de ma vie inquiète* (Paris: Editions Pierre Jean Oswald, 1973). Boltanski's brother, Luc Boltanski, has worked with Pierre Bourdieu on photography in Pierre Bourdieu, *Un art moyen: essai sur les usages sociaux de la photographie* (Paris: Éditions de Minuit, 1965); translated as *Photography: A Middle-Brow Art,* trans. Shaun Whiteside (Stanford, Calif.: Stanford University Press, 1990).

53. Between 1969 and 1974, Boltanski embarked on several "mail art" projects wherein he recopied scores of times the same letters; sometimes, these were requests for help, as in "Il faut que vous m'aidiez . . ." (You must help me . . .) (1970) and at other times they were statements explaining (or deepening) the contradictions in his work as in "Lettre manuscrite dans laquelle j'explique les directions contradictoires dans lesquelles mon travail s'engage" (Letter in which I explain the contradictory directions that my work has taken) (1970). No matter what the content, these letters were an attempt to engage spectators, friends, and some randomly chosen recipients in his life-work in ways that eroded the producer-imbiber relationship of most artistic production.

54. As we saw above, Kiefer demonstrates an abiding interest in alchemy, yet while Boltanski does not actively share this interest, some commentators describe the hope that Boltanski's ordinary objects could be alchemically transformed: "there remained the hope that he [Boltanski] as artist-alchemist could endow these common materials with significance and transform poor substances into meaningful works" (Mary Jane Jacob, "Introduction," *Christian Boltanski: Lessons of Darkness* [Chicago: Museum of Contemporary Art, 1988], 10); Gilbert Lascault also discusses the alchemical tone of some of Boltanski's works in Musée national d'art moderne, *Boltanski*, 92–93; Semin et al., *Christian Boltanski*, 16.

55. "Christian Boltanski," interview with Demosthènes Davvetas, *Flash Art* 124 (October–November 1985): 82–83.

56. Semin et al., *Christian Boltanski*, 8.

57. See Anne-Madeleine Durez, Dorothée Gravoueille, and Franck Lepin, "Christian Boltanski," in *Une scène parisienne: 1968–1972* (Rennes: Centre d'histoire de l'art contemporain, 1991); on Boltanski's humor see the short comment by Maria Stangret in *Dialog* (Stockholm: Moderna Musset, 1985), 51.

58. Quoted in Jacques Clayssen, *Identité/Identifications* (Bordeaux: Centre d'Arts Plastiques Contemporains, 1976), 60. Boltanski's work often appears alongside Messager's; see, for example, *La photographie et au-delà: nouvelles expressions en France* (Paris: Association Française d'Action Artistique, 1995).

59. See, respectively: Andrew Graham-Dixon, "Much Possessed by Death," *Independent* [London], April 10, 1990: 15; Michael Bracewell, "Beyond These Four Walls: Do Today's Artists Have Anything to Say about Society?" *Independent* [London], February 13, 1996: 9; Adrian Searle, "Up the Workers: A Travelling French Artist Takes His Cue from Rusty Biscuit Tins, Inspirational Carpets, a Town's Forgotten Past and Trouble at T'Mill," *Independent* [London], July 11, 1995: 8; Robert Clark, "Christian Boltanski: Dean Clough, Halifax," *Guardian* [London], June 28, 1995: T10; Marianne MacDonald, "Q: Which Photo Shows a Work of Conceptual Art and Which a Jumble Sale?" *Independent* [London], March 25, 1995: 3; Tim Hilton, *Guardian* [London], April 18, 1990.

60. Kenneth Baker, "Pictures Worth a Thousand Pages," *San Francisco Chronicle*, October 11, 1998: 12; Cate McQuaid, "Christian Boltanski: Favorite Objects," *Boston Globe*, April 20, 2000: F5; Genevieve Breerette, "Christian Boltanski, un guide sur les chemins de la mémoire," *Le Monde*, May 14, 1998.

61. In addition to his installation in the Bundestag and *La maison manquante*, Boltanski has done a number of works in Germany; see, for example, Olivier Schmitt, "Les reminiscences d'un siècle de violence dans un sanitorium allemand," *Le Monde*, June 30, 1999; and for Boltanski's comments on the fall of the Berlin Wall see "Christian Boltanski: Peut-on encore croire à l'utopie?" *Le Monde*, June 10, 1996; for Boltanski's piece at the Jewish Museum in Paris see Alan Riding, "Selective French Homage

to Jewish History; Scant Mention of Holocaust in a New Museum," *New York Times,* December 28, 1998: E1. For more on Botlanski's reception see also Eunice Lipton, "The Glory That Was Paris: How Did France Lose Its Grip on the Art World?" *Guardian* [London], January 19, 2002: 5; Judith H. Dobrzynski, "France Playing Catch-Up in the Arts?" *New York Times,* March 4, 1999: E1; and Edmund White holds Boltanski up as the only internationally known French artist today in "Paris Is Perfect for the Aimless Stroller," *Daily Telegraph* [London]: 01.

62. Quoted in Clayssen, *Identité,* 24. For an examination of "vernacular photography"—or the use of ordinary photos, see Geoffrey Batchen, "Vernacular Photographies," *History of Photography* 24:3 (Autumn 2000): 262–71; for a review of an interesting show of vernacular photographs at the Griffin Museum in Wincester, Massachusetts, see Vicki Goldberg, "The Photo Booth: A Portrait Studio of One's Own," *New York Times,* August 3, 2002, sec. 2: 1, 27. See also Roland Barthes, *Camera Lucida: Reflections on Photography,* trans. Richard Howard (New York: Hill and Wang, 1981).

63. Portions of the Lycée Chases images were also exhibited in "Art after Auschwitz" at the Imperial War Museum, London (1995) and other venues; for a review of the Imperial War Museum show see Adrian Searle, "Art and the Aftermath," *Independent* [London], March 21, 1995: 25; see also Genevieve Breerette, "Monuments à l'enfance morte; Christian Boltanski expose à Grenoble des tableux qui disent le potentiel criminel de l'homme," *Le Monde,* February 11, 1991.

64. Stella Klein Lön, "Le lycée Chajes," in Ruth Beckerman, *Vienne rue du Temple: Le quartier juif 1918–1938,* trans. Françoise Samson (Paris: Fernand Hazan, 1986), 116. Originally published in German as *Die Mazzesinsel: Juden in der Wiener Leopoldstadt* (Vienna: Loecker Verlag, 1984).

65. Christian Boltanski, *Classe Terminale du Lycée Chases en 1931: Castelgasse-Vienne* (Düsseldorf: Kunstverein für die Reinlande und Westfalen, 1987), unpaginated. In another artist's book, *Kaddish,* which includes photos from an exhibition at the Musée d'Art Moderne de la Ville de Paris in 1998, Boltanski echoed this sense of not knowing: "On ne sait plus rien d'eux. Ils sont à égalité. Ils ont appartenu à la chose humaine, c'est tout ce qu'on peut en dire" (One does not know anything about them. They are all the same. All one can say is that they are part of humanity) (Breerette, "Un guide"). Kenneth Baker, in reviewing the book version of the exhibit, suggests that the book "is the form his art was meant to take" ("Pictures," 12). With Bertrand Lavier, Boltanski organized another show at the same museum in 2000; see Genevieve Breerette, "Voila, les archives impossibles du temps present," *Le Monde,* June 29, 2000.

66. Musée national d'art moderne, *Boltanski,* 92; "Christian Boltanski: Interview by Suzanne Pagé," in *Statements New York 82: Leading Contemporary Artists from France* (Paris: Les Presses Artistiques, 1982), 26. Jean Clair notes that "Boltanski imagine les *traces* d'un événement *futur:* catapultant ainsi deux catégories temporelles

contradictoires, il abolit la réalité même du temps. Il escamote la mort" (Boltanski imagines *traces* of a *future* event: thus catapulting two contradictory temporal categories, he abolishes the reality of time itself. He spirits death away.) (Ministère des affaires culturelles, *Douze ans d'art contemporain en France* [Paris: Éditions des Musées Nationaux, 1972], unpaginated).

67. Marianne Hirsch, *Family Frames: Photography, Narrative, and Postmemory* (Cambridge, Mass.: Harvard University Press, 1997), 260; van Alphen, *Caught by History*, 99; David Bonetti, "Photographic Art Personalizes Jewish History," *San Francisco Chronicle*, November 23, 2001: C1; Susan Gubar, *Poetry after Auschwitz*, 132. Marjorie Perloff and Nancy M. Shawcross also discuss *Le Lycée Chases* in Perloff's "'What Has Occurred Only Once': Barthes Winter Garden/Boltanski's Archives of the Dead" and Shawcross's "The Filter of Culture and the Culture of Death: How Barthes and Boltanski Play the Mythologies of the Photograph," both in Jean Michel Rabaté, ed., *Writing the Image after Roland Barthes* (Philadelphia: University of Pennsylvania Press, 1997), 32–58; 59–70.

68. Lynn Gumpert, *Christian Boltanski* (Paris: Flammarion, 1994), 161. Many thanks to Matti Bunzl, an expert on Austrian Jewish history, for rounding out this information on the Chajes school. See also the following web sources: http://www.zpc.nwy.at/zpcgesch.htm; http://www.aeiou.at./aeiou.encyclop.j/j740384.htm.

69. Telephone conversation, July 30, 2003.

70. Telephone conversation, October 2004; many thanks to Kurt Glückselig for putting me in touch with Nina. For more on Leo Glückselig, see Albert Lichtblau, *Leo Glückselig: Gottlob kein Held und Heiliger! Ein Wiener >>Jew-boy<< in New York* (Vienna: Picus Verlag, 1999).

71. I requested a copy of this letter (which is not included in the exhibition catalogue) several times from Robert Rainwater at the New York Public Library, but at press time I had not yet received it.

72. Phone conversation with Janet Gerson, January 21, 2005. For a portrait of Glückselig (and also of Boltanski) see Reiner Leist, *American Portraits, 1910–2001* (Munich: Prestel, 2001).

73. Susan Sontag, *On Photography* (New York: Farrar, Straus and Giroux, 1973), 70.

74. Boltanski has said that "small memory" concerns him (see Semin et al., *Christian Boltanski*, 19, and Moure, *Boltanski*, 107). Genevieve Breerette echoes this when she finds that Boltanski's images "permettent à chacun d'imaginer une histoire. Une petite histoire, ou un pan d'histoire" (allow each [viewer] to imagine a story. A little story or a morsel of a story) ("Carte blanche à Christian Boltanski," *Le Monde*, May 28, 1999).

75. Hirsch, *Family Frames*, 264.

76. Boltanski, *La vie impossible,* unpaginated.

77. In the same interview with Delphine Renard, Boltanski continues, "essayer de

dire une chose et son contraire, jouer avec un code . . . constituent chez moi une attitude politique" (trying to say one thing and its opposite, playing with a code . . . amounts to, for me, a political attitude) (Renard, "Entretien avec Christian Boltanski," 73).

78. Semin et al., *Christian Boltanski*, 23.

79. Boltanski, *La vie impossible,* unpaginated.

80. Davvetas, "Boltanski," 82.

81. Elisabeth Lebovici, "Entretien: Christian Boltanski," *Beaux Arts* 37 (July–August 1986): 29–30.

82. Georgia Marsh, "The White and the Black: An Interview with Christian Boltanski," *Parkett* 22 (December 1989): 36–40, 37.

83. Christian Boltanski, "Les utopies perdues de Christian Boltanski" (interview with Genevieve Breerette), *Le Monde,* March 3, 1993; see also Marie Helene Exel, "Perec, Boltanski, et MC Solaar," *Le Cabinet d'amateur* 7–8 (December 1998): 81–86.

84. Boltanski quoted in Sharon Waxman, "Lost and Found in Grand Central Station," *Forward,* May 12, 1995: 10.

85. Moure, *Boltanski*, 105.

86. Jean-Louis Pinte, "Christian Boltanski; Sauver la mémoire," *Le Figaro,* June 10, 1998.

87. Boltanski displayed a version of "Lost Property" at the Douglas Hyde Gallery in Dublin in 1994; see Brian Fallon, "Moving Work in a Rather Desolate Way," *Irish Times,* July 26, 1994: 10. His displays of anonymous people's personal effects have been done in many museums globally, including Charleston; see *Places with a Past: New Site-Specific Art at Charleston's Spoleto Festival* (New York: Rizzoli, 1991).

88. An exhibit in Bourgogne in 2001 was accompanied by Mahler's Third Symphony; see Marie-Guy Baron, "Arts Plastiques Invite des 'Nouvelles Scenes de Dijon,'" *Le Figaro,* December 4, 2001; and an exhibit in Gers in 1997 used tape-recorded voices to highlight the sense of loss; see Philippe Dagen, "L'école fantôme de Christian Boltanski," *Le Monde,* August 25, 1997.

89. For a review, see Mark Stevens, "Orphan Spaces," *New York,* May 29, 1995: 56.

90. Elizabeth Hess, "Packing, Unpacking," *Village Voice,* 40:22 (May 30, 1995); many thanks to Mayuri Amuluru of the Public Art Fund for a press packet about Boltanski's project. See also Bruce Weber, "Just Stuff. Just Art?" *New York Times,* May 10, 1995: B1, B10; Carol Vogel, "Inside Art," *New York Times,* April 21, 1995; Bill Bell, "Lost-and-Found Is Where His Art Is," *Daily News,* May 8, 1995; Deborah Solomon, "In America's Cluttered Attic," *Wall Street Journal,* May 12, 1995; Holland Cotter, "Lost, Found and Somewhere in between," *New York Times,* May 26, 1995: C26; Michael Kimmelman, "Dusting Off the Past, Inviting In the Future," *New York Times,* May 12, 1995: C1.

91. Bob Morris, *New York Times,* May 21, 1995: 45.

92. Amei Wallach, "A Portrait of the City, in 4 Parts," *New York Newsday,* May 18, 1995: B15.

93. Waxman, "Lost and Found," 10.

94. This piece is featured in the video *Christian Boltanski,* produced and directed by Gerald Fox (London Weekend Television, 1994).

95. See Grace Glueck, "A Life Cut Short by the Nazis Endures in a Painted 'Opera,'" *New York Times,* August 25, 2000: E2, 33; Christine Temin, "Charlotte Salomon, Life? or Theater?" *Boston Globe,* August 11, 2000: D1; and Julia Watson, "Charlotte Salomon's Memory Work in the 'Postscript' to *Life? or Theatre?*" *Signs: Journal of Women in Culture and Society* 28:1 (2002).

96. Peter Stallybrass, "Worn Worlds: Clothes, Mourning, and the Life of Things," *Cultural Memory and the Construction of Identity,* ed. Dan Ben-Amos and Lilliane Weissberg (Detroit: Wayne State University Press, 1999), 28, 30; see also Ann Rosalind Jones and Peter Stallybrass, *Renaissance Clothing and the Materials of Memory* (New York: Cambridge University Press, 2000).

97. Marsh, "White and the Black," 36–37. In speaking of Boltanski, José Jiménez echoes this sentiment: "Old clothes. Used. Vestments. A part of ourselves, when we wear them they retain a trace of life, even when the person who wore them no longer exists. And thus, this second skin of the human being becomes a metonymic emblem of an absent presence" ("Theatre of Metamorphosis," in Moure, *Boltanski,* 51).

98. On Beuys see Caroline Tisdall, *Joseph Beuys* (New York: Thames and Hudson, 1979). Boltanski cites Beuys also in his many "actions" that refer to Beuys' similarly untraditional projects, and in his donning, in his *Clowns* series, of a hat reminiscent of Beuys's famously ubiquitous felt hat. While *Bathtub* (1960) for Beuys was an important symbol of what he terms the wound of birth, Kiefer used it in a series of paintings mocking the German invasions during the war and Boltanski used it as a repeated image in *Menschlich.* Boltanski mentions Kiefer as part of a mythological triad of Boltanski, Kiefer, Kantor, where each artist has a place. This mythical place is a "great plain where armies crashed and where the Jews of my culture lived"; while Boltanski flees and Kantor ironizes in this place, "Kiefer is the one who occupies it, he is the army, present by a sort of physical weight, obvious, hitting you over the head." Boltanski wishes to distance himself from the heavy monumentality embodied by Kiefer and stresses that "My clothing is not made of lead, but of real cloth that will rot" (Marsh, "White and the Black," 37).

99. Smith et al., *Life Death,* 122.

100. Raul Hilberg, *The Destruction of the European Jews* (New York: Holmes and Meier, 1985), 254, 303.

101. Christian Boltanski, "Vêtements," Danilo Eccher, ed., *Christian Boltanski* (Milan: Charta, 1997), 151. And in an interview Boltanski explains that "for me there is a direct relationship between a piece of clothing, a photo and a dead body" (Semin et al., *Christian Boltanski,* 19); Boltanski has used clothing in many of his installation pieces, including *Lake of the Dead* (1990), *Holy Week* (1994), and *Reserves: The Purim Holiday* (1989).

102. In commenting on the Holocaust resonance of *Canada,* Didier Semin notes that "With *Canada* and the works related to it, it is just as if a phantom had entered the artist's consciousness." Semin describes this phantom as a repressed "family secret" that had not necessarily been made explicit, and he argues that the discovery of this Holocaust phantom "induces a retrospective reading of Boltanski's works starting from an exploration of genocide" (Semin et al., *Christian Boltanski,* 80).

103. Danto, *Encounters,* 260, 259.

104. Van Alphen, *Caught by History,* 115; Boltanski notes that *Les Habits de François C* "is particularly close to the concentration camp museums and I'm sure it was about that, although when I made it it was impossible for me to focus my mind on the subject" (Morgan, "Little Christians," 49).

105. Guillame Pô, for example, claims that Boltanski's work is overwhelmingly about the Holocaust: "Né en 1944, Boltanski n'a pas vraiment connu la guerre, mais son œuvre tout entière—qui prend des formes très différentes: installations, cinéma, peinture, art postal, etc.—témoigne d'un profond traumatisme causé par les horreurs de celle-ci" (Born in 1944, Boltanski never really knew the war, but his entire œuvre—which takes very different forms: installations, films, paintings, postal art, etc.—bears witness to a profound trauma caused by the horrors of [the war].) ("Perec et Boltanski, de la rue Vilin à la rue de Vaugirard," *Le Cabinet d'amateur* 7–8 [December 1998]: 75–79, 75). Many commentators take this tack; see, for example, Mel Gussow, "The Art of Aftermath, Distilled in Memory," *New York Times,* November 14, 2001: E1; Cate McQuaid notes that "Boltanski is best known for work he has created from photographs of children during the Holocaust," yet, as far as I know, Boltanski has never used photos of children taken *during* the Holocaust (McQuaid, "Boltanski," F5). Similarly, Christine Temin notes that Boltanski incorporates "photographs of murdered Jews" into his installations ("Art for Life's Sake," *Boston Globe,* September 19, 1999: D6). Other critics find a more balanced view of Boltanski's incorporation of Holocaust loss with a more general reflection on loss. See, for example, Melissa E. Feldman, *Face-Off: The Portrait in Recent Art* (Philadelphia: Institute of Contemporary Art/University of Pennsylvania, 1994), 33; Nancy Marmer, "Boltanski: The Uses of Contradiction," *Art in America* 77:10 (October 1989): 169–235, 170; Guy Schraenen, *D'une oeuvre l'autre: Le livre d'artiste dans l'art contemporain* (Mariemont: Musée Royal de Mariemont, 1996), 13; Semin et al., *Christian Boltanski,* 35; Moure, *Boltanski,* 31–32.

106. John Czaplicka, "History, Aesthetics, and Commemorative Practice in Berlin," *New German Critique* 65 (Spring–Summer 1995): 155–87, 167.

107. Ibid., 172.

108. Richard Dorment, "Wrong Number: Christian Boltanski's Installation of 3,000 Telephone Directories Is Intriguing and Beautiful, but Magic Is Lacking," *Daily Telegraph* [London], April 17, 2002: 19.

109. Adam Gopnik, "Lost and Found," *New Yorker,* February 20, 1989: 107–11, 109.

110. Van Alphen, *Caught by History,* 3.

CHAPTER 5: AESTHETIC POLLUTION

1. It is sometimes hard to grasp the precise difference between the terms "monument" and "memorial." Marita Sturken suggests that monuments are anonymous and offer less in the way of narrative, whereas memorials tend to list names of the dead and to be more pedagogically inclined; Marita Sturken, *Tangled Memories: The Vietnam War, the AIDS Epidemic, and the Politics of Remembering* (Berkeley: University of California Press, 1997), 48. Agreement tends to land with James Ingo Freed, the designer of the United States Holocaust Memorial Museum, who "prefers 'memorial' to 'monument,' feeling the latter is more celebratory and, therefore, inappropriate" (Jim Murphy, "Memorial to Atrocity," *Progressive Architecture* 74 [February 1993]: 61–69). This is no doubt why many contemporary designers and architects have chosen to create counter-monuments rather than counter-memorials. Memorials have maintained closer ties to their traditional fore-figures because they are not as threatened by the fear of reproducing the monumentality associated with fascist architecture. That is, while the fear of aesthetic pollution haunts the creation of memorials, because they are less abstract and more specific the pollutant is less likely to be fascism and more likely to be traditions of the glorification of war heroes. For the most part I have chosen the term "commemorative sites" as a more general way of indicating three-dimensional spaces, except in cases where the term "memorial" or "monument" is part of the title of a piece.

2. See Eric Michaud, *Un art de l'éternité: l'image et le temps du national-socialisme* (Paris: Gallimard, 1996).

3. Roger Cohen, "A Shrine to Power: Is Berlin Ready?" *New York Times,* February 16, 2001: A3; Martin Filler, "Berlin: The Lost Opportunity," *New York Review of Books,* November 1, 2001: 28–31.

4. Rolf J. Goebel, "Berlin's Architectural Citations: Reconstruction, Simulation, and the Problem of Historical Authenticity," *PMLA* 118:5 (October 2003): 1268–89, 1287.

5. I cannot do justice here to the long and tortured history of debate that haunts the reconstruction of Berlin, both after the war and then again due to the relocation of the capital from Bonn. I refer readers to the excellent collection of architectural essays to be found in Thorsen Scheer, Joseph Paul Kleihues, and Paul Kahlfeldt, eds., *City of Architecture, Architecture of the City: Berlin 1900–2000* (Berlin: Nicolai, 2000); to Michael Z. Wise, *Capital Dilemma: Germany's Search for a New Architecture of Democracy* (New York: Princeton Architectural Press, 1998); to Brian Ladd's *The Ghosts of Berlin: Confronting German History in the Urban Landscape* (Chicago: Uni-

versity of Chicago Press, 1997); as well as to Beatrice Hanssen, "Christo's Wrapped Reichstag: Globalized Art in a National Context," *Germanic Review* 73:3 (Fall 1998): 351–67.

6. Although arguing that "individual architectural forms cannot be accorded the attribute 'fascist,'" Andrea Mesecke nonetheless suggests that there are "universal effect mechanisms which make a style of architecture appear 'violent.'" Mesecke thus helps us understand why the fear of aesthetic pollution has been strident enough to transform the aesthetics of many contemporary commemorative sites (Scheer et al., *Architecture of the City*, 187).

7. Many fascinating commemorative sites have been left out of this chapter. On Hrdlicka's "Monument against War and Fascism" in Vienna, for example, see James Young, *The Texture of Memory: Holocaust Memorials and Meaning* (New Haven, Conn.: Yale University Press, 1993), and Matti Bunzl, "On the Politics and Semantics of Austrian Memory: Vienna's Monument against War and Fascism," *History and Memory* 7:2 (1996): 7–40; for Libeskind's Jewish Museum, see the video-recording *Berlin's Jewish Museum: A Personal Tour with Daniel Libeskind* (Michael Blackwood Productions, 2000); Julia Klein, "The Jewish Museum Berlin: Amid Clutter, at Odds with Itself," *Chronicle of Higher Education*, November 9, 2001: B15–B17; and David Clark, *Developing Jewish Museums in Europe* (London: Institute for Jewish Policy Research, 1999); for a survey of monuments and memorials see Sybil Milton and Ira Nowinski, *In Fitting Memory: The Art and Politics of Holocaust Memorials* (Detroit: Wayne State University Press, 1991); on Rachel Whiteread's monument in Vienna see notes to chapter 3.

8. Paul Goldberger, "Down at the Mall: The New World War II Memorial Doesn't Rise to the Occasion," *New Yorker*, May 31, 2004: 82–84, 84.

9. Thomas Keenan, "The Greatest Veneration: The Architect for the Controversial National World War II Memorial on Why His Design Isn't Fascist—and Why the War's Legacy Is Far from Settled," *New York Times Magazine*, July 1, 2001: 23.

10. Robert Harbison, "Half-Truths and Misquotations: A Skeptical Look at Monuments," and Nancy Levinson, editor's introduction, *Harvard Design Magazine* (Fall 1999): 20, 2.

11. Young, *Texture*, 27.

12. Ladd, *Ghosts*, 139.

13. Barbara Miller Lane, *Architecture and Politics in Germany, 1918–1945* (Cambridge: Harvard University Press, 1968), 185–91. See also Paul B. Jaskot, *The Architecture of Oppression: The SS, Forced Labor and the Nazi Monumental Building Economy* (New York: Routlege, 2000).

14. Ladd, *Ghosts*, 141.

15. Wise, *Capital Dilemma*, 16.

16. Lane, *Architecture*, 185.

17. Walter Benjamin, *Illuminations*, 241.

18. Ibid., 241.

19. Philippe Lacoue-Labarthe, *La fiction du politique* (Paris: Christian Bourgois, 1987), 92 (English translation cited in note 27, chap. 1); see also Lacoue-Labarthe and Jean-Luc Nancy, *Le mythe nazi* (La Tour d'Aigues: Editions de l'aube, 1991); Marc Redfield, *The Politics of Aesthetics: Nationalism, Gender, Romanticism* (Stanford, Calif.: Stanford University Press, 2003); Richard J. Golsan, ed., *Fascism, Aesthetics, and Culture* (Hanover, N.H.: University Press of New England, 1992); and Alice Yaeger Kaplan, *Reproductions of Banality: Fascism, Literature, and French Intellectual Life* (Minneapolis: University of Minnesota Press, 1986).

20. For an intentionalist approach see Eberhard Jäckel, *Hitler's Weltanshauung: A Blueprint for Power*, trans. Herbert Arnold (Middletown, Conn.: Wesleyan University Press, 1972); for a functionalist approach see Hans Mommsen, "The Realization of the Unthinkable," *From Weimar to Auschwitz*, trans. Philip O'Connor (Princeton, N.J.: Princeton University Press, 1991); for an approach that combines the two see Friedländer, *Nazi Germany and the Jews.*

21. Benjamin, *Illuminations,* 242.

22. Construction on the memorial began in April 2003, and it opened on May 10, 2005. For a detailed account of the debates over this memorial see *Der Denkmalstreit—das Denkmal?: Die Debatte um das "Denkmal für die ermordeten Juden Europas"* (Berlin: Philo Verlagsgesellschaft, 1999); in this collection critics, artists, historians, and architects such as Daniel Libeskind, James Young, Eberhard Jäckel, Jürgen Habermas, Michael Naumann, Lea Rosh, Peter Eisenman, Richard Serra, Jochen Gerz, Rebecca Horn, Gesine Weinmiller, Horst Hoheisel, and Martin Walser discuss and debate the memorial at great length. See also Jacques Derrida and Peter Eisenman, *Choral Works* (New York: Montacelli Press, 1997).

23. "Were the Nazis poststructuralists and deconstructors *avant la lettre* in their desire 'never to utter the words that would be appropriate to the action being taken'?" Elaine Marks, "Cendres juives: Jews Writing in French 'After Auschwitz,'" *Auschwitz and After,* 37.

24. Michael Naumann, in conversation with James Young, cited in Young, *Memory's Edge,* 216; Christopher Phillips, "Go-Ahead for Berlin Holocaust Memorial?" *Art in America* (March 1999): 29.

25. For analyses of this monument, see James Young, *Memory's Edge,* and Caroline Wiedmer, *The Claims of Memory: Representations of the Holocaust in Contemporary Germany and France* (Ithaca, N.Y.: Cornell University Press, 1999).

26. See Edmund Andrews, "Serra Quits Berlin's Holocaust Memorial Project," *New York Times,* June 4, 1998: E1; and Roger Cohen, "Wiesel Urges Germany to Ask Forgiveness," *New York Times,* January 28, 2000: A3.

27. Derrida and Eisenman, *Choral Works,* 46–47.

28. Young documents these changes in *Memory's Edge,* 184–223.

29. Email correspondence with Cynthia Davidson at Eisenman Architects, August 27, 2004.

30. The Master Architect Series, *Eisenman Architects: Selected and Current Works* (Mulgrave, Australia: Images Publishing Group, 1995).

31. Jeffrey Karl Ochsner, in an article on the USHMM exemplifies acceptance of the desire for an aesthetics unique to the Holocaust when he claims there are "particular difficulties in creating a museum specific to the Holocaust." He further notes that there is a "special set of problems unique to the Holocaust" in designing a museum to commemorate the event. "Understanding the Holocaust through the U.S. Holocaust Memorial Museum," *Journal of Architectural Education* 48:4 (May 1995): 240–49.

32. Young, *Texture*, 28, 31.

33. Ibid., 31.

34. Stephan Schmidt-Wulffen, "The Monument Vanishes: A Conversation with Esther and Jochen Gerz," *The Art of Memory: Holocaust Memorials in History*, ed. James Young (Munich and New York: Prestel-Verlag/Jewish Museum, 1994), 73.

35. Dannatt, *Freed*, 5.

36. Edward T. Linenthal, *Preserving Memory: The Struggle to Create America's Holocaust Museum* (New York: Viking, 1995), 78, 83. For more analyses of the USHMM see Oren Baruch Stier, *Committed to Memory: Cultural Mediations of the Holocaust* (Amherst: University of Massachusetts Press, 2003); Tim Cole, *Selling the Holocaust: From Auschwitz to Schindler. How History Is Bought, Packaged, and Sold* (New York: Routledge, 2000); Peter Novick, *Holocaust in American Life.*

37. Dannatt, *Freed*, 10.

38. James S. Russell, "The National Memorial Dilemma," *Harvard Design* (Fall 1999): 35. For an account of Freed's accommodation see *Progressive Architecture* 74 (February 1993): 61–69.

39. James Ingo Freed, "The United States Holocaust Memorial Museum," in Young, *Art of Memory*, 89.

40. Ibid., 95, 100.

41. Andreas Huyssen, "Monumental Seduction," *Acts of Memory: Cultural Recall in the Present*, ed. Mieke Bal, Jonathan Crewe, and Leo Spitzer (Hanover, N.H.: University Press of New England, 1999), 199.

42. Mary Douglas, *Purity and Danger: An Analysis of Concepts of Pollution and Taboo* (New York: Frederick A. Praeger, 1966). For other interesting arguments about purity and pollution see Mireille Rosello, "Contamination et pureté: pour un protocole de cohabitation," *L'Esprit Créateur* 37:3 (Fall 1997): 3–13; Vincent Buckley, "Poetry and Pollution," *Quadrant* 73:15:5 (September–October 1971): 39–50; Martin Danahay, "Matter Out of Place: The Politics of Pollution in Ruskin and Turner," *CLIO* 21:1 (Fall 1991): 61–77; David Carroll, "Pollution, Defilement, and the Art of

Decomposition," *Ruskin and Environment: The Storm-Cloud of the Nineteenth Century,* ed. Michael Wheeler (Manchester: Manchester University Press, 1995), 58–75.

43. Omer Bartov, *Mirrors of Destruction: War, Genocide, and Modern Identity* (Oxford: Oxford University Press, 2000), 143.

44. Ladd, *Ghosts,* 140.

45. Zygmunt Bauman, *Modernity and the Holocaust* (Ithaca, N.Y.: Cornell University Press, 1989), 66.

46. Andreas Huyssen, "Monument and Memory in a Postmodern Age," in Young, *Art of Memory,* 10.

47. Susan Sontag, "Regarding the Torture of Others," *New York Times Magazine,* May 23, 2004: 25–29, 42, 28.

48. Michael Light, *100 Suns: 1945–1962* (New York: Alfred A. Knopf, 2003), unpaginated. For an example of a review that finds that *100 Suns* is "visually fascinating" and "will leave readers changed," see *Publisher's Weekly Reviews,* October 6, 2003: 77 (no author given).

49. The comparison of Nachtwey to a war surgeon was offered by Hans-Hermann Klare. For reviews that find Natchtwey's work in this film and in his coffee-table-sized book, *Inferno,* "haunting," "profoundly affect[ing]," and "beautifully reproduced," see A. O. Scott, "Witnessing the Witness: Looking over a Shoulder at War's Deprivation," *New York Times,* June 19, 2002: E1; Stan Grossfeld, "'Inferno' Images Sear the Mind," *Boston Globe,* April 13, 2001: D16; Jym Wilson, "Haunting Images Give Voices to the Silenced," *USA Today,* June 1, 2001: 5D.

Tisdall, Caroline, 199n98
Tobias, Rochelle, 178n26
"Todesfuge" (Celan), 13, 20–36, 59, 80, 109, 115, 117, 121
Tokyo, 140, 159–60
Tolanksy, Ethel, 180n51
totalitarianism, 156, 166
trauma: and beauty, 35, 170; and concentration camps, 28; experience of, 14, 20, 33, 85; in Freud, 43–44; and memory, 36, 41, 53, 70, 75, 160; surviving, 36, 40, 47, 167; transhistorical, 107

uncanny, 59, 133, 171
United States. *See* America
United States Holocaust Memorial Museum (USHMM, Washington, D.C., Freed), 5, 16, 152, 162–63, plate 8
unwanted beauty, 1–16, 155, 167–71; and Boltanski; 107–9, 147; and Celan, 20, 26, 30, 32–33, 36, 51, 115; and commemorative sites, 151; and Delbo, 20, 51; and Jabès, 76, 79, 99–102, 105; and Kiefer, 107–10, 125, 147, and Semprun, 54, 70. *See also* beauty

van Alphen, Ernst, 12, 132, 144, 148; *Caught by History,* 12
Vernon, Kathleen, 183n17
La vie impossible (Boltanski), 109, 135–37
Vienna, 23–24, 89–90, 131–33; Viennese Jews, 131–34

Waldrop, Rosmarie, 79, 84, 93–94, 99; *Lavish Absence,* 84

Wallis, Brian, 175n35
War Photographer (Frei), 169–70
Washington, D.C., 16, 152, 153, 156
Weimar, Karl, 177n10
Weinberg, Judy, 120
Weissberg, Liliane, 11
Weissman, Gary, 19
Weitzman, Lenore, 180n52
We're Not out of the Woods Yet (Silas), 125–26
White, Allon, 141
White, Edmund, 181n63
White, Hayden, 4
Whiteread, Rachel, 89–90; *Holocaust Memorial* (Vienna), 89–90
Wiedmer, Caroline, 203n25
Wiesel, Eli, 4–5, 65–66
Wise, Michael, 153–54, 164; *Capital Dilemma,* 154
Wisenberg, S. L., 180n52
Wisse, Ruth, 64, 87, 94, 100
Wolosky, Shira, 187n40
Woollacot, Angela, 180n52
World War II, 2, 10, 19, 41, 54, 84, 110, 122, 123, 127, 138, 153, 156, 158

Yad Vashem, 136
Ydessa Hendeles Foundation, Toronto, 143
Yerushalmi, Yosef Hayim, 187n36
Young, James, 5–6, 90, 153, 158, 161, 202n7
Your Blond Hair, Margarete (Kiefer), 112

Zimmerman, Ernst, 188n4
Žižek, Slavoj, 175n25
Zweite, Armin, 190n17, 192n38

BRETT ASHLEY KAPLAN received her Ph.D. from the Rhetoric Department at the University of California, Berkeley, and is currently an assistant professor in the Programs in Comparative and World Literature and Jewish Culture and Society at the University of Illinois, Urbana-Champaign. She has published articles in *Journal of Modern Jewish Studies, Comparative Literature Studies, International Studies in Philosophy, Comparative Literature, Philip Roth Studies,* and other venues. Her current book project is titled *Landscapes of Holocaust Postmemory.*

The University of Illinois Press
is a founding member of the
Association of American University Presses.

Composed in 10.5/13.5 Minion
with Meta capitals display
by Celia Shapland
for the University of Illinois Press
Designed by Dennis Roberts
Manufactured by Thomson-Shore, Inc.

University of Illinois Press
1325 South Oak Street
Champaign, IL 61820-6903
www.press.uillinois.edu